WITH FULL MILITARY HONORS

Civil War Generals Buried at Arlington National Cemetery

David L. Callihan

HERITAGE BOOKS
2009

HERITAGE BOOKS
AN IMPRINT OF HERITAGE BOOKS, INC.

Books, CDs, and more—Worldwide

For our listing of thousands of titles see our website
at
www.HeritageBooks.com

Published 2009 by
HERITAGE BOOKS, INC.
Publishing Division
100 Railroad Ave. #104
Westminster, Maryland 21157

Copyright © 2009 David L. Callihan

Other books by the author:
They Did Their Work Bravely: Civil War Generals Buried in Pennsylvania

All rights reserved. No part of this book may be reproduced or transmitted in any form or by any means, electronic or mechanical, including photocopying, recording or by any information storage and retrieval system without written permission from the author, except for the inclusion of brief quotations in a review.

International Standard Book Numbers
Paperbound: 978-0-7884-4934-5
Clothbound: 978-0-7884-8186-4

Dedicated

To My Dear Friend

Robert G. Morgan,

Who Now Lies Buried

At Arlington National Cemetery

TABLE OF CONTENTS

Introduction ix

Alexander Sandor Asboth 1
Christopher Columbus Augur 3
Romeyn Beck Ayres 5
Absalom Baird 7
Joseph Jackson Bartlett 9
William Worth Belknap 11
Luther Prentice Bradley 13
John Rutter Brooke 15
Stephen Gano Burbridge 17
William Wallace Burns 19
Cyrus Bussey 21
William Thomas Clark 23
Powell Clayton 25
Thomas Turpin Crittenden 27
George Crook 29
John Wynn Davidson 31
Frederick Tracy Dent 33
Abner Doubleday 35
Alexander Brydie Dyer 37
John Edwards 39
Charles Ewing 41
George Washington Getty 43
John Gibbon 45
Lawrence Pike Graham 47
Walter Quintin Gresham 49
William Alexander Hammond 51
William Selby Harney 53
Joseph Abel Haskin 55
John Porter Hatch 57
William Babcock Hazen 59
Charles Edward Hovey 61
Rufus Ingalls 63
August Valentine Kautz 65
Philip Kearny 67
Benjamin Franklin Kelley 69
John Haskell King 71

Wladimir Bonawentura Krzyzanowski..73
John Sanford Mason..75
James Winning McMillan...77
Montgomery Cunningham Meigs...79
Nelson Appleton Miles..81
John Franklin Miller..83
Robert Byington Mitchell..85
Joseph Anthony Mower..87
Edward Otho Cresap Ord...89
Thomas Ogden Osborn..91
Halbert Eleazer Paine..93
Innis Newton Palmer..95
Gabriel Rene Paul..97
William Henry Penrose...99
Thomas Gamble Pitcher..101
Joseph Bennett Plummer...103
Orlando Metcalfe Poe..105
Green Berry Raum...107
John Aaron Rawlins...109
Joseph Jones Reynolds...111
Americus Vespucius Rice..113
James Brewerton Ricketts...115
William Starke Rosecrans..117
Lovell Harrison Rousseau..119
Daniel Henry Rucker..121
Rufus Saxton...123
John McAllister Schofield...125
Philip Henry Sheridan..128
Daniel Edgar Sickles...131
Green Clay Smith..133
Morgan Lewis Smith..135
William Farrar Smith..137
Julius Stahel..139
Charles John Stolbrand...141
Samuel Davis Sturgis..143
Wager Swayne..145
Stewart Van Vliet...147
Louis Douglass Watkins..149
Joseph Rodman West...151
Frank Wheaton..153

Joseph Wheeler..155
William Denison Whipple...157
Orlando Bolivar Willcox..159
Horatio Gouverneur Wright...161
Marcus Joseph Wright...163

Appendix 1: Burials Listed By Section Numbers................................165

Appendix 2: Union Brevet Generals Listed By Section Numbers.............169

Endnotes..173

Bibliography..207

INTRODUCTION

Arlington National Cemetery is located in Arlington, Virginia, directly across the Potomac River from Washington, D.C. It is one of the most famous cemeteries in the world. Each year hundreds of thousands of Americans and visitors from all over the world come to Arlington. Some walk its tranquil and sacred grounds, while others merely ride the tour bus. Most visits to Arlington consist of taking a tour of Arlington House, watching the changing of the guard at the Tomb of the Unknowns, and standing silently at the grave site of President John Fitzgerald Kennedy. Many of those visitors leave Arlington without realizing that many other notables are buried there, such as: another United States president (William Howard Taft), explorers, astronauts, inventors, manufacturers, actors, writers, journalists, sports figures, many United States Supreme Court Justices and Chief Justices, many Cabinet officials, and yes, many famous American military figures. After all, Arlington is a military cemetery. Veterans of all our wars, from the American Revolution to the present time, are buried there. Among the thousands of soldiers and officers buried at Arlington are 79 full rank or substantive Union Civil War generals and two Confederate generals. This book presents the stories of these 81 Civil War generals, as well as photographs of their grave markers at Arlington.

Arlington became a military cemetery during the Civil War.[1] Prior to the war Arlington had been an estate owned by the Custis family of Virginia. George Washington Parke Custis, the adopted son of our first president, George Washington, owned the estate and in 1802 construction began on Arlington House. When Custis died in 1857 his only surviving child, Mary Anna Custis Lee, inherited the house and estate. She was the wife of Robert Edward Lee, then a colonel in the United States army. With the outbreak of the Civil War in April 1861, Robert E. Lee chose to side with his native state of Virginia. He resigned his commission in the United States army and soon accepted a commission in the army of the Confederacy. Eventually Robert E. Lee became the South's most successful general during the Civil War.

Mrs. Lee evacuated the estate on May 15, 1861. Later that month, shortly after the Virginia ordinance of secession was ratified, Union forces crossed the Potomac and took possession of the house and estate. Several forts were built on the estate itself. In June 1862 a law was enacted wherein the United States government could impose taxes on real estate located in "insurrectionary" districts, which was just a transparent ploy to legalize the confiscation of property owned by Confederate sympathizers. A tax of some $92 was eventually imposed on the Arlington estate. The law also required that the actual owner of the real estate personally pay the tax. Mrs. Lee was unable to go to Washington, D.C. and personally pay the tax, and so the federal government declared the taxes delinquent. The government then purchased the property in January 1864 for its assessed value of $26,800, although no money was given to Mrs. Lee. Finally in 1883 George Washington Custis Lee, the eldest son of the then deceased Robert E. and Mary Custis Lee, ended a complicated court case by deeding the property to the federal government in return for a payment of $150,000.

During the Civil War many hospitals were located in Washington, D.C. and many of the patients in those hospitals died. Although several national cemeteries were created in the immediate Washington, D.C. area during the war, by 1864 more cemeteries were needed. In June 1864 the Quartermaster General of the Army, Montgomery Cunningham

Meigs, suggested that the confiscated Arlington estate be the site of an additional national cemetery. Although the 1,100 acres of the estate would certainly provide sufficient land for a national cemetery, Meigs' suggestion was mainly motivated by his hatred of Robert E. Lee, whom Meigs regarded as a traitor. Meigs wanted to be certain that the Lees would never want to return to their estate, and turning their estate into a national cemetery seemed to be an ideal means of achieving that objective. In fact by the time Meigs made his suggestion in June 1864, several Union soldiers had already been buried on the estate, beginning with Private William Christman on May 13, 1864. Meigs' suggestion was quickly approved and 200 acres of the estate were set aside for the cemetery. In the summer of 1864 hundreds of Union soldiers were buried on the estate. When he visited the grounds at Arlington in August 1864 Meigs insisted that some of the burials take place adjacent to the house in Mrs. Lee's rose garden, thereby assuring that the Lees would never again live at Arlington. Through the years more land from the estate was added to the area of the cemetery, until today the cemetery consists of more than 600 acres.

At first only common Union soldiers were buried at Arlington. By the end of the Civil War some 16,000 Union soldiers were buried there. But during the next several decades, as more and more soldiers and officers were buried at Arlington, the families of some of the Civil War's more notable officers chose Arlington as the final resting place for those officers. As time went by, Arlington became more prestigious, until today it is regarded as both a national cemetery and a national shrine. Some of the most famous Union Civil War generals were buried there, including Philip Henry Sheridan, William Starke Rosecrans, George Crook, and Philip Kearny. And Montgomery Cunningham Meigs, whose desire for revenge against a perceived traitor helped create this national treasure, was also buried there, appropriately enough in Section 1, Lot 1.

In all 79 substantive Union Civil War generals were buried at Arlington. And two Confederate generals – Joseph Wheeler, who served as a major general during the Spanish – American War, and Marcus Joseph Wright, who spent almost four decades collecting and preserving Confederate war records for publication by the United States government – were also buried there. Although some of these 81 generals are not well known today, all of their stories deserve to be told. And anyone visiting Arlington today should get off the tour bus, walk around the cemetery, and discover some or all of these 81 grave sites. The visitor will not only come away with a deeper appreciation for these men, but by visiting these grave sites the visitor will also be honoring Americans, both blue and gray, who fought and sometimes died for what they believed in.

The arrangement of the book is simple. The 81 generals are presented in alphabetical order. For those interested in visiting these grave sites, Appendix 1 presents a listing of the 81 generals by cemetery section numbers. As can be seen, all but three of the generals are buried in sections 1, 2, or 3, which simplifies finding these grave sites. A map of the cemetery can be obtained at the cemetery visitor center and there are markers on the cemetery grounds showing the section numbers. With the photographs in the book, the visitor should have little trouble finding these grave sites.

There are an additional 105 Union officers buried at Arlington who attained the grade of brigadier general or major general by brevet only, either during the Civil War itself or after the war for their Civil War services. Appendix 2 contains a listing by cemetery section numbers of these 105 Union officers. All but two of these 105 grave sites are located in sections 1, 2, or 3, and thus it is likely that the cemetery visitor will find many of these grave sites as well while looking for the grave sites of the substantive generals.

Through the years I have spent many hours walking the beautiful grounds of Arlington National Cemetery, finding and photographing the grave sites of these generals, as well as the grave sites of many other notables. I hope that readers of this book will journey to Arlington and discover these and other grave sites of men who were buried "with full military honors."

David L. Callihan
October 2008

ALEXANDER SANDOR ASBOTH

Born: December 18, 1811
Died: January 21, 1868

General Asboth was born in Keszthely, Hungary. After graduating from the Academy of Selmecbanya he served in the Austrian Army and worked as an engineer. He sided with the revolutionary Lajos Kossuth during the Hungarian Revolution of 1848. When the revolution failed, Asboth was forced to flee to Turkey. In 1851 he moved to the United States and by 1861 he had become a citizen of his adopted country.[1]

In the summer of 1861 Maj. Gen. John C. Fremont, commander of the Western Department, named Asboth as his chief of staff and on September 3, 1861, Fremont appointed Asboth brigadier general of volunteers. Asboth commanded two different divisions in the Army of the Southwest between September 24, 1861, and May 9, 1862. He ably led his division on March 7 – 8, 1862, at the Battle of Pea Ridge. He was severely wounded in the right arm on March 7, but continued in command of his division. In March 1862 the Senate negated his appointment as brigadier general of volunteers, because Fremont lacked the authority to appoint anyone as a general. On March 22, 1862, Asboth was properly appointed brigadier general of volunteers by the president. The Senate confirmed his nomination two days later and his commission ranked from March 21, 1862.[2]

Asboth commanded several brigades and a division in the Army of the Mississippi from May 25 until July 30, 1862, when health problems and ongoing complications with his wound forced him to take an extended medical leave. Finally on January 11, 1863, he was able to assume command of the District of Columbus, and from March 31 to September 21, 1863, he commanded several divisions in the Army of the Tennessee. On November 9, 1863, Asboth was placed in command of the District of West Florida. He was severely wounded in the left arm and the left cheekbone on September 27, 1864, while leading a cavalry charge during an engagement at Marianna, Florida. He permanently lost the use of his left arm and the wound to his cheek never fully healed. Surgeons were unable to remove the ball from his cheek, and eventually the wound impaired his sense of smell, sight, and hearing. And he still suffered pain and complications from his previous wound in his right arm.[3]

Asboth was brevetted major general of volunteers on March 13, 1865, and on August 24, 1865, he was mustered out of the volunteer service. In 1866 he was named United States minister to the Argentine Republic and Uruguay. Frail and sickly from his wounds and health problems, Asboth accepted the appointment and faithfully carried out his diplomatic duties for the next two years, until his death in Buenos Aires, Argentina. He was originally buried in Buenos Aires in the British Cemetery in the Victorian District. In 1989 a descendant found the general's will, which contained the sentence, "It is in the free soil of America in which I wish to rest in eternal peace." On October 23, 1990, Asboth's wish was belatedly fulfilled when his remains were reinterred, with full military honors, at Arlington National Cemetery. The top photo shows the government marker originally placed at his grave site in Section 2 at Arlington and the bottom photo shows the new marker that replaced that original marker. The inscriptions on both markers imply that Asboth was brevetted major general in the regular army, whereas he was never in the regular army and was brevetted major general of volunteers.[4]

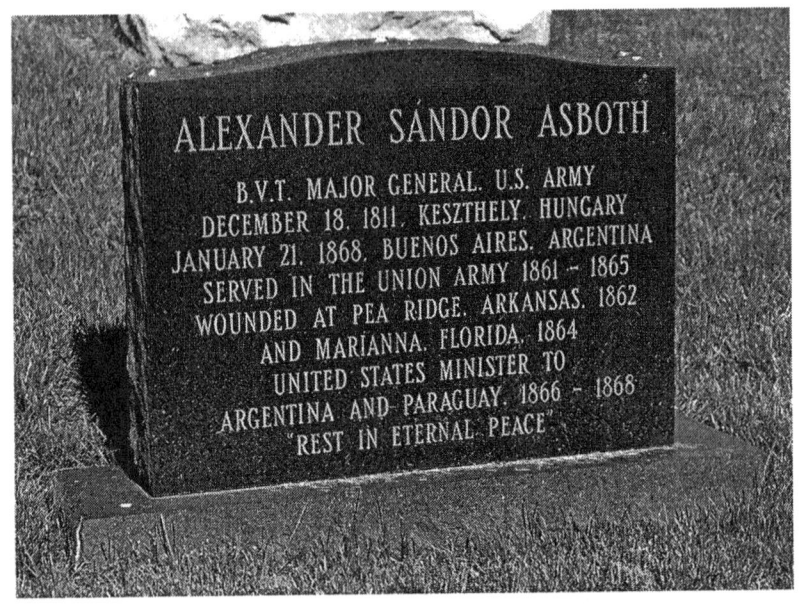

CHRISTOPHER COLUMBUS AUGUR

Born: July 10, 1821
Died: January 16, 1898

General Augur was born in Kendall, New York. His widowed mother moved the family to Michigan when he was less than a year old. He graduated from West Point in 1843, ranked 16th out of 39. He served on the frontier and was promoted to second lieutenant on September 12, 1845. During the Mexican War he served as an aide-de-camp on the staffs of Brig. Gen. Enos D. Hopping and Brig. Gen. Caleb Cushing, and he was promoted to first lieutenant on February 16, 1847. After the war he performed routine garrison duty, mainly on the frontier. On August 1, 1852, he was promoted to captain and on May 14, 1861, he was promoted to major in the regular army. From August 26 to December 5, 1861, he served as commandant of cadets at West Point. On November 12, 1861, he was appointed brigadier general of volunteers.[1]

On December 5, 1861, Augur was given command of a brigade in Brig. Gen. Irvin McDowell's division, which in March 1862 became a part of the newly created First Corps of the Army of the Potomac. The Senate confirmed his nomination on February 3, 1862, and his commission as brigadier general of volunteers ranked from November 12, 1861. Augur's brigade saw no combat during the Peninsula Campaign, being assigned to duty along the Rappahannock River. Augur commanded the forces that captured Fredericksburg, Virginia, on April 21, 1862. Then on June 26, 1862, Augur was placed in command of a brigade in the newly formed Army of Virginia and on July 7 he was given command of a division in that army. On August 9, 1862, during the Battle of Cedar Mountain, he was wounded in the right hip moments after his horse was shot. He went home to recover from his wound. He was brevetted colonel in the regular army on August 9, 1862, for his performance at Cedar Mountain.[2]

Augur returned to duty in September 1862 and was assigned to a military commission in Washington, D.C. On November 14, 1862, he was appointed major general of volunteers. That autumn Maj. Gen. Nathaniel P. Banks asked that Augur be assigned to his forces in Louisiana, and in January 1863 Augur went to Louisiana to take command of a division in the 19th Corps. The Senate confirmed his nomination on March 10, 1863, and his commission as major general of volunteers ranked from August 9, 1862. During the siege of Port Hudson Augur commanded the left wing of Banks' army. He was promoted to lieutenant colonel in the regular army on July 1, 1863. After the surrender of the Confederate forces at Port Hudson Augur, suffering from dysentery, went back north on sick leave. In August 1863 he again returned to duty and was assigned to another military commission in Washington, D.C. He commanded the 22nd Corps, which was assigned to garrison duty at the nation's capital, from October 14, 1863, through the end of the war. He commanded the District of Washington from December 15, 1864, until April 26, 1865. On March 13, 1865, he was brevetted brigadier general in the regular army for his performance at Port Hudson and major general in the regular army for his war service.[3]

On March 5, 1866, Augur was placed in command of the Department of the Platte and ten days later he was promoted to colonel in the regular army. He was mustered out of the volunteer service on September 1, 1866. During the next nineteen years he commanded various military departments in the West and South, and on March 4, 1869, he was promoted to brigadier general. He retired on July 10, 1885, having reached the mandatory retirement age of sixty-four. He died in Washington, D.C. and was buried in Section 1 at Arlington National Cemetery. The inscription on his grave marker correctly indicates the highest substantive and brevet grades Augur attained in the regular army, but there is no inscription concerning his service in the volunteers during the Civil War.[4]

BRIGADIER GENERAL AND
BREVET MAJOR GENERAL
CHRISTOPHER C. AUGUR U.S.A.
BORN JULY 10, 1821
DIED JAN. 16, 1898

ROMEYN BECK AYRES

Born: December 20, 1825
Died: December 4, 1888

General Ayres was born in East Creek, New York. He graduated from West Point in 1847, ranked 22nd out of 38. He was immediately sent to Mexico, where he was engaged in garrison duties until the end of the Mexican War. He was promoted to second lieutenant on September 22, 1847. Between the Mexican War and the Civil War he was assigned to various posts on the frontier and in the eastern United States, including two years at the Fort Monroe Artillery School in Virginia. He was promoted to first lieutenant on March 16, 1852, and captain in the regular army on May 14, 1861.[1]

During the First Manassas Campaign Ayres commanded Battery E, Third Artillery, which was assigned to the brigade of Col. William T. Sherman. On July 21 during the fighting at Manassas Ayres' guns were placed on the north side of Bull Run near the Stone Bridge and later that day his battery helped cover the Union retreat from that field. His efficient handling of his guns during that disastrous first major battle of the war caught the attention of his superiors. On October 3, 1861, he was placed in command of the artillery assigned to Brig. Gen. William F. Smith's division. Smith commended Ayres for his performance during the early stages of the 1862 Peninsula Campaign. When Smith was given command of a Sixth Corps division on May 18, 1862, Ayres was assigned as artillery chief for Smith's division. Ayres earned the praise of his superiors for his conduct throughout the remainder of the Peninsula Campaign and during the fighting at Crampton's Gap and Antietam in September 1862. On November 16, 1862, his excellent performance on these battlefields was rewarded when he was placed in command of the artillery of the entire Sixth Corps. His performance during the Battle of Fredericksburg on December 13, 1862, earned him additional praise. His consistent fine performance on many battlefields, and the fact that he was a West Point graduate, earned him a nomination as brigadier general of volunteers on March 4, 1863. The Senate confirmed his nomination five days later and his commission ranked from November 29, 1862.[2]

Ayres was given command of an infantry brigade in the Fifth Corps on April 21, 1863, which he led at Chancellorsville the next month. On June 28, 1863, he was advanced to command of a Fifth Corps division, which he ably led at Gettysburg and throughout the remaining actions of 1863. He was brevetted major in the regular army on

July 2, 1863, for his performance at Gettysburg. With the reorganization of the Army of the Potomac in the spring of 1864, Ayres, based on seniority, was given command of a Fifth Corps brigade, which he led in the various engagements from The Wilderness through Cold Harbor. He was brevetted lieutenant colonel in the regular army on May 5, 1864, for his performance at The Wilderness. On June 6, 1864, he was given command of a Fifth Corps division, which he led through the end of the war. He was brevetted major general of volunteers on August 1, 1864, for his performance during the Overland Campaign and at Petersburg. On March 13, 1865, he was brevetted colonel, brigadier general, and major general in the regular army. It is unclear why he did not receive promotion to substantive major general of volunteers, because his combat record indicates that he deserved such a promotion.[3]

Ayres was mustered out of the volunteer service on April 30, 1866, but he remained in the regular army. On July 28, 1866, he was promoted to lieutenant colonel in the 28th Infantry. He was subsequently assigned to the 19th Infantry and then to the Third Artillery. He was promoted to colonel of the Second Artillery on July 18, 1879. He continued to serve at various posts until his death at Fort Hamilton, New York. Ayres was buried in Section 1 at Arlington National Cemetery. The inscription on his grave marker does not clearly indicate that Ayres was brevetted major general in both the regular army and the volunteers.[4]

ABSALOM BAIRD

Born: August 20, 1824
Died: June 14, 1905

General Baird was born in Washington, Pennsylvania. He attended Washington College in his native city and he graduated from West Point in 1849, ranked ninth out of 43. Before the Civil War he served in Florida in actions against the Seminoles, he spent several months in Europe on sick leave, he taught mathematics at West Point for six years, and he engaged in garrison duties in Texas. On April 1, 1850, he was promoted to second lieutenant and he was promoted to first lieutenant on December 24, 1853.[1]

During the First Manassas Campaign Baird served as assistant adjutant general on the staff of Col. Daniel Tyler. He was promoted to captain of staff in the regular army on August 3, 1861, and on November 12, 1861, he was promoted to major of staff in the regular army. In March 1862 he was assigned to the Fourth Corps in the Army of the Potomac as chief of staff and assistant inspector general. On April 12, 1862, he was given command of a brigade in the Army of the Ohio and five days later he was nominated brigadier general of volunteers. The Senate confirmed his nomination on April 28, 1862, and his commission ranked from April 28, 1862. Baird spent the rest of the war in the Western Theater, where he earned a reputation as an excellent brigade and division commander. He ably led his brigade until November 1862, when he was advanced to command of a division in the Army of Kentucky. In February 1863 he was given command of a division in the Department of the Cumberland and between June 8 and August 11, 1863, he commanded a division in the Army of the Cumberland's Reserve Corps.[2]

On August 23, 1863, Baird was placed in command of a 14th Corps division, which he ably led at Chickamauga the next month. His division was one of the units that held its position at Chickamauga on September 20, thereby preventing the destruction of the Army of the Cumberland. He was brevetted lieutenant colonel in the regular army on September 20, 1863, for his performance at Chickamauga. On October 10, 1863, Baird was given command of a different 14th Corps division, which he commanded for the remainder of the war. He proved to be a solid, dependable division commander in the Chattanooga and Atlanta Campaigns, during the March to the Sea, and in the Carolinas Campaign. He was brevetted colonel in the regular army on November 24, 1863, for his performance at

Chattanooga. On September 1, 1864, he was brevetted major general of volunteers for his performance at Resaca, Jonesboro, and Savannah. And on March 13, 1865, he was brevetted brigadier general and major general in the regular army. He was never appointed a substantive major general of volunteers, although his army commander, Maj. Gen. William S. Rosecrans, recommended that Baird receive such a promotion after his performance at Chickamauga. There is certainly nothing in the records to explain why he was never advanced to a substantive major general of volunteers.[3]

Baird was mustered out of the volunteer service on September 1, 1866, but he remained in the regular army. On June 13, 1867, he was promoted to lieutenant colonel and named assistant inspector general. He served in the latter capacity for various military departments until he was promoted to colonel and named army inspector general on March 11, 1885. On September 22, 1885, he was promoted to brigadier general. He continued to serve as army inspector general until his retirement on August 20, 1888, having reached the mandatory retirement age of sixty-four. In 1896 he was awarded the Medal of Honor for his conduct at Jonesboro, Georgia, on September 1, 1864, where he "voluntarily led a detached brigade in an assault upon the enemy's works." Baird died near Relay, Maryland and was buried in Section 1 at Arlington National Cemetery. The inscription on his grave marker correctly indicates that Baird was brevetted major general in the regular army, but there is no inscription concerning his service in the volunteers during the Civil War. Although there is no inscription concerning the Medal of Honor on his grave marker, the symbol of the Medal of Honor is located at the top of the front of his grave marker.[4]

JOSEPH JACKSON BARTLETT

Born: November 21, 1834
Died: January 14, 1893

General Bartlett was born in Binghamton, New York.[1] In 1858 he began to practice law in Elmira, New York, however, three years later his career was cut short with the beginning of the Civil War. He quickly enlisted in the 27th New York Infantry, which was raised in Elmira and was called "The Union Regiment." Soon Bartlett was elected captain and given command of a company in the regiment. On May 21, 1861, Henry W. Slocum was elected colonel of the regiment and Bartlett was elected major. During the Battle of First Manassas on July 21, 1861, Slocum was wounded in the right thigh and command of the regiment devolved on Bartlett. His regiment maintained good order at the end of that chaotic battle and the regiment helped cover the retreat of the Union army from that field. Three times during the retreat he had his men stop, form a line, and fire at the pursuing Confederates. In his after action report Bartlett's brigade commander, Col. Andrew Porter, commended Bartlett for "his enthusiasm and valor" which kept the regiment "in action and out of the panic." Slocum was promoted to brigadier general of volunteers in August 1861 and Bartlett was promoted to colonel of the regiment on September 21, 1861.[2]

On May 13, 1862, Bartlett was given command of a brigade in the Sixth Corps, which he ably led until November 1863. On September 14, 1862, he was appointed brigadier general of volunteers, but the Senate failed to act on his nomination before the current congressional session ended on March 4, 1863. By operation of law the appointment expired without confirmation and Bartlett reverted back to the grade of colonel of volunteers. On November 6, 1863, Bartlett was given command of a division in the Fifth Corps. He was renominated brigadier general of volunteers on December 31, 1863. The Senate confirmed his nomination on April 20, 1864, and his commission ranked from March 30, 1863. With the reorganization of the Army of the Potomac in the spring of 1864 Bartlett reverted, based on seniority, to command of a Fifth Corps brigade. From then to the end of the war he moved back and forth from command of his brigade to command of his division, based on seniority of the officers present. Bartlett was present at and participated conspicuously in every battle involving the Army of the Potomac, from

First Manassas to Appomattox, with two exceptions. Bartlett was not present at Fredericksburg, being away on sick leave, and Bartlett and the Sixth Corps were not present at Second Manassas. The inscription on Bartlett's grave marker incorrectly includes both of these battles. His superiors consistently commented on his command skills and leadership abilities.[3]

On August 1, 1864, Bartlett was brevetted major general of volunteers for his performance during the Richmond Campaign. He was never appointed a substantive major general of volunteers, possibly because he was not a West Point graduate or career soldier. But in recognition of his excellent war record he and his division were given the honor of representing the Union forces during the formal surrender ceremonies of the Army of Northern Virginia at Appomattox Courthouse on April 12, 1865. Bartlett was mustered out of the volunteer service on January 15, 1866. He served as United States minister to Norway and Sweden from 1867 to 1869. He then resumed his law practice, and later he served as a deputy pension commissioner. He died in Baltimore, Maryland and was buried in Section 2 at Arlington National Cemetery. The inscription on his grave marker does not clearly indicate that Bartlett attained the grades of brigadier general and brevet major general in the volunteers, and not in the regular army.[4]

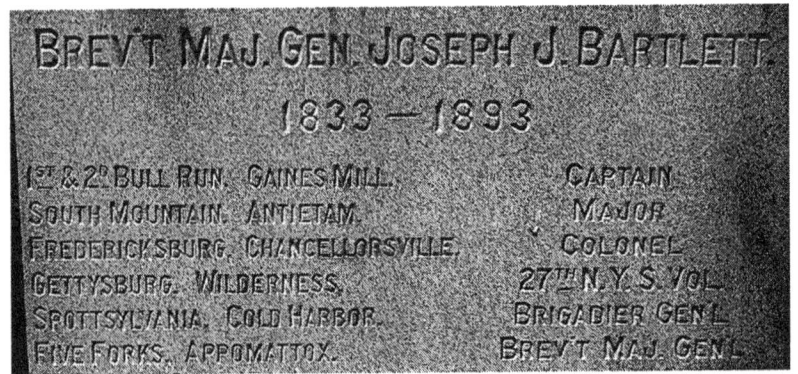

WILLIAM WORTH BELKNAP

Born: September 22, 1829
Died: October 13, 1890

General Belknap was born in Newburgh, New York. After attending Princeton University he studied law, briefly practiced law in Washington, D.C., and then in 1851 moved to Keokuk, Iowa, where he began a successful law practice. He was elected to one term in the Iowa legislature in 1857. Although he was a Democrat Belknap vigorously supported the Union war effort.[1]

On December 7, 1861, Belknap was named major of the 15th Iowa Infantry. He served in this regiment for the next two and a half years, being promoted to lieutenant colonel on August 20, 1862, and to colonel of the regiment on June 3, 1863. During the fighting at Shiloh on April 6, 1862, his horse was shot from under him and Belknap was slightly wounded, but he remained on the field and carried out his duties on foot. He earned a reputation as a brave and gallant officer, particularly for his actions at Corinth, Vicksburg, and Atlanta. On July 30, 1864, he was appointed brigadier general of volunteers. The next day he was given command of a 17th Corps brigade in the Army of the Tennessee, which he ably led for the remainder of the Atlanta Campaign, during the March to the Sea, and in the Carolinas Campaign. The Senate finally confirmed his nomination on February 14, 1865, and his commission as brigadier general of volunteers ranked from July 30, 1864. He was brevetted major general of volunteers on March 13, 1865, and was mustered out of the volunteer service on August 24, 1865.[2]

Belknap was one of the many Union generals with no previous military training or experience who proved to be a talented and capable officer. Unfortunately his post war career was marred with scandal and controversy. Soon after leaving the army he was appointed collector of internal revenue in Iowa. He held this position until his appointment as United States Secretary of War under President Ulysses S. Grant in 1869. In early 1876 he was accused of accepting thousands of dollars in bribes from a post trader at Fort Sill in return for immunity from removal. On March 2, 1876, Belknap resigned his Cabinet post. That same day the United States House of Representatives voted unanimously to impeach Belknap. A trial was held in the Senate, but Belknap was acquitted. Many senators believed they lacked jurisdiction because Belknap had already resigned his position, and so they voted for acquittal. Nevertheless, Belknap was presumed by many to be guilty and his reputation was now ruined.[3]

Belknap briefly lived in Philadelphia, and then he practiced law in Washington, D.C. He died in the latter city and was buried in Section 1 at Arlington National Cemetery. Fittingly, his comrades of the Army of the Tennessee's Iowa Brigade erected his impressive grave marker, for although his name is forever associated with the corruption of the Grant administration, Belknap should also be remembered as an able and gallant Civil War officer.[4]

LUTHER PRENTICE BRADLEY

Born: December 8, 1822
Died: March 13, 1910

General Bradley was born in New Haven, Connecticut. He served in the Connecticut militia, rising to the grade of captain, before he moved to Chicago, Illinois in 1855. There he worked as a bookkeeper and salesman, and he served in the Illinois militia, rising to the grade of lieutenant colonel. His many years of training in the militia would serve him well during the Civil War.[1]

On November 6, 1861, Bradley was named lieutenant colonel of the 51st Illinois Infantry. During the next year he served bravely with his regiment, seeing action at Island No. 10 and New Madrid. On October 15, 1862, he was promoted to colonel of his regiment. He commanded a 14th Corps brigade in the Army of the Cumberland during the Battle of Stones River (December 31, 1862 – January 3, 1863), suffering a minor injury to his foot during the fighting. From January 9 to September 28, 1863, he commanded a 20th Corps brigade. He was severely wounded in the right hip and right arm on September 19, 1863, on the first day of the Battle of Chickamauga. He was away from the army, recovering from his wounds, during the Chattanooga Campaign.[2]

By the summer of 1864 Bradley was finally able to return to the field. He was given command of a Fourth Corps brigade on June 27, 1864, which he led for the remainder of the Atlanta Campaign. On July 30, 1864, he was appointed brigadier general of volunteers. That autumn the Fourth Corps was sent to Tennessee to oppose the invasion of that state by the Army of Tennessee. On November 29, 1864, during fighting at Spring Hill, Tennessee, Bradley was severely wounded in the left shoulder. He was not present during the subsequent battles of Franklin and Nashville. The shoulder wound caused him considerable pain and eventually his left arm became useless. The Senate confirmed his nomination on February 14, 1865, and his commission as brigadier general of volunteers ranked from July 30, 1864. He sufficiently recovered from his wound to be able to serve as president of a court-martial from April to May 1865.[3]

On June 30, 1865, Bradley resigned from the volunteer service. He was named lieutenant colonel of the 27th Infantry on July 28, 1866. On March 2, 1867, he was brevetted colonel in the regular army for his performance at Chickamauga and brigadier general in the regular army for his performance at Resaca, Georgia. On March 20, 1879, he was promoted to colonel of the Third Infantry and on December 8, 1886, he retired, having reached the mandatory retirement age of sixty-four. Bradley moved to Tacoma, Washington. On April 23, 1904, he was placed on the retired list of the army as a brigadier general. He died in Tacoma six years later and was buried in Section 2 at Arlington National Cemetery. His grave site is marked by a slightly damaged government marker. The inscription on his grave marker correctly indicates that Bradley was placed on the retired list as a brigadier general in the regular army, but there is no inscription concerning his service in the volunteers during the Civil War.[4]

JOHN RUTTER BROOKE

Born: July 21, 1838
Died: September 5, 1926

General Brooke was born in Montgomery County, Pennsylvania. He was attending local schools when the Civil War began. He quickly joined the Fourth Pennsylvania Infantry, a three-month regiment, and on April 20, 1861, he was named a captain in the regiment. The regiment did not distinguish itself during the First Manassas Campaign. The day before the battle of July 21 the regiment marched away from the battlefield, its three-month enlistment having expired that day. Fortunately this incident did not adversely affect Brooke's reputation or subsequent career. On November 7, 1861, he was named colonel of the 53rd Pennsylvania Infantry.[1]

Brooke ably led his regiment during the 1862 Peninsula Campaign. He was wounded in the right hand on June 1, 1862, during the Battle of Fair Oaks, which resulted in the loss of the end of his right index finger. He commanded a Second Corps brigade from June 20 until October 6, 1862, leading the brigade in action at Antietam on September 17. He briefly returned to command of his own regiment, which he led during the Fredericksburg Campaign of December 1862. From December 29, 1862, until March 20, 1863, he commanded a Second Corps brigade. On April 13, 1863, he was given command of a different Second Corps brigade, which he ably led at Chancellorsville in May 1863 and at Gettysburg in July 1863. On July 2, 1863, a spent ball bruised his left ankle while his brigade was engaged in The Wheatfield at Gettysburg. From December 29, 1863, until March 26, 1864, he commanded a convalescent camp at Harrisburg, Pennsylvania.[2]

In late March 1864 Brooke returned to command of his Second Corps brigade, which he ably led during the early combat of the Overland Campaign. Finally his excellent combat record was rewarded when he was appointed brigadier general of volunteers. The Senate confirmed his nomination on May 13, 1864, and his commission ranked from May 12, 1864. He saw his last action less than a month later, for on June 3 during the bloody attacks at Cold Harbor Brooke was severely wounded and was carried from the field unconscious. He was brevetted major general of volunteers on August 1, 1864, for his performance at Totopotomoy Creek and Cold Harbor. After many months of recuperation he was assigned on April 2, 1865, to command of a division in the Shenandoah Valley, which he led through the end of the war.³

Brooke resigned from the volunteer service on February 1, 1866. He was named lieutenant colonel of the 37th Infantry on July 28, 1866. On March 2, 1867, he was brevetted colonel in the regular army for his performance at Gettysburg and brigadier general in the regular army for his performance at Spotsylvania. He was promoted to colonel of the 13th Infantry on March 20, 1879, to brigadier general on April 6, 1888, and to major general on May 22, 1897. During the Spanish-American War he first commanded a training camp at Chickamauga, Georgia and later he participated in the Puerto Rican Campaign. He served as military governor of Puerto Rico in 1898 and military governor of Cuba from 1898 to 1900. He retired from the army on July 21, 1902, having reached the mandatory retirement age of sixty-four. Brooke spent the last twenty-four years of his life in Philadelphia. When he died there in 1926 only one other substantive Union general, Adelbert Ames, survived him. Brooke was buried in Section 2 at Arlington National Cemetery. The inscription on his grave marker correctly indicates the highest substantive grade Brooke attained in the regular army, but there is no inscription concerning his service in the volunteers during the Civil War.⁴

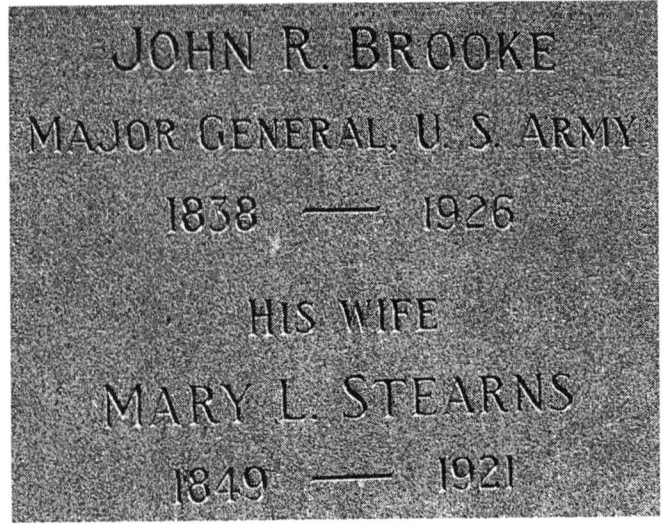

STEPHEN GANO BURBRIDGE

Born: August 19, 1831
Died: November 30, 1894

General Burbridge was born in Scott County, Kentucky. After attending Georgetown College (Kentucky) and Kentucky Military Institute he became a lawyer and a farmer. In the summer of 1861 he raised the 26th Kentucky (Union) Infantry and on August 27, 1861, he was named colonel of the regiment. He ably led the regiment during the second day of fighting at Shiloh on April 7, 1862. On May 3, 1862, he was nominated brigadier general of volunteers, presumably because, in part, the Lincoln Administration sought to reward and encourage loyalty by Kentuckians. The Senate confirmed his nomination on June 9, 1862, and his commission ranked from June 9, 1862.[1]

Between August 23 and October 16, 1862, Burbridge commanded a brigade in the Department of the Ohio and then he commanded a division in the Army of Kentucky from October 16 to November 13, 1862. He commanded a brigade that participated in the successful expedition against Arkansas Post in January 1863 and he commanded a 13th Corps brigade during the Vicksburg Campaign. From August 17 to December 5, 1863, he commanded at first a brigade and later a division in the Department of the Gulf.[2]

On February 15, 1864, Burbridge was placed in command of the District of Kentucky. His predecessor, Brig. Gen. Jeremiah Boyle, had alienated many citizens of that crucial border state with his unpopular civilian policies, but Burbridge managed, in one year, to make the citizens of Kentucky wish for the return of Boyle. Burbridge had vast civil and military authority, and he used those powers harshly. He arrested anyone suspected of disloyalty, including many people who merely opposed the reelection of Abraham Lincoln. He also created a system whereby Kentucky farmers were required to sell their goods to the Federal government at prices below market prices in nearby Cincinnati, Ohio. And he expanded Boyle's unpopular policy regarding guerilla raids by creating a system of reprisals against civilians for guerilla activities in their area. Finally the furor over his policies was so great that on February 22, 1865, he was relieved of his command.[3]

Burbridge was involved in several military actions during his tenure in Kentucky. In early June 1864 Confederate cavalry, under the command of Brig. Gen. John Hunt

Morgan, invaded Kentucky. Burbridge personally led the Union forces that defeated Morgan's raiders in fighting at Mount Sterling and Cynthiana, thereby ending the raid. On July 4, 1864, Burbridge was brevetted major general of volunteers for his repulse of Morgan's raid. In early October 1864 Burbridge led a raid against the valuable Confederate salt mining operations at Saltville, in southwestern Virginia. His attacks were repulsed, and when he withdrew back to Kentucky, Burbridge left behind hundreds of wounded Federal soldiers. The victorious Confederates massacred about one hundred wounded black soldiers left on the field. In December 1864 Burbridge participated in (but did not command) another raid against Saltville and this time the salt works were captured and destroyed.[4]

On December 1, 1865, Burbridge resigned his commission in the volunteers. When he returned home to Kentucky he soon discovered that his harsh policies while in command in Kentucky had made him a pariah in his home state. He and his family moved to Brooklyn, New York, where he died many years later. He was buried in Section 1 at Arlington National Cemetery. The inscription on his grave marker does not indicate that Burbridge only attained the grade of major general of volunteers by brevet.[5]

WILLIAM WALLACE BURNS

Born: September 3, 1825
Died: April 19, 1892

General Burns was born in Coshocton, Ohio. He graduated from West Point in 1847, ranked 28th out of 38. Immediately after graduation he was assigned to recruiting duties and was promoted to second lieutenant on September 8, 1847. After the Mexican War he performed the usual garrison duties at posts on the frontier. He was promoted to first lieutenant on August 12, 1850, and he served as regimental quartermaster from November 1, 1856, to August 18, 1858. On November 3, 1858, he was promoted to captain of staff and named assistant commissary of subsistence. At the start of the Civil War he was named chief commissary for the Department of the Ohio and on August 3, 1861, he was promoted to major of staff in the regular army.[1]

On September 28, 1861, Burns was appointed brigadier general of volunteers. From October 22, 1861, to March 13, 1862, he commanded two different brigades in the Army of the Potomac while the army was stationed at Washington, D.C. On March 13, 1862, he was given command of a Second Corps brigade, which he led during the 1862 Peninsula Campaign. The Senate finally confirmed his nomination on April 10, 1862, and his commission as brigadier general of volunteers ranked from September 28, 1861. He received a wound in his right cheek on June 29, 1862, during fighting at Savage's Station. Despite the wound, he remained in command of his brigade, leading it in the repulse of an enemy attack. The next day, during fighting at Glendale, he was thrown from his horse when it jumped a ditch. Burns suffered injuries to his back and neck as a result of the fall, and the wound in his cheek was slow to heal. He spent the next several months in a hospital in Philadelphia. Burns himself stated that he "was prostrated with my wound, malaria, and twenty-eight days of constant strain." He also suffered from rheumatism. He was brevetted lieutenant colonel in the regular army on June 29, 1862, for his performance at Savage's Station and colonel in the regular army on June 30, 1862, for his performance at Glendale. Burns was able to return to his brigade at Harpers Ferry in October 1862. He was given command of a Ninth Corps division on November 12, 1862, which he led during the Fredericksburg Campaign, although his division was held in reserve during the battle itself.[2]

On March 20, 1863, Burns resigned his commission in the volunteers and reverted to his regular army grade of major of staff in the Commissary of Subsistence. Some sources state that Burns took this action because he preferred his staff duties in the Commissary of Subsistence to his duties in field command. It is also likely that the effects of his wound, rheumatism, and his bout with malaria made staff work preferable to field command. He served as chief commissary in the Department of the Northwest from September 1863 through the end of the war. He was brevetted brigadier general in the regular army on March 13, 1865.[3]

After the war Burns remained in the army, serving as chief commissary for various military departments. He was promoted to lieutenant colonel of staff on June 23, 1874, and colonel on November 9, 1884. He retired on September 3, 1889, having reached the mandatory retirement age of sixty-four. In his last years he suffered from rheumatism, a constant cold feeling, and pains in his neck and back. The latter symptoms were most likely related to his fall at Glendale. He died at Beaufort, South Carolina and was buried in Section 2 at Arlington National Cemetery. His grave site is marked with a simple government marker.[4]

CYRUS BUSSEY

Born: October 5, 1833
Died: March 2, 1915

General Bussey was born in Hubbard, Ohio. His family moved to Indiana in 1837. By the time he was fourteen he was working as a clerk in a dry goods store and two years later he opened his own dry goods store in Dupont, Indiana. He moved to Bloomfield, Iowa in 1855 and in 1858 he was elected to the Iowa Senate. He was a delegate at the 1860 Democratic National Convention, where he supported the nomination of Stephen A. Douglas for president. At the beginning of the Civil War Samuel J. Kirkwood, Iowa's governor, appointed Bussey a lieutenant colonel in the state militia, with command of the state militia in the southeastern part of the state. It is uncertain if Bussey had any prior experience with the militia, although Governor Kirkwood's actions seem to indicate that he might have.[1]

On August 10, 1861, Bussey was named colonel of the Third Iowa Infantry and on September 5, 1861, he was named colonel of the Third Iowa Cavalry. During the Battle of Pea Ridge on March 7 – 8, 1862, he ably commanded his own regiment, plus portions of three other cavalry regiments and half of a battery. After the battle the lieutenant colonel of the Third Iowa Cavalry accused Bussey of running from the field and abandoning his command during the battle. The enlisted men of the regiment were so incensed by this bogus accusation that they purchased and gave Bussey a presentation sword inscribed "Pea Ridge."[2]

Bussey commanded a brigade of cavalry in the Department of the Missouri from November 2, 1862, until January 21, 1863. He commanded a 13th Corps cavalry brigade from January 31 to April 3, 1863. During the Vicksburg Campaign he commanded at first a 13th Corps cavalry division and later two different 13th Corps cavalry brigades. Immediately after the surrender of Vicksburg he commanded the cavalry accompanying Maj. Gen. William T. Sherman's expedition against Jackson, Mississippi. In November 1863 Bussey was sent to Arkansas, where, for the remainder of the war, he commanded at various times a brigade and a division of cavalry, and a brigade and division of infantry. On January 5, 1864, he was nominated brigadier general of volunteers. The Senate confirmed his nomination on April 7, 1864, and his commission ranked from January 5, 1864. On March 13, 1865, he was brevetted major general of volunteers.[3]

Bussey was mustered out of the volunteer service on August 24, 1865. He worked as a merchant, first in St. Louis, then in New Orleans, and finally in New York City. He served as president of the New Orleans Chamber of Commerce for six years and he was instrumental in the building of the jetty system that protected the mouth of the Mississippi River. After the war Bussey became a Republican and he was a delegate to the Republican National Conventions in 1868 and 1884. He served as the assistant Secretary of the Interior from 1889 to 1893 during the Benjamin Harrison administration. In the latter position he was involved in generously awarding pensions to many Union veterans of the Civil War. He practiced law in Washington, D.C. from 1893 until his death there twenty-two years later. He was buried in Section 3 at Arlington National Cemetery.[4]

WILLIAM THOMAS CLARK

Born: June 29, 1831
Died: October 12, 1905

General Clark was born in Norwalk, Connecticut. In 1854 he began to practice law in New York and two years later he moved to Davenport, Iowa, where he again practiced law. In the summer of 1861 he helped recruit the 13th Iowa Infantry. On November 2, 1861, he was named first lieutenant of the regiment. He was promoted to captain and assistant adjutant general on March 6, 1862. From that time until almost the end of the war Clark ably served in staff positions rather than in field command. He was promoted to major on November 24, 1862, and lieutenant colonel on February 10, 1863.[1]

In July 1863 Clark was named assistant adjutant general for the 13th Corps and in January 1864 he was named assistant adjutant general for the Army of the Tennessee. In both of these assignments he proved to be an efficient aide to his commander, Maj. Gen. James B. McPherson. Clark was brevetted brigadier general of volunteers on July 22, 1864, for his performance in the Atlanta Campaign. On January 26, 1865, he was given command of a 15th Corps brigade, which he led through the end of the war. His valuable services during the war were not rewarded until May 31, 1865, when he was appointed a substantive brigadier general of volunteers.[2]

On August 1, 1865, Clark was given command of a 25th Corps division, which was assigned to the Department of Texas. While stationed there he recommended that the United States purchase Matamoros in order to stop the scheming of Maximilian in Mexico. Although both Ulysses S. Grant and William T. Sherman endorsed the proposal, the powers that be in Washington rejected the idea. Clark was brevetted major general of volunteers on November 24, 1865, and he commanded his division until January 8, 1866. He was mustered out of the volunteer service on February 1, 1866. The Senate finally confirmed his nomination on February 23, 1866, and his commission as a substantive brigadier general of volunteers ranked from May 31, 1865.[3]

Clark had served his country well during the war, but unfortunately his post war activities tarnished his reputation. Clark decided to remain in Texas, where he basically functioned as a carpetbagger during Reconstruction. He helped organize a national bank in Galveston and in 1869 he was elected to the United States House of Representatives, largely with the backing of the black voters in Galveston. Clark advocated the sale of west Texas lands, which would benefit railroads that Clark had an interest in. He was defeated in his bid for reelection in 1871, but the Republican governor of Texas certified Clark as the winner after the governor threw out thousands of votes for Clark's Democratic opponent. This farce was soon ended when, by unanimous vote, Clark was expelled from the House of Representatives on May 13, 1872. He soon landed on his feet, though, obtaining a position at the Bureau of Internal Revenue. He worked for the Bureau until his death in New York City thirty-three years later. He was buried in Section 3 at Arlington National Cemetery. The inscription on his grave marker implies that Clark was brevetted major general in the regular army, whereas he was never in the regular army and was brevetted major general of volunteers.[4]

POWELL CLAYTON

Born: August 7, 1833
Died: August 25, 1914

General Clayton was born in Delaware County, Pennsylvania. He attended a military academy in Bristol, Pennsylvania and an engineering school in Wilmington, Delaware. In 1855 he moved to Leavenworth, Kansas where he worked as a civil engineer. He became the city engineer for Leavenworth in 1859. On April 29, 1861, he was named captain in command of a company of Kansas militia at Fort Leavenworth. Exactly one month later he was named captain of the Leavenworth Light Infantry, which became a part of the First Kansas Infantry. He and his regiment saw action at the Battle of Wilson's Creek on August 10, 1861. On December 28, 1861, he was promoted to lieutenant colonel of the Fifth Kansas Cavalry and he became the regiment's colonel on March 7, 1862. During the next year the regiment was mainly engaged in garrison duties in Kansas, Missouri, and Arkansas.[1]

In April 1863 Clayton was given command of a cavalry brigade in the District of East Arkansas and from August 19, 1863, to January 6, 1864, he commanded a cavalry brigade in the Army of Arkansas. From April 1864 until May 1865 he commanded the post at Pine Bluff, Arkansas. On August 1, 1864, he was appointed brigadier general of volunteers. In October 1864 he led the forces that repulsed an attack against Pine Bluff. The Senate confirmed his nomination on February 23, 1865, and his commission as brigadier general of volunteers ranked from August 1, 1864. He was mustered out of the volunteer service on August 24, 1865.[2]

After the war Clayton remained in Arkansas, where he purchased a cotton plantation near Pine Bluff and got deeply involved in Reconstruction politics. He was elected governor of Arkansas in 1868. Unfortunately his term in office was marked with corruption and carpetbag politics. He spent $300,000 for a Negro militia, to be employed in combating the Ku Klux Klan. He supported a $10 million increase in the state's bonded debt. In 1871, after he had been elected United States Senator, he paid the Arkansas Secretary of State $30,000 to resign, so that Clayton could appoint to that post the lieutenant governor (whom Clayton did not want to succeed him as governor). In 1876, amid numerous charges of corruption and election fraud, he was defeated in his bid for reelection to the Senate.[3]

The remainder of Clayton's post war activities was remarkably free of taint and scandal. He moved to Eureka Springs, Arkansas, where he was president of The Eureka Springs Railroad. He served as United States Ambassador to Mexico from 1897 until 1905. In 1912 he moved to Washington, D.C., where he died two years later. He was buried in Section 3 at Arlington National Cemetery.[4]

THOMAS TURPIN CRITTENDEN

Born: October 16, 1825
Died: September 5, 1905

General Crittenden was born in Huntsville, Alabama. When he was very young his family moved to Texas. Shortly thereafter his father, who was a brother of Senator John J. Crittenden, died and his mother raised the family near Galveston. Thomas studied law at Transylvania University in Lexington, Kentucky and afterwards began to practice law in Hannibal, Missouri. During the Mexican War he served as a second lieutenant in the Missouri volunteers from August 3, 1846, until he was mustered out of the army on September 28, 1847. After the war he moved to Madison, Indiana, where he again practiced law.[1]

On April 19, 1861, Crittenden was named captain in the Sixth Indiana Infantry and eight days later he was named colonel of this three-month regiment. He led the regiment during the (West) Virginia Campaign of the summer of 1861, seeing action at the small battles of Philippi on June 3 and Carrick's Ford on July 13. The regiment was mustered out on August 2, 1861, but a month later it reenlisted (as the Sixth Indiana Infantry) for three years. Crittenden was named colonel of the regiment on September 20, 1861. The regiment was sent to Kentucky where it spent the winter of 1861 – 1862, having been assigned to the Army of the Ohio. On March 27, 1862, he was nominated brigadier general of volunteers. He led his regiment at the Battle of Shiloh, where it was engaged on April 7, 1862. The Senate confirmed his nomination on April 28, 1862, and his commission as brigadier general of volunteers ranked from April 28, 1862.[2]

Up to this point in the war Crittenden had built a good record for himself, but that would all change with his next assignment. On July 8, 1862, he was directed to take command of the post at Murfreesboro, Tennessee. He arrived there on July 11 and took command of the post the next day. On July 13 his post was attacked without warning by enemy forces commanded by Col. Nathan B. Forrest. Crittenden and most of his command were captured. In August 1862 Crittenden was exchanged. His commander, Maj. Gen. Don Carlos Buell, referred to the surrender as "a most disgraceful affair" and he stated that it was an example of "neglect of duty and lack of good conduct." With such strong condemnations being placed in the official records, it is not surprising that

Crittenden requested that a court of inquiry be convened "to investigate and give an opinion" concerning this episode. The court convened on December 17, 1862, and a month later, on January 24, 1863, the court issued its findings. The court concluded that Crittenden "did all that should be expected of a vigilant commander from the time he took command until the surrender. We find no evidence that impugns his skill or courage." The court placed great weight on the fact that Crittenden "was an entire stranger" to his post and that he had been assured by his predecessor in command at Murfreesboro "that there was no danger of an attack and that no enemy of importance was nearer than Chattanooga." A review of the record supports the court's findings, particularly in light of the fact that Crittenden had only been present at Murfreesboro one day before his command was surprised and captured. Vindicated by the court of inquiry, Crittenden was given command of a brigade in the 20th Corps on March 9, 1863. Two months later, on May 5, 1863, he resigned from the army. There is no indication in the record as to why he resigned, although the stigma of the episode at Murfreesboro was most likely the reason.[3]

After his resignation from the army Crittenden resumed his law practice. He moved to Washington, D.C. in 1868. When he retired as a lawyer in 1885 he moved to San Diego, California, where he worked as a real estate agent and developer. He died in the Hawthorne Inn in East Gloucester, Massachusetts while on vacation. He was originally buried at Rock Creek Cemetery in Washington, D.C., however, in 1931 his remains were reinterred in Section 7 at Arlington National Cemetery. He was a first cousin of both Union Maj. Gen. Thomas Leonidas Crittenden and Confederate Maj. Gen. George Bibb Crittenden.[4]

GEORGE CROOK

Born: September 8, 1828
Died: March 21, 1890

General Crook was born in or near Dayton, Ohio.[1] He graduated from West Point in 1852, ranked 38th out of 43. He served on garrison duty at various posts in California and the Pacific Northwest until the start of the Civil War. He was promoted to second lieutenant on July 7, 1853, and first lieutenant on March 11, 1856. On June 10, 1857, at Pit River Canyon, California, he was wounded in the right hip by an arrow during a skirmish with hostile Indians. He managed to pull out the shaft, but the arrowhead remained in his hip for the remainder of his life. He was promoted to captain in the regular army on May 14, 1861.[2]

On September 13, 1861, Crook was named colonel of the 36th Ohio Infantry, which was sent to (West) Virginia. He was given command of a brigade in the Mountain Department on March 11, 1862, and during fighting at Lewisburg, (West) Virginia on May 23, 1862, he was slightly wounded in the foot by a spent ball. He was brevetted major in the regular army on May 23, 1862, for his performance at Lewisburg. On September 7, 1862, he was appointed brigadier general of volunteers. He commanded a Ninth Corps brigade during the fighting at South Mountain and Antietam later in September. He was brevetted lieutenant colonel in the regular army on September 17, 1862, for his performance at Antietam.[3]

In early 1863 Crook was sent to the Western Theater of the war. From February to July 1863 he commanded two different infantry brigades in the Army of the Cumberland. The Senate confirmed his nomination on March 11, 1863, and his commission as brigadier general of volunteers ranked from September 7, 1862. Between July 29, 1863, and February 3, 1864, he commanded a division of cavalry in the Army of the Cumberland. He ably led his cavalry division during the Chickamauga Campaign in September 1863. He was brevetted colonel in the regular army on October 7, 1863, for his performance at Farmington, Tennessee, where his command defeated Confederate cavalry. In February 1864 he was sent back east to take command of an infantry division in the Department of Western Virginia. On May 9, 1864, he led the Union forces that defeated the Confederates at Cloyd's Mountain, Virginia. He was brevetted major general of volunteers on July 18,

1864. From July 25, 1864, until March 22, 1865, he commanded the Department of Western Virginia and from August 8 to December 19, 1864, he commanded the Army of West Virginia. He participated in the successful 1864 Shenandoah Valley Campaign, where his Army of West Virginia served as a corps under Maj. Gen. Philip Sheridan in the fighting at Winchester, Fisher's Hill, and Cedar Creek. On October 21, 1864, he was appointed major general of volunteers. The Senate confirmed his nomination on February 14, 1865, and his commission ranked from October 21, 1864.[4]

On February 21, 1865, Crook and Brig. Gen. Benjamin F. Kelley were captured during a daring raid on Union headquarters in Cumberland, Maryland. Crook was exchanged on March 20, 1865. Despite this embarrassing episode, on March 13, 1865, Crook was brevetted brigadier general and major general in the regular army. From March 27, 1865, through the end of the war he commanded a cavalry division in the Army of the Potomac. He was mustered out of the volunteer service on January 15, 1866, but he remained in the regular army for the remainder of his life. On July 18, 1866, he was promoted to major and ten days later he was promoted to lieutenant colonel. During the next twenty-four years he earned a reputation as one of the most successful Indian fighters in the army. He was promoted to brigadier general on October 29, 1873, and major general on April 6, 1888. He commanded the Division of the Missouri from 1888 until his death in Chicago two years later. He was buried in Section 2 at Arlington National Cemetery. The inscription on his grave marker correctly indicates the highest substantive grade Crook attained in the regular army, but there is no inscription concerning his service in the volunteers during the Civil War.[5]

JOHN WYNN DAVIDSON

Born: August 18, 1824
Died: June 26, 1881

General Davidson was born in Fairfax County, Virginia. It is not surprising that he pursued a military career, considering that a grandfather had been an officer in the American Revolution and his father had graduated from West Point in 1815. John graduated from West Point in 1845, ranked 27th out of 41. For the next sixteen years he served in the First Dragoons. He was promoted to second lieutenant on April 21, 1846. He participated in the Mexican War, serving in California in the Army of the West, and was promoted to first lieutenant on January 8, 1848. After the war he served on the western frontier, where he was involved in numerous engagements with hostile Indians. He served as regimental quartermaster in December 1850 and as regimental adjutant from January 1 to September 30, 1851. On March 30, 1854, he was wounded during a fight with Apaches in New Mexico Territory. He was promoted to captain on January 20, 1855, and at the beginning of the Civil War he was stationed at Fort Tejon near Los Angeles, California.[1]

It is believed that in the early days of the war Davidson was offered a commission in the Confederate army, based on the fact that he was a Virginia native, but that he declined the offer. After making his way back east he was given command of a brigade in the Washington, D.C. defenses on October 26, 1861. He was promoted to major in the regular army on November 14, 1861. On January 14, 1862, he was nominated brigadier general of volunteers. The Senate confirmed his nomination on February 3, 1862, and his commission ranked from February 3, 1862. Between March 13 and May 18, 1862, he commanded a Fourth Corps brigade and from the latter date to July 1862 he commanded a Sixth Corps brigade. He ably led his brigades in several engagements during the Peninsula Campaign. He was brevetted lieutenant colonel in the regular army on June 27, 1862, for his performance at Gaines' Mill, and colonel in the regular army on June 28, 1862, for his performance at Golding's Farm. Unfortunately he suffered sunstroke during this campaign, and for the remainder of his life he would be susceptible to sunstroke whenever he was exposed to hot weather.[2]

In the summer of 1862 Davidson was sent to the Western Theater of the war, where he served for the remainder of the war. He commanded the District of St. Louis from August 6, 1862, to June 16, 1863, and the District of Southeast Missouri from June 16 to July 20, 1863. Between June 1863 and February 13, 1864, he commanded several different cavalry divisions in Missouri and Arkansas. On February 15, 1864, he was given command of the cavalry depot in St. Louis. From January 3 to June 3, 1865, he commanded the District of Natchez. On March 13, 1865, he was brevetted brigadier general and major general in the regular army, as well as major general of volunteers.[3]

Davidson was mustered out of the volunteer service on January 15, 1866, but he remained in the regular army until his death fifteen years later. He was promoted to lieutenant colonel of the Tenth Cavalry on December 1, 1866. He served for a while in the inspector general's department. Between 1868 and 1871 he was a professor of military science and tactics at Kansas Agricultural College. Afterward he served on the frontier, where he continued to have problems with sunstroke as well as malaria, and on March 20, 1879, he was promoted to colonel of the Second Cavalry. On February 7, 1881, he was severely injured while in command at Fort Custer, Montana, when his horse slipped on ice and fell down a twenty-foot embankment. Davidson suffered two broken ribs and internal injuries from the fall and from being struck by the saddle. He died four months later while on sick leave in St. Paul, Minnesota. He was buried in Section 2 at Arlington National Cemetery.[4]

FREDERICK TRACY DENT

Born: December 17, 1820
Died: December 23, 1892

General Dent was born on a farm near St. Louis, Missouri. He graduated from West Point in 1843, ranked 33rd out of 39. Dent was a friend and classmate of Ulysses S. Grant, who later married Dent's sister Julia. Before the Mexican War Dent engaged in routine garrison duties on the frontier and was promoted to second lieutenant on March 30, 1846. During the Mexican War he performed bravely in several battles, being brevetted first lieutenant on August 20, 1847, for his performance at both Contreras and Churubusco and captain on September 8, 1847, for his performance at Molino del Rey. During the latter battle he was severely wounded. He was promoted to first lieutenant on September 11, 1847. After the war he continued to serve on the western frontier and was promoted to captain on March 3, 1855.[1]

When the Civil War began Dent was stationed with the Ninth Infantry at San Francisco. He remained at that post until he was promoted to major in the regular army on March 9, 1863, and ordered to report for duty at New York City. There he briefly commanded four companies of the Fourth Infantry as they helped enforce the conscription laws and he served on a military commission to try prisoners of state. In early March 1864 Dent's brother-in-law, Ulysses S. Grant, was promoted to lieutenant general and made general-in-chief of the Union army. On March 29, 1864, Dent was promoted to lieutenant colonel of staff in the regular army and was assigned to Grant's staff as an aide-de-camp, in which capacity he ably served throughout the 1864 – 1865 campaigns in Virginia. He was brevetted lieutenant colonel in the regular army on May 7, 1864, for his performance at The Wilderness and colonel in the regular army on July 30, 1864, for his performance at Petersburg. He was brevetted colonel of volunteers on February 24, 1865, and brigadier general in the regular army on March 13, 1865. On April 5, 1865, he was appointed a substantive brigadier general of volunteers. It is likely that this appointment was primarily the result of the fact that Dent was Grant's brother-in-law, for although he had ably served on Grant's staff during the previous year, his limited involvement in the war did not justify such an appointment.[2]

After the surrender of the Army of Northern Virginia Dent briefly served as military governor of Richmond, Virginia, and then he commanded the garrison in the defenses at Washington, D.C. The Senate confirmed his nomination on February 23, 1866, and his commission as a substantive brigadier general of volunteers ranked from April 5, 1865. He was mustered out of the volunteer service on April 30, 1866, but he remained in the regular army. He was promoted to lieutenant colonel of staff on May 3, 1866, and colonel of staff on July 25, 1866. He continued to serve as an aide-de-camp to Grant until the latter became president on March 4, 1869, and then as an aide-de-camp to Grant's successor as army commander, Gen. William T. Sherman. In 1873 Dent was placed in command of Fort Trumbull, Connecticut. He was promoted to colonel of the First Artillery on January 2, 1881. He was compelled to retire from the army on December 1, 1883, because of complications from a stroke he had previously suffered. He lived in Washington, D.C. for five years, and then in 1888 he moved to Denver, Colorado, where a son was practicing law. He died in Denver four years later and was buried in Section 2 at Arlington National Cemetery. The inscription on his grave marker correctly indicates the highest substantive grade Dent attained in the regular army, but there is no inscription concerning his service in the volunteers during the Civil War.[3]

ABNER DOUBLEDAY

Born: June 26, 1819
Died: January 26, 1893

General Doubleday was born in Ballston Spa, New York. He graduated from West Point in 1842, ranked 24th out of 56. Assigned to the artillery, he performed routine garrison duties on the frontier before the Mexican War and was promoted to second lieutenant on February 24, 1845. He saw action during that war and was promoted to first lieutenant on March 3, 1847. After the war he again served at various posts in Texas, Florida, and on the eastern seaboard. He was promoted to captain on March 3, 1855. He was stationed at Fort Sumter in Charleston harbor in April 1861 and it is believed that he fired the first artillery shot in defense of the fort when Confederate forces fired on the fort.[1]

On May 14, 1861, Doubleday was promoted to major in the regular army. He commanded the artillery in the Department of Pennsylvania from June 18 to July 19, 1861, and the artillery in the Department of the Shenandoah from the latter date to August 17, 1861. From that date until March 1862 he commanded the artillery in a division in the Army of the Potomac. On January 17, 1862, he was nominated brigadier general of volunteers. The Senate confirmed his nomination on February 3, 1862, and his commission ranked from February 3, 1862. Between March and May 1862 he commanded that part of the defenses at Washington, D.C. located north of the Potomac River. He commanded a brigade in the Army of Virginia from June 26 to August 30, 1862, and then a division in that army from August 30 to September 12, 1862. He ably led his commands during the Second Manassas Campaign. With the reorganization of the Union forces after Second Manassas, Doubleday was given command of a First Corps division in the Army of the Potomac, which he led during the fighting at South Mountain and Antietam in September 1862. At the latter battle he was injured from a fall resulting from a shell exploding near his horse. He was brevetted lieutenant colonel in the regular army on September 17, 1862, for his performance at Antietam. His division saw limited combat during the Fredericksburg Campaign of December 1862.[2]

Doubleday was given command of a different First Corps division on January 18, 1863. Eight days later he was nominated major general of volunteers. The Senate confirmed his nomination on March 9, 1863, and his commission ranked from November

29, 1862. He led his division during the Chancellorsville Campaign of April - May 1863, although it saw limited combat. On the morning of July 1, 1863, during the first day's fighting at Gettysburg, his corps commander, Maj. Gen. John F. Reynolds, was killed and command of the corps devolved on Doubleday as the senior officer in the First Corps. Despite the fact that Doubleday ably commanded the corps that day, Maj. Gen. George G. Meade, the army commander, questioned Doubleday's command abilities. That night Meade decided to assign command of the corps to Maj. Gen. John Newton, a division commander in the Sixth Corps. Doubleday reverted to command of his division for the remainder of the battle. He was brevetted colonel in the regular army on July 2, 1863, for his performance at Gettysburg. He was promoted to lieutenant colonel in the regular army on September 20, 1863.[3]

The Gettysburg Campaign marked the last time Doubleday commanded troops in the field during the war. He spent the remainder of the war in Washington, D.C., assigned to administrative duties and military commissions, except in July 1864 when he briefly commanded a portion of the Washington, D.C. defenses when an enemy force threatened the nation's capital. He was brevetted brigadier general and major general in the regular army on March 13, 1865, and he was mustered out of the volunteer service on August 24, 1865. He remained in the regular army, being promoted to colonel of the 35th Infantry on September 15, 1867. He retired on December 11, 1873, and lived in San Francisco, where he created the first cable car company in the United States. Later he moved to New Jersey, where he lived until his death in Mendham, New Jersey. He was buried in Section 1 at Arlington National Cemetery. It is a myth that he invented the game of baseball.[4]

ALEXANDER BRYDIE DYER

Born: January 10, 1815
Died: May 20, 1874

General Dyer was born in Richmond, Virginia. He graduated from West Point in 1837, ranked sixth out of 50. He was sent as a second lieutenant in the Third Artillery to Florida, where he saw action during the Second Seminole War. On July 9, 1838, he was assigned to the ordnance department. During the Mexican War he was chief of ordnance for the American forces operating in New Mexico Territory. He actually was involved in some combat in that region and was wounded during fighting at Canada, New Mexico Territory on February 4, 1847. He was promoted to first lieutenant on March 3, 1847, and was brevetted captain on March 16, 1848, for his performance at Santa Cruz de Rosales. He remained in the ordnance department between the Mexican War and the Civil War. On March 3, 1853, he was promoted to captain.[1]

In August 1861 Dyer was placed in charge of the Springfield Arsenal in Massachusetts. Under his administration the arsenal soon quadrupled its production of rifles. In January 1862 he was offered the position of chief of ordnance, but he declined out of respect for the current chief, Brig. Gen. James W. Ripley. On March 3, 1863, Dyer was promoted to major in the regular army. Finally in September 1863 Ripley retired, but the position of chief of ordnance went to Brig. Gen. George D. Ramsay instead of Dyer. A year later, on September 12, 1864, Ramsay retired and the next day Dyer was appointed brigadier general in the regular army and named chief of ordnance. The Senate confirmed his nomination on February 23, 1865, and his commission ranked from September 12, 1864. Dyer competently administered the ordnance department for the remainder of the war. He also aided the Union cause with his invention of the twenty-four pounder "Dyer Shell" or "Dyer Projectile," which was a reliable artillery shell for rifled ordnance. He was brevetted major general in the regular army on March 13, 1865.[2]

After the war Dyer remained chief of ordnance. Through the years some people objected to the way he managed the department, particularly some inventors who believed they were ignored by Dyer and some contractors who did not win contracts with the department. Many of these people complained about Dyer to their local Congressmen, which resulted in pressure being put on Dyer to change the way he ran the department.

Finally he requested that a court of inquiry look into his administration of the ordnance department. The court approved of his administration of the department and his handling of inventors and contracts. Although he started to experience health problems in 1869, he remained as chief of ordnance until his death five years later in the hospital at the Washington Arsenal in Washington, D.C. He was buried in Section 1 at Arlington National Cemetery. For thirty-seven years he had served his country well, behind the scenes in the often overlooked but vitally important ordnance department. He proved to be one of the unsung heroes of the Union cause in the war. As a native Virginian, he chose to remain loyal to the Union. And he greatly assisted the nation's ability to fight and win the Civil War through his commendable management of the Springfield Arsenal and his able administration of the ordnance department.[3]

JOHN EDWARDS

Born: October 24, 1815
Died: April 8, 1894

General Edwards was born in Louisville, Kentucky. He practiced law in Indiana. Like so many others of his time he moved to California in 1849 during the gold rush. After working as a justice of the peace for several years in California, he moved back to Indiana, where he served in both houses of the state legislature. Later he moved to Iowa, where he was a member of the Iowa constitutional convention. After Iowa was admitted to the Union in 1846 he served in the Iowa legislature and was speaker from 1858 to 1860. He also founded and edited a newspaper, *The Patriot*.[1]

On May 21, 1861, Edwards was named lieutenant colonel and aide-de-camp on the staff of Iowa governor Samuel J. Kirkwood. There is nothing in the records to indicate that Edwards had any prior involvement in the state militia, so it assumed that his assignment to the governor's staff as an officer was based solely on his political influence and stature in Iowa. Edwards was mustered into the Federal service as colonel of the 18th Iowa Infantry on August 8, 1862. The regiment was sent to southwest Missouri, where it spent the next year performing routine garrison duties in and near Springfield, Missouri. In October 1863 Edwards and his regiment were sent to Fort Smith, Arkansas, where they again were mainly engaged in garrison duties. Beginning in December 1863 Edwards commanded several different brigades in the District of the Frontier. He ably led his brigade during several engagements in Arkansas in the spring of 1864. On September 26, 1864, he was appointed brigadier general of volunteers. He briefly commanded a division in the Department of Arkansas from December 3, 1864, to January 5, 1865, and then he reverted back to command of a brigade in that department. The Senate confirmed his nomination on February 14, 1865, and his commission as brigadier general of volunteers ranked from September 26, 1864. He was mustered out of the volunteer service on January 15, 1866, without a brevet of major general of volunteers, probably because he had been involved in little combat during the war.[2]

Later in 1866 Edwards was named assessor of internal revenue at Fort Smith, Arkansas, where he had taken up residence. He ran for a seat in the United States House of Representatives in 1870 as a Liberal Republican against the moderate incumbent, Thomas

Boles, who was a native of Arkansas and a former Confederate officer. The results of the election were uncertain, but Edwards contended that he had won, he presented to the House evidence of his victory, and on March 4, 1871, he took his seat in Congress. Meanwhile Boles was busy contesting the election results. Finally on February 9, 1872, Boles was deemed the winner of the election and he replaced Edwards in the House. This ended Edwards' political career. He chose to remain in Washington, D.C., where he practiced law. He died in Washington, D.C. and was buried in Section 1 at Arlington National Cemetery.[3]

CHARLES EWING

Born: March 6, 1835
Died: June 20, 1883

General Ewing was born in Lancaster, Ohio. His father, Thomas Ewing, had a distinguished political career, serving as a United States Senator and holding several Cabinet positions. His brothers, Hugh B. Ewing and Thomas Ewing, Jr., also became substantive Union brigadier generals during the Civil War. And his foster brother, William T. Sherman, became his brother-in-law before the war. Charles attended the University of Virginia, studied law, and then practiced law in St. Louis, Missouri.[1]

Ewing was named captain in the newly formed 13th U. S. Infantry on May 14, 1861. The regiment did not see any fighting until late 1862, being assigned before then to routine garrison duties in Alton, Illinois and Memphis, Tennessee. On December 29, 1862, the regiment was engaged in the unsuccessful Union assaults at Chickasaw Bluff, Mississippi and on January 10 – 11, 1863, the regiment was involved in the capture of Fort Hindman at Arkansas Post, Arkansas. Later in January 1863 the regiment was assigned to the 15th Corps and it was engaged in several actions during the Vicksburg Campaign. On May 22, 1863, during the second major Union assault against the Confederate defenses at Vicksburg, command of the first battalion of the regiment devolved on Ewing when the battalion commander was wounded. After three color bearers had been killed or wounded during the attack, Ewing carried the colors of the battalion up to the parapets before the assault was repulsed. Ewing was slightly wounded in the hand during this attack. His brigade commander, Col. Giles A. Smith, recommended Ewing's promotion "for gallantry on the field as well as [his] eminent fitness for higher commands."[2]

On June 22, 1863, Ewing was promoted to lieutenant colonel of staff in the regular army and named assistant inspector general for the 15th Corps, which was commanded by his brother-in-law, Maj. Gen. William T. Sherman. Ewing was brevetted major in the regular army on July 4, 1863, for his performance during the Vicksburg Campaign. When Sherman became commander of the Army of the Tennessee in October 1863, Ewing remained on his staff as assistant inspector general for the army. And when Sherman became commander of the Military Division of the Mississippi in March 1864, Ewing again remained on his staff, as assistant inspector general for the military division. Ewing was brevetted lieutenant colonel in the regular army on September 1, 1864, for his performance in the Atlanta Campaign. On March 8, 1865, he was nominated brigadier general of volunteers. The Senate confirmed his nomination two days later and his commission ranked from March 8, 1865. On March 13, 1865, he was brevetted colonel in the regular army. He was given command of a 17th Corps brigade on April 3, 1865, which he commanded through the end of the war. It is certain that his promotion to substantive brigadier general of volunteers was based, in part, on his being a son of Thomas Ewing and a brother-in-law of William T. Sherman. But it can be argued that his gallantry and performance during the war justified his promotion.[3]

Ewing resigned from the volunteer service on December 1, 1865, but he briefly remained in the regular army with the substantive grade of captain. On September 21, 1866, he was assigned to the 22nd Infantry and on July 31, 1867, he resigned from the army. He then practiced law in Washington, D.C., where he died sixteen years later. He was buried in Section 4 at Arlington National Cemetery.[4]

GEORGE WASHINGTON GETTY

Born: October 2, 1819
Died: October 1, 1901

General Getty was born in Washington, D.C. He graduated from West Point in 1840, ranked 15th out of 42. He served on the frontier before the Mexican War, being named second lieutenant in the Fourth Artillery on July 1, 1840, and promoted to first lieutenant on October 31, 1845. He saw action during the Mexican War and was brevetted captain on August 20, 1847, for his performance at Contreras and Churubusco. After the war he served on the frontier and was involved in fighting against the Seminole Indians in Florida. He was promoted to captain on November 4, 1853.[1]

On September 28, 1861, Getty was promoted to lieutenant colonel of staff in the regular army and named an aide-de-camp on the staff of Maj. Gen. George B. McClellan. The next month Getty was given command of the artillery in a division in the Army of the Potomac. He ably commanded four batteries during the Peninsula Campaign. In August 1862 he was named commander of the Ninth Corps artillery, which he led at South Mountain and Antietam in September 1862. On September 25, 1862, he was appointed brigadier general of volunteers. He was given command of a Ninth Corps division on October 4, 1862, which he led during the Fredericksburg Campaign of December 1862. The Senate confirmed his nomination on March 12, 1863, and his commission as brigadier general of volunteers ranked from September 25, 1862. On March 21, 1863, he was named commander of a Seventh Corps division stationed at Suffolk, Virginia. He was brevetted lieutenant colonel in the regular army on April 19, 1863, for his performance during the Suffolk Campaign and he was promoted to major in the regular army on August 1, 1863. Getty spent the remainder of 1863 in southeast Virginia, commanding at various times an 18th Corps division and the Union forces stationed at Norfolk and Portsmouth.[2]

On January 27, 1864, Getty was named acting inspector general for the Army of the Potomac, which position he held until he was given command of a Sixth Corps division on March 25, 1864. He was severely wounded in the shoulder on May 6, 1864, during fighting at The Wilderness. He was brevetted colonel in the regular army on May 4, 1864, for his performance at The Wilderness. In late June 1864 he was able to return to command of his division at Petersburg, which he ably led in the 1864 Shenandoah Valley

Campaign and during the pursuit of the Confederate army in April 1865 from Petersburg to Appomattox Courthouse. He was brevetted major general of volunteers on August 1, 1864, for his performance at Winchester and Fisher's Hill. On March 13, 1865, he was brevetted brigadier general in the regular army for his performance at Petersburg and major general in the regular army for his war service. His combat record justified a commission as a substantive major general of volunteers, but he never received such a promotion.[3]

Getty was promoted to colonel of the 37th Infantry on July 28, 1866. He was mustered out of the volunteer service on October 9, 1866, but he remained in the regular army. He served in the infantry until December 31, 1870, when he transferred to the Third Artillery. He commanded the artillery school at Fort Monroe, Virginia for six years and he served on the board that in 1879 reversed Maj. Gen. Fitz John Porter's 1863 court-martial conviction. He retired from the army on October 2, 1883, having reached the mandatory retirement age of sixty-four. He died at his farm at Forest Glen, Maryland and was buried in Section 1 at Arlington National Cemetery. The inscription on his grave marker correctly indicates the highest substantive grade Getty attained in the regular army, but it does not indicate that he was brevetted major general in the regular army and there is no inscription concerning his service in the volunteers during the Civil War.[4]

JOHN GIBBON

Born: April 20, 1827
Died: February 6, 1896

General Gibbon was born in Philadelphia, Pennsylvania. When he was young his family moved to Charlotte, North Carolina. He graduated from West Point in 1847, ranked 20th out of 38. He was sent to Mexico soon after his graduation and was promoted to second lieutenant on September 13, 1847. After the Mexican War he served on the frontier and saw action in Florida against the Seminole Indians. He also spent five years at West Point as an artillery instructor. He was promoted to first lieutenant on September 12, 1850, and captain on November 2, 1859. In 1860 his book, *The Artillerist's Manual*, was published. Although three of his brothers fought for the Confederacy, Gibbon chose to fight for the Union.[1]

From October 1861 to May 1862 Gibbon commanded the artillery of a division in the Department of the Rappahannock. On April 21, 1862, he was nominated brigadier general of volunteers. The Senate confirmed his nomination on May 2, 1862, and his commission ranked from May 2, 1862. Five days later he was given command of a brigade in the Department of the Rappahannock. On June 26, 1862, he was given command of a brigade that first served in the Army of Virginia before being assigned to the First Corps of the Army of the Potomac. The brigade, which was made up of one Indiana and three Wisconsin regiments, earned a reputation as one of the best combat brigades in the Union army. Gibbon ably led the brigade in fighting at Second Manassas, South Mountain, and Antietam. Soon the brigade became known as "The Iron Brigade." Gibbon was brevetted major in the regular army on September 17, 1862, for his performance at Antietam.[2]

On November 5, 1862, Gibbon left the Iron Brigade to take command of a First Corps division, which he led during the Fredericksburg Campaign. He was wounded in the right wrist and hand on December 13, 1862, during the fighting at Fredericksburg. He was brevetted lieutenant colonel in the regular army on December 13, 1862, for his performance at Fredericksburg. He was able to return to the field in April 1863, at which time he was given command of a Second Corps division. His division was held in reserve during the fighting at Chancellorsville in May 1863. He gallantly led his division, and temporarily the Second Corps itself, at Gettysburg, where he was severely wounded in the left arm and shoulder on July 3, 1863, as his men were repelling Pickett's Charge. He was brevetted colonel in the regular army on July 4, 1863, for his performance at Gettysburg.[3]

His Gettysburg wounds were slow to heal, but in November 1863 Gibbon was able to take command of the Cleveland, Ohio draft depot. In late December 1863 he returned to command of his division, which he ably led during the 1864 Overland Campaign. On May 26, 1864, he was nominated major general of volunteers. The Senate confirmed his nomination on June 13, 1864, and his commission ranked from June 7, 1864. From January 15, 1865, through the end of the war he commanded the 24th Corps in the Army of the James. On March 13, 1865, he was brevetted brigadier general in the regular army for his performance at Spotsylvania and major general in the regular army for his performance at Petersburg. His excellent combat record earned him the honor of being named one of the Union commissioners who received the surrender of the Army of Northern Virginia at Appomattox Courthouse in April 1865.[4]

Gibbon was mustered out of the volunteer service on January 15, 1866, but he remained in the regular army. He was promoted to colonel of the 36th Infantry on July 28, 1866. He spent the post war years mainly in the west, where he was involved in many engagements with hostile Indians. He was promoted to brigadier general on July 10, 1885, and he retired on April 20, 1891, having reached the mandatory retirement age of sixty-four. He died in Baltimore, Maryland five years later and was buried in Section 2 at Arlington National Cemetery.[5]

LAWRENCE PIKE GRAHAM

Born: January 8, 1815
Died: September 12, 1905

    General Graham was born in Amelia County, Virginia. He received his education through private tutors. On October 13, 1837, he was directly commissioned in the army as a second lieutenant in the Second Dragoons. It is hardly surprising that he decided to pursue a career in the military. His father, a physician, was a veteran of both the American Revolution and the War of 1812, and three of his brothers were West Point graduates. There is no explanation in the records as to why Lawrence did not attend the academy, but having entered the army, he remained in the army for the next thirty-three years. He served in Florida during the Second Seminole War and was promoted to first lieutenant on January 1, 1839, and captain on August 31, 1843. During the Mexican War he was brevetted major on May 9, 1846, for his performance at Palo Alto and Resaca de la Palma. On June 14, 1858, he was promoted to major. When the Civil War began he was stationed at Carlisle Barracks, Pennsylvania. Although he was a native Virginian, Graham refused to side with the Confederacy.[1]

    Graham was appointed brigadier general of volunteers on August 31, 1861. It is likely that he received such an appointment so early in the war, without a West Point education, because the Lincoln administration wanted to encourage and reward loyalty by native Virginians. He was given command of a brigade in the newly formed Army of the Potomac and on October 1, 1861, he was promoted to lieutenant colonel in the regular army. The Senate confirmed his nomination on March 7, 1862, and his commission as brigadier general of volunteers ranked from August 31, 1861. In the spring of 1862 his brigade was assigned to the Fourth Corps and he led his brigade during the siege of Yorktown, Virginia during the early stages of the Peninsula Campaign. Unfortunately in late April 1862 he contracted typhoid fever and the next month he had to go on sick leave. He never again commanded troops in the field during the war. In June 1862 he was able to take command of the cavalry instruction camp at Annapolis, Maryland. Then in September 1862 he was sent to St. Louis, Missouri to serve as president of a general court-martial. Afterwards he returned to Annapolis, where he served as president of a board for the examination of disabled officers. He was promoted to colonel of the Fourth U. S.

Cavalry on May 9, 1864, and was brevetted brigadier general in the regular army on March 13, 1865.[2]

Graham was mustered out of the volunteer service on August 24, 1865, but he remained in the regular army. During the next five years he served with his regiment at various posts on the frontier. On December 15, 1870, he retired from the army. After his retirement he acquired a reputation as a Shakespearean scholar. In 1877 he moved to Washington, D.C., where he lived for the remaining twenty-eight years of his life. In July 1905 he fractured his hip and two months later he died in a Washington, D.C. hospital at the age of ninety. He was buried in Section 1 at Arlington National Cemetery. The inscription on his grave marker correctly indicates that Graham was brevetted brigadier general in the regular army, but there is no inscription concerning his service in the volunteers during the Civil War.[3]

WALTER QUINTIN GRESHAM

Born: March 17, 1832
Died: May 28, 1895

General Gresham was born in Lanesville, Indiana. He attended Corydon Seminary in Indiana and Indiana University. He worked as a teacher and as a clerk for several county officials. Later he studied law and began to practice law in New Albany, Indiana in 1854. A successful lawyer, he wanted to get involved in local politics. After several unsuccessful attempts to be elected to local offices, wherein he was affiliated with several different political parties, he was finally elected to the Indiana legislature in 1860, running as a Republican. Unfortunately he had a falling out with Republican governor Oliver P. Morton, so that when the Civil War began Morton rejected Gresham's request for a commission. Undaunted, Gresham raised a company and enlisted as a private in the 38th Indiana Infantry. On September 18, 1861, he was named lieutenant colonel of the regiment. He was named colonel of the newly formed 53rd Indiana Infantry on March 10, 1862.[1]

Gresham's regiment was not engaged in the fighting at Shiloh in April 1862, however, it did participate in the subsequent advance on Corinth, Mississippi. Eventually assigned to the 16th Corps, the regiment saw considerable action during the 1863 Vicksburg Campaign. On August 11, 1863, Gresham was appointed brigadier general of volunteers. Fifteen days later he was given command of a brigade in the 17th Corps, which he commanded until May 27, 1864. The Senate confirmed his nomination on April 1, 1864, and his commission as brigadier general of volunteers ranked from August 11, 1863. On May 27, 1864, he was given command of a 17th Corps division. He ably led his division during the advance to Atlanta in the spring and summer of 1864. On July 20, 1864, during the fighting near Atlanta, he was severely wounded in the left leg by a sharpshooter's bullet. The shinbone was badly broken several inches below the knee. The limb was not amputated, but doctors removed bone fragments from the wound. Unfortunately the wound was very slow to heal and Gresham spent many months convalescing. For the remainder of his life he had to use a cane or crutches to get around, because of the loss of bone and the inability of the limb to support his weight. He never commanded troops again, although he was brevetted major general of volunteers on March 13, 1865. He was mustered out of the volunteer service on April 30, 1866.[2]

After the war Gresham resumed his law practice in New Albany, Indiana. Twice he unsuccessfully ran for a seat in the United States House of Representatives and once he was defeated for election to the United States Senate. Although unsuccessful in winning elections, Gresham found his niche with Federal appointments. He served as United States Postmaster General from April 3, 1883, until September 25, 1884, and then United States Secretary of the Treasury from the latter date until October 29, 1884. His tenure as treasury secretary ended abruptly when he was appointed a United States circuit judge. He was viewed as a possible presidential candidate in 1884, 1888, and 1892. His support for Grover Cleveland in the 1892 election was rewarded when Gresham served as Cleveland's Secretary of State from March 6, 1893, until his death two years later in Washington, D.C. He was buried in Section 2 at Arlington National Cemetery.[3]

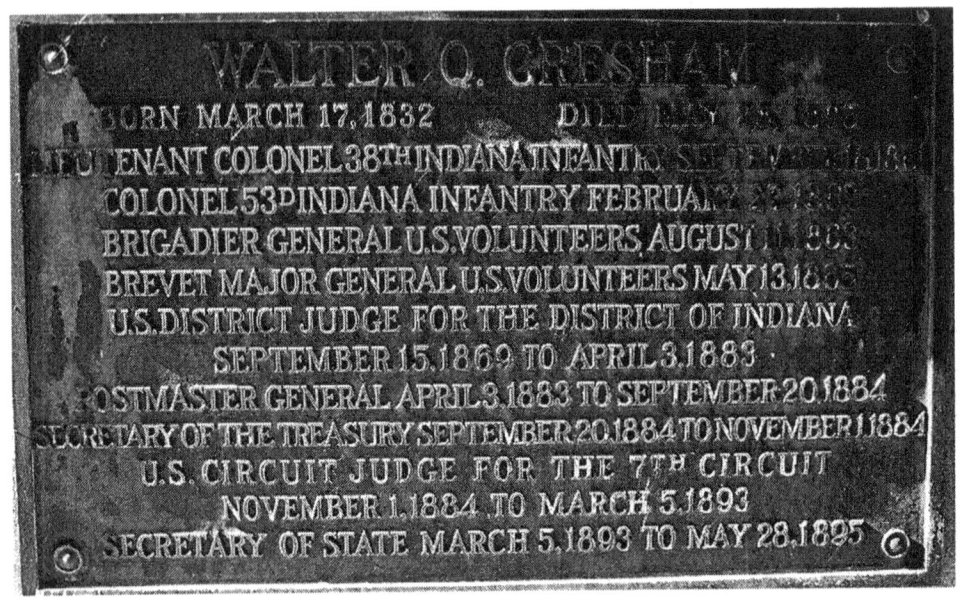

WILLIAM ALEXANDER HAMMOND

Born: August 28, 1828
Died: January 5, 1900

General Hammond was born in Annapolis, Maryland. He subsequently lived in Pennsylvania and New York. In 1848 he graduated from New York University Medical School. On June 29, 1849, he was named assistant surgeon in the army and he spent the next eleven years at various posts on the frontier. In 1857 he wrote a well-received book concerning nutrition. He resigned from the army on October 31, 1860, in order to assume his duties as a professor of anatomy and physiology at the University of Maryland.[1]

On May 28, 1861, Hammond returned to the army as an assistant surgeon, but he lost credit for his previous service and so for purposes of seniority was placed at the bottom of the list of assistant surgeons. During the summer and autumn of 1861 he worked as an inspector of camps and hospitals. His tireless efforts to improve conditions impressed the U. S. Sanitary Commission, and that organization as well as other groups and individuals lobbied for his appointment as surgeon general. Their efforts paid off, for on April 18, 1862, Hammond was nominated brigadier general in the regular army. The Senate confirmed his nomination seven days later and his commission ranked from April 25, 1862. Hammond was also named surgeon general, effective April 25, 1862. Quickly he strove to reorganize and reenergize the Medical Department. Reforms were adopted and bureaucracy was reduced. Younger doctors were placed in positions of authority. A general hospital service and an ambulance corps were created. Hammond pushed for dramatic increases in appropriations for the Medical Department, and he helped create the Army Medical Museum, which started to collect valuable information about the medical and surgical history of the war.[2]

Hammond succeeded in bringing much needed reforms and improvements to the Medical Department, but as with anyone who creates changes, he ruffled some feathers. By 1864 he had a falling out with Edwin M. Stanton, the powerful and caustic Secretary of War. When Hammond was ordered away from Washington, D.C. and an acting successor was named to replace him, Hammond demanded a court-martial to clear his name. The court-martial found him guilty of ungentlemanly conduct in connection with some liquor contracts and on August 18, 1864, he was dismissed from the army.[3]

Hammond easily adapted to civilian life. He worked as a physician, he helped pioneer the treatment of nervous and mental ailments, he wrote extensively on a vast array of medical topics, and from 1867 to 1876 he was the editor of *The American Psychological Journal*. By an Act of Congress on March 15, 1878, restoration of Hammond to the service was permitted if justice so indicated. On August 27, 1879, he was acquitted of the bogus charges against him from 1864 and restored to the service. He was placed on the retired list as brigadier general on March 16, 1886. Accordingly, when he died in Washington, D.C. fourteen years later, he was eligible for burial at Arlington National Cemetery. He was buried there in Section 1.[4]

WILLIAM SELBY HARNEY

Born: August 27, 1800
Died: May 9, 1889

General Harney was born in Haysboro, Tennessee. On February 13, 1818, he was directly commissioned in the army as a second lieutenant in the First Infantry. He was promoted to first lieutenant on January 7, 1819, and captain on May 14, 1825. He participated in the Black Hawk War and was promoted to major in the paymaster department on May 1, 1833. He fought gallantly in Florida during the Second Seminole War, gaining promotion to lieutenant colonel in the Second Dragoons on August 15, 1836. He was brevetted colonel on December 7, 1840, for his performance in the fighting in Florida. On June 30, 1846, he was promoted to colonel of the Second Dragoons. During the Mexican War he was relieved of his command by Maj. Gen. Winfield Scott, who lacked confidence in Harney's judgment. President James K. Polk reversed Scott's action. Harney was returned to command of his cavalry force and he distinguished himself at Cerro Gordo, for which he was brevetted brigadier general on April 18, 1847. Between the Mexican War and the Civil War Harney saw action on the frontier against hostile Indians. On June 14, 1858, he was promoted to brigadier general.[1]

When the Civil War started Harney was one of only four generals of the line in the United States army. He was in command of the Department of the West, with his headquarters in St. Louis, Missouri. Accordingly he was in a position of great power and authority, in a slave state that was teetering between staying loyal to the Union and joining the Confederacy. He entered into an agreement with Maj. Gen. Sterling Price of the pro-Confederate Missouri State Guard that he would take no actions against the Guard as long as Price and the Guard took no actions against the Federal authorities in Missouri. Now Harney's loyalty to the Union was in doubt, based on his Southern birth, his marriage into a wealthy Southern family, and his pacifist actions in Missouri in the early days of the war. Uncertain if Harney was pro-Southern or merely trying to avoid bloodshed in Missouri, the Lincoln administration succumbed to pressure from pro-Union forces in Missouri and relieved Harney of his command on May 31, 1861.[2]

Harney was given no other assignments and so on August 1, 1863, he retired from the army. He had gallantly served his country for over forty-five years, and in the end there is no evidence that he was pro-Confederate or that he committed any disloyal acts while in command in Missouri. He was brevetted major general in the regular army on March 13, 1865. After the war he lived in Pass Christian, Mississippi and in St. Louis. He died in Orlando, Florida and was buried in Section 1 at Arlington National Cemetery. The inscription on his grave marker does not clearly indicate that Harney attained the substantive grade of brigadier general in the regular army, as well as the grade of major general in the regular army by brevet.[3]

JOSEPH ABEL HASKIN

Born: June 21, 1818
Died: August 3, 1874

General Haskin was born in Troy, New York. He graduated from West Point in 1839, ranked tenth out of 31. He spent five years in garrison duties along the Canadian border and was promoted to first lieutenant on August 31, 1844. He fought bravely during the Mexican War, being brevetted captain on April 18, 1847, for his performance at Cerro Gordo and major on September 13, 1847, for his performance at Chapultepec. During the latter battle he was severely wounded during the storming of the enemy defenses. His left arm had to be amputated at the shoulder, but the stump continued to bother him until the bullet was removed nine years later. Haskin remained in the army during the period between the Mexican War and the Civil War. He served in the quartermaster department from August 12, 1848, to February 22, 1851, and he was promoted to captain on the latter date.[1]

Haskin was in command of the arsenal and barracks at Baton Rouge, Louisiana during the secession crisis of late December 1860. On January 10, 1861, the governor of Louisiana informed Haskin that he wanted Haskin to surrender to him all of the Federal property under Haskin's control in Baton Rouge. The governor had at his command a much larger force than Haskin and so Haskin believed he had no alternative but to comply. This episode did not seem to adversely affect his career, for on February 20, 1862, Haskin was promoted to major in the regular army. On June 26, 1862, he was promoted to lieutenant colonel of staff in the regular army and named an aide-de-camp on the staff of Maj. Gen. John E. Wool. In August 1862 he was given command of that part of the defenses of Washington, D.C. located north of the Potomac River. He took an active role in defending Fort Stevens and defeating Confederate forces that threatened to capture the nation's capital in July 1864. From July 13, 1864, through the end of the war he commanded the artillery of the 22nd Corps in the defenses of Washington, D.C. On August 5, 1864, he was appointed brigadier general of volunteers, most likely as a result of his vigorous defense of Washington, D.C. the previous month. The Senate confirmed his nomination on February 14, 1865, and his commission ranked from August 5, 1864. On March 13, 1865, he was brevetted lieutenant colonel, colonel, and brigadier general in the regular army.[2]

On April 30, 1866, Haskin was mustered out of the volunteer service, but he remained in the regular army. He was promoted to lieutenant colonel of the First Artillery on July 26, 1866. He commanded Fort Independence in Boston harbor in 1866 and from 1866 to 1870 he commanded Forts Schuyler and Wood in New York harbor. He retired from the army on December 15, 1870, and took up residence in Oswego, New York. After contracting tuberculosis several years later he moved to Charleston, South Carolina in hopes of recuperating from the disease. Unfortunately within two years he died in Oswego. He was originally buried at Riverside Cemetery in Oswego, but in October 1894 his remains were reinterred in Section 1 at Arlington National Cemetery. The inscription on his grave marker implies that Haskin attained the grade of brigadier general in the regular army, whereas he was a brigadier general of volunteers and a brevet brigadier general in the regular army.[3]

JOHN PORTER HATCH

Born: January 9, 1822
Died: April 12, 1901

General Hatch was born in Oswego, New York. He graduated from West Point in 1845, ranked 17th out of 41. During the Mexican War he was conspicuous for his bravery and was promoted to second lieutenant in the Mounted Rifles on April 18, 1847. He was brevetted first lieutenant on August 20, 1847, for his performance at both Contreras and Churubusco and captain on September 13, 1847, for his performance at Chapultepec. He served as regimental adjutant from November 1, 1847, to May 1, 1850. Between the Mexican War and the Civil War he performed routine garrison duties on the frontier, mainly in Texas, Oregon Territory, and New Mexico Territory. He was promoted to first lieutenant on June 30, 1851, and captain on October 30, 1860.[1]

When the Civil War started Hatch was stationed in the Department of New Mexico. Soon he was sent back east and on September 28, 1861, he was appointed brigadier general of volunteers. The Senate confirmed his nomination on February 3, 1862, and his commission ranked from September 28, 1861. During the winter of 1861 – 1862 he commanded several different cavalry units in the Army of the Potomac. From April 4 to June 26, 1862, he commanded a cavalry brigade in the Department of the Shenandoah. When the Army of Virginia was formed on June 26, 1862, Hatch was given command of a cavalry brigade in that army. A month later, on July 27, he was placed in command of an infantry brigade in the Army of Virginia. After leading his brigade in the early fighting of the Second Manassas Campaign, on August 28 he advanced to command of his division, which he led for the remainder of that campaign. He was slightly wounded on August 30 but remained in command of his division on the field. He was brevetted major in the regular army on August 30, 1862, for his performance at Second Manassas.[2]

With the reorganization of the Army of the Potomac after Second Manassas, Hatch was given command of a First Corps brigade on September 12, 1862. He succeeded to command of his division two days later during the fighting at South Mountain, Maryland. During that battle he was severely wounded in the right leg and was carried from the field. Never again did he see combat during the war. He was brevetted lieutenant colonel in the regular army on September 14, 1862, for his performance at South Mountain. He went home to Oswego to recuperate, but the wound was slow to heal. Finally in February 1863 he was able to serve on several courts-martial in Washington, D.C. In July 1863 he was given command of the draft depot in Philadelphia and on October 27, 1863, he was promoted to major in the regular army. In December 1863 he was given command of the cavalry depot in St. Louis. From March 28, 1864, through the end of the war he commanded several different military districts and departments in the occupied areas of the Deep South. On March 13, 1865, he was brevetted colonel and brigadier general in the regular army, as well as major general of volunteers.[3]

Hatch was mustered out of the volunteer service on January 15, 1866, but he remained in the regular army, serving at various frontier posts in the west. He was promoted to lieutenant colonel on January 15, 1873, and colonel of the 2nd Cavalry on June 26, 1881. On January 9, 1886, he retired from the army, having reached the mandatory retirement age of sixty-four. He resided in New York City until his death there fifteen years later. In 1893 he was awarded the Medal of Honor for his gallantry at South Mountain, where he "was severely wounded while leading one of his brigades in the attack under heavy fire from the enemy." He was buried in Section 1 at Arlington National Cemetery. The inscription on his grave marker does not clearly indicate that Hatch was brevetted major general in the volunteers and not in the regular army. Also, there is no notation or marker at his grave site concerning the Medal of Honor.[4]

WILLIAM BABCOCK HAZEN

Born: September 27, 1830
Died: January 16, 1887

General Hazen was born in West Hartford, Vermont. His family moved to Hiram, Ohio when he was three years old. There he became a friend of future Civil War major general and United States President James A. Garfield. He graduated from West Point in 1855, ranked 28th out of 34. He spent the next four years performing routine garrison duties on the frontier, mainly in Texas and the Pacific Northwest. He was promoted to second lieutenant on September 4, 1855, and on May 16, 1859, he was brevetted first lieutenant for his performance in fighting hostile Indians. On November 3, 1859, he was severely wounded during a fight with Comanches near the Llano River in Texas. A bullet went through his right hand and entered his right side between two ribs. The bullet remained in his body for the remainder of his life. He was on sick leave until February 1861, when he became an assistant instructor of infantry tactics at West Point, a position he held until September 1861. He was promoted to first lieutenant in the regular army on April 1, 1861, and captain in the regular army on May 14, 1861.[1]

On October 29, 1861, Hazen was named colonel of the 41st Ohio Infantry, in part because of the recommendation of his friend, James Garfield. He was given command of a brigade in the Army of the Ohio on January 3, 1862. He ably led his brigade in fighting at Shiloh on April 7, 1862, and at Perryville on October 8, 1862. On December 31, 1862, while in command of a 14th Corps brigade at the Battle of Stones River, he was slightly wounded in the shoulder. During that day's fighting the Union right collapsed, but Hazen and his men held the Union center at the Round Forest, preventing the collapse of the rest of the Union line. On January 8, 1863, he was nominated brigadier general of volunteers. The next day he was given command of a brigade in the 21st Corps. The Senate confirmed his nomination on March 9, 1863, and his commission as brigadier general of volunteers ranked from November 29, 1862. Hazen led his brigade during the Tullahoma Campaign in the summer of 1863 and at Chickamauga in September 1863. He was brevetted major in the regular army on September 20, 1863, for his performance at Chickamauga. On October 10, 1863, he was given command of a Fourth Corps brigade, which he ably led at

Chattanooga. He was brevetted lieutenant colonel in the regular army on November 24, 1863, for his performance at Chattanooga.[2]

Hazen commanded his brigade throughout the advance to Atlanta in the spring and summer of 1864. On August 17, 1864, he was placed in command of a 15th Corps division, which he led through the end of the war. He was brevetted colonel in the regular army on September 1, 1864. On January 23, 1865, he was nominated major general of volunteers. The Senate confirmed his nomination on February 14, 1865, and his commission ranked from December 13, 1864. On March 13, 1865, he was brevetted brigadier general in the regular army for his performance at Fort McAllister near Savannah, Georgia and major general in the regular army for his war service. On many battlefields he had proven to be a solid, reliable brigade and division commander. He was mustered out of the volunteer service on January 15, 1866, but he remained in the regular army, being promoted to colonel of the 38th Infantry on July 28, 1866. He spent some time on the frontier and was in Europe in the early 1870s as an observer during the Franco-Prussian War. On December 13, 1880, he was promoted to brigadier general and was named chief signal officer. Six years later he died in Washington, D.C. and was buried in Section 1 at Arlington National Cemetery.[3]

CHARLES EDWARD HOVEY

Born: April 26, 1827
Died: November 17, 1897

General Hovey was born in Thetford, Vermont. Working as a teacher in order to finance his education, he graduated from Dartmouth College in 1852. He had an impressive career as an educator and school administrator before the Civil War. He worked as the principal of a high school in Framingham, Massachusetts, the principal of a high school in Peoria, Illinois, superintendent of the Peoria school system, president of the Illinois state teachers' association, a member of the first Illinois state board of education, and a founder and president of the first state teachers' university at Normal, Illinois.[1]

With the outbreak of the Civil War Hovey raised and organized the 33rd Illinois Infantry. The regiment was mostly comprised of students and teachers from the Illinois Normal School and was called "The Normal Regiment." Hovey was named colonel of the regiment on August 15, 1861. The regiment was sent to Missouri and was engaged in several minor fights in Missouri and Arkansas between the autumn of 1861 and the summer of 1862. On July 7, 1862, Hovey was slightly wounded during fighting at Cache River, Arkansas. He was appointed brigadier general of volunteers on September 5, 1862, although his background and combat experience by that date does not seem to justify such an appointment. Based on his appointment he was given command of a brigade in the Department of the Missouri on November 2, 1862, and from December 1862 to January 1863 he commanded two different 13th Corps brigades in the Army of the Tennessee. He ably commanded a brigade in the Army of the Mississippi that was involved in the capture of Fort Hindman at Arkansas Post, Arkansas. On January 11, 1863, during the assault against that Confederate fort he was wounded by shell fragments. He suffered a deep flesh wound in the right arm and a more serious wound just below the left knee. He refused to leave the field despite his two wounds. On January 12, 1862, he was given command of a 15th Corps brigade in the Army of the Tennessee.[2]

In the spring of 1863 it was learned that the Senate had failed to act on Hovey's nomination as a brigadier general of volunteers before the current congressional session ended on March 4, 1863. By operation of law, the appointment expired without confirmation and Hovey reverted back to colonel. He was not reappointed brigadier general of volunteers. As of May 22, 1863, he was no longer in command of his brigade, and he took no further part in the war. He was brevetted major general of volunteers on March 13, 1865, for his performance at Arkansas Post. He lived in Washington, D.C., where he became quite successful as a lawyer and a pension lobbyist. He died in Washington, D.C. and was buried in Section 1 at Arlington National Cemetery. The inscription on his grave marker implies that he was commissioned a substantive brigadier general of volunteers, whereas Hovey was only appointed and nominated to that grade without confirmation by the Senate.[3]

CHARLES EDWARD HOVEY
1827   1897
FOUNDER AND FIRST PRESIDENT
ILLINOIS STATE NORMAL UNIVERSITY
PRIVATE AND COL. 33D ILL. VOL. INFANTRY
BRIG. GEN. AND BVT. MAJOR GEN. U.S.V.
MEMBER OF BAR, SUPREME COURT, U.S.
EDUCATION. ARMS. LAW.
HIS WIFE
HARRIETTE F. SPOFFORD
1834   1916

RUFUS INGALLS

Born: August 23, 1818
Died: January 15, 1893

General Ingalls was born in Denmark, Maine. He graduated from West Point in 1843, ranked 32nd out of 39. Initially he performed routine garrison duties on the frontier, being promoted to second lieutenant in the First Dragoons on March 17, 1845. During the Mexican War he saw action in New Mexico Territory and was brevetted first lieutenant on February 4, 1847, for his performance at Embudo and Taos. He was promoted to first lieutenant on February 16, 1847. On January 12, 1848, he was promoted to captain and was named assistant quartermaster. He would serve with distinction in that branch of the service for the next thirty-five years. From 1848 until the beginning of the Civil War he served as quartermaster at various posts in the west and at Washington, D.C.[1]

Between April and July 1861 Ingalls was stationed at Fort Pickens, near Pensacola, Florida. On September 28, 1861, he was promoted to lieutenant colonel of staff in the regular army and was named an aide-de-camp on the staff of Maj. Gen. George B. McClellan. He was promoted to major in the regular army on January 12, 1862. On July 10, 1862, he replaced Brig. Gen. Stewart Van Vliet as chief quartermaster of the Army of the Potomac. Ingalls held this position for the remainder of the war. Several different men served as commander of that army during that time period, but Ingalls ran his department with such competence and efficiency that he remained as chief quartermaster through all the turmoil and change. On May 23, 1863, he was appointed brigadier general of volunteers. The Senate confirmed his nomination on May 7, 1864, and his commission ranked from May 23, 1863. On June 16, 1864, his powers were increased when his friend and classmate at West Point, Lt. Gen. Ulysses S. Grant, named him chief quartermaster of all the Union armies in Virginia operating against Richmond, including the Army of the Potomac. Ingalls created and efficiently operated the huge depot at City Point, Virginia, which supplied the needs of those armies during the last year of the war. He was brevetted brigadier general in the regular army on July 6, 1864. On March 13, 1865, he was brevetted lieutenant colonel, colonel, and major general in the regular army, as well as major general of volunteers.[2]

On July 29, 1866, Ingalls was promoted to colonel in the regular army and was named assistant quartermaster general. He was mustered out of the volunteer service on September 1, 1866. Between 1866 and 1882 he served as chief quartermaster for the Division of the Pacific, then the Division of the Missouri, and finally the depot at New York City. On February 23, 1882, he was promoted to brigadier general and named quartermaster general of the army. He retired from the army on July 1, 1883, and died in New York City more than nine years later. He was buried in Section 1 at Arlington National Cemetery. The inscription on his grave marker does not clearly indicate that Ingalls had attained the substantive grade of brigadier general in both the regular army and the volunteers, as well as the grade of major general by brevet only in both the regular army and the volunteers. His name is unfamiliar to many people today, but Ingalls served his country well during the Civil War, competently handling the important duties of a chief quartermaster of a major army.[3]

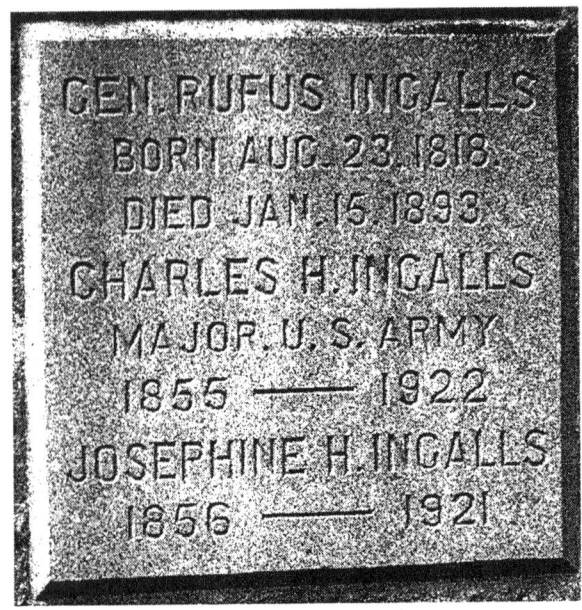

AUGUST VALENTINE KAUTZ

Born: January 5, 1828
Died: September 4, 1895

General Kautz was born in or near Pforzheim, Baden. Shortly after his birth his family moved to Baltimore, Maryland, and then to Georgetown, Ohio. On June 8, 1846, he enlisted as a private in the First Ohio Infantry, in which regiment he served during the early part of the Mexican War. He was mustered out of the army on June 14, 1847. The next year he was appointed to West Point. He graduated in 1852, ranked 35th out of 43. He spent the next nine years serving on the frontier, where he was engaged in numerous fights with hostile Indians. He was promoted to second lieutenant on March 24, 1853. On October 25, 1855, he was wounded in the right chest during a fight with hostile Indians in Oregon Territory. Fortunately two books in his pocket stopped the bullet from penetrating his body. He was promoted to first lieutenant on December 4, 1855. On March 1, 1856, he was wounded in the leg in another Indian fight, this time in Washington Territory.[1]

Kautz was promoted to captain in the Third Cavalry on May 14, 1861 and on August 3, 1861, he was transferred to the Sixth Cavalry. He and his regiment saw action during the 1862 Peninsula Campaign. On September 2, 1862, he was named colonel of the Second Ohio Cavalry, which was serving in the Department of Kansas. Between October and December 1862 the regiment served in the Army of the Frontier. Then in December 1862 the regiment was sent to Columbus, Ohio and Kautz briefly commanded Camp Chase in Columbus. In March 1863 Kautz and his regiment were sent to Kentucky. Between April 27 and June 24, 1863, Kautz commanded a cavalry brigade in the District of Central Kentucky. He was brevetted major in the regular army on June 9, 1863, for his performance in a fight at Monticello, Kentucky. He then commanded a cavalry brigade in the Army of the Ohio from June 24 to August 6, 1863, during which time he participated in the pursuit and capture of the Confederate cavalry raider Brig. Gen. John Hunt Morgan. From August 11 to December 1863 he served as commander of the cavalry in the 23rd Corps.[2]

In early 1864 Kautz was sent back east and on April 28, 1864, he was given command of an 18th Corps cavalry division in the Army of the James. He ably led his division in numerous engagements in the spring and summer of 1864, mainly involving the railroads leading in and out of Petersburg and Richmond, Virginia. On April 16, 1864, he was appointed brigadier general of volunteers. The Senate confirmed his nomination on May 7, 1864, and his commission ranked from May 7, 1864. He was brevetted lieutenant colonel in the regular army on June 9, 1864, for his performance at Petersburg and colonel in the regular army on October 7, 1864, for his performance at Darbytown Road. He was brevetted major general of volunteers on October 28, 1864, for his performance in various actions around Richmond. On March 13, 1865, he was brevetted brigadier general and major general in the regular army. Two weeks later, on March 27, he was given command of an infantry division in the 25th Corps, which he led through the end of the war. In the summer of 1865 he served as a member of the military commission that tried and convicted eight members of the Lincoln assassination conspiracy.[3]

On January 15, 1866, Kautz was mustered out of the volunteer service, but he remained in the regular army, being promoted to lieutenant colonel in the 34th Infantry on July 28, 1866. He mainly served on the western frontier and was promoted to colonel of the 8th Infantry on June 8, 1874. On April 20, 1891, he was promoted to brigadier general and less than a year later, on January 5, 1892, he retired, having reached the mandatory retirement age of sixty-four. He died in Seattle, Washington, and was buried in Section 2 at Arlington National Cemetery.[4]

PHILIP KEARNY

Born: June 2, 1815
Died: September 1, 1862

General Kearny was born in New York, New York.[1] He was orphaned when he was nine years old and was raised after that by his wealthy grandfather. Young Kearny wanted to pursue a career in the military, in part because his uncle, Stephen Kearny, was a dragoon in the United States army. But his grandfather forbade it. After attending private schools Philip graduated from Columbia University in 1833. He studied law and traveled during the next few years. When he inherited a fortune from his grandfather in 1836, he decided to pursue the military career he had always dreamed about.[2]

On March 8, 1837, Kearny was directly commissioned in the army as a second lieutenant in the First Dragoons. He was promoted to first lieutenant on July 22, 1839. That same year he was on leave in order to study at the Royal Cavalry School in Saumur, France. From 1839 to 1840 he served in the French Army as a voluntary aide-de-camp with the First Chasseurs d'Afrique and as such experienced combat in Algiers. He was promoted to captain on December 6, 1846, and during the Mexican War he served as an aide-de-camp on the staff of Maj. Gen. Winfield Scott. On August 20, 1847, during fighting at Churubusco, he was severely wounded in the left arm by grapeshot and the arm was amputated. He was brevetted major on August 20, 1847, for his performance at Churubusco. Between May 1848 and August 1851 he served on recruiting duty and on October 9, 1851, he resigned from the army. He lived at his estate in New Jersey until 1859, when he went to Europe and served as a member of the French Imperial Guard, seeing action during the Italian War.[3]

When he learned of the start of the Civil War Kearny quickly returned to the United States. On July 30, 1861, he was nominated brigadier general of volunteers. The Senate confirmed his nomination on August 3, 1861, and his commission ranked from May 17, 1861. On August 20, 1861, he was given command of a brigade that later was assigned to the First Corps in the Army of the Potomac. On April 30, 1862, he was placed in command of a Third Corps division, which he ably led in several engagements during the 1862 Peninsula Campaign. On June 30, 1862, during fighting at Charles City Crossroads, a shell exploded above Kearny and he was struck in the chest by several fragments, but he did not suffer any serious injury. On July 25, 1862, he was appointed major general of volunteers. He was given command of a different Third Corps division on August 5, 1862, and he ably led his division during the Battle of Second Manassas. On September 1, 1862, during fighting in a torrential rainstorm at Chantilly, Virginia, Kearny mistakenly rode into the Confederate lines. Ignoring demands for his surrender, he tried to quickly ride away, but was instantly killed when struck in the hip and spine by a bullet. The Senate confirmed his nomination on March 9, 1863, and his posthumous commission as major general of volunteers ranked from July 4, 1862. He was originally buried in Trinity Churchyard in Manhattan, New York, however, in 1912 his remains were reinterred in Section 2 at Arlington National Cemetery. Two years later an equestrian statue was placed at his grave site, one of only two such grave markers at Arlington. The inscription on his grave marker does not clearly indicate that Kearny was a major general of volunteers and not a major general in the regular army.[4]

Although he died early in the war, Kearny left his mark on the Union army. In 1862 he created a red diamond badge to be worn by members of his division, so that they could be easily identified. Known as the Kearny Patch, the idea caught on and by the end of the war all Union infantrymen wore distinctive badges signifying their division and corps. This was the forerunner of the modern day shoulder patch.[5]

BENJAMIN FRANKLIN KELLEY

Born: April 10, 1807
Died: July 16, 1891

General Kelley was born in New Hampton, New Hampshire. After attending the Partridge Military Academy he moved to Wheeling, (West) Virginia in 1826. He worked in Wheeling as a merchant until 1851, when he became a freight agent for the Baltimore & Ohio Railroad. When the Civil War began he raised the First (West) Virginia Infantry and on May 22, 1861, he was named colonel of this three-month regiment. During the fighting at Philippi, (West) Virginia on June 3, 1861, he commanded a column consisting of his own regiment as well as two other regiments. During that battle Kelley was chasing a retreating Confederate down a street when the man turned and fired his pistol at Kelley, severely wounding him in the right shoulder. His collarbone was broken and he lost a considerable amount of blood. Although at first it was believed his wound was fatal, by August 1861 he was able to return to the field. In his after action report Maj. Gen. George B. McClellan, commander of the Department of the Ohio, stated that Kelley "conducted the movement on Philippi with marked ability and zeal" and he "exhibited in an eminent degree the qualities of an efficient commander." McClellan recommended that Kelley be promoted to brigadier general. On July 31, 1861, Kelley was nominated brigadier general of volunteers. The Senate confirmed his nomination on August 5, 1861, and his commission ranked from May 17, 1861.[1]

Kelley spent the remainder of the war in western Maryland and Virginia (later West Virginia). Throughout that time his major task was to guard the valuable but vulnerable Baltimore & Ohio Railroad from Confederate raiding parties. Between August 3 and December 20, 1861, he commanded the District of Grafton. He commanded the Department of Harpers Ferry and Cumberland from October 22 to December 20, 1861. On the latter date he was placed in command of the Railroad District. On June 27, 1862, he was given command of an Eighth Corps division in the Middle Department, and he commanded several different divisions in that department until June 26, 1863. On June 28, 1863, he was placed in command of the Department of West Virginia, which he commanded until March 10, 1864. Between April 1864 and February 1865 he commanded various forces in the field and he led Union forces that successfully repelled Confederate raiders in early August 1864 at Cumberland, Maryland, at New Creek, West Virginia, and at Moorefield, West Virginia. Kelley was brevetted major general of volunteers on August 5, 1864.[2]

Kelley had established a good, though hardly noteworthy, record in the war, but that came to an abrupt end on February 21, 1865, when he and Maj. Gen. George Crook were captured during a daring raid on Union headquarters in Cumberland, Maryland. Kelley was exchanged on March 20, 1865, but he did not receive a new assignment. He resigned from the army on June 1, 1865, and spent the remainder of his life working at various Federal jobs. In 1866 he was named collector of internal revenue for West Virginia and in 1876 he was named superintendent of the military reservation located at Hot Springs, Arkansas. In 1883 he was made an examiner of pensions. He died in Oakland, Maryland, and was buried in Section 1 at Arlington National Cemetery.[3]

JOHN HASKELL KING

Born: February 19, 1820
Died: April 7, 1888

General King was born in Sackets Harbor, New York. He grew up in Michigan. On December 2, 1837, he was directly commissioned in the army as a second lieutenant in the First Infantry. He saw action in Florida during the Second Seminole War and was promoted to first lieutenant on March 2, 1839. He served on the frontier and was promoted to captain on October 31, 1846. During the Mexican War he again saw action, although he did not earn any brevets. The beginning of the Civil War found him on duty in Texas, from where he brought nine companies of Regulars back east.[1]

On May 14, 1861, King was promoted to major in the 15th Infantry and sent to Cincinnati, where for the next several months he was busy trying to find recruits for this newly created regular army regiment. In November 1861 four companies of the regiment, formed as a battalion and led by King, were sent to Kentucky. The battalion was assigned to the Army of the Ohio and it was engaged during the second day of combat at Shiloh on April 7, 1862. The battalion participated in the subsequent advance to Corinth, Mississippi. King bravely led his battalion at the Battle of Stones River on December 31, 1862, until he was wounded twice in the left arm and once in the left hand. He then fell from his horse, dislocating his shoulder. On March 4, 1863, he was nominated brigadier general of volunteers. The Senate confirmed his nomination on March 9, 1863, and his commission ranked from November 29, 1862.[2]

King's wounds and injured shoulder were slow to heal, but on May 6, 1863, he was given command of the brigade of Regulars in the Army of the Cumberland. He was promoted to lieutenant colonel in the regular army on June 1, 1863. He gallantly led his brigade of Regulars at Chickamauga in September 1863. During the second day of that battle the brigade helped maintain the Union position at Horseshoe Ridge, staving off defeat for the portion of the army still on the field. Unfortunately the brigade's stout fighting came with a price – the highest percentage loss of any brigade in the Union army at that bloody battle. King was brevetted colonel in the regular army on September 20, 1863, for his performance at Chickamauga. He was on sick leave and was not present during the fighting at Chattanooga in November 1863.[3]

During the 1864 Atlanta Campaign King commanded the Regular Brigade, and sporadically a division in the 14th Corps, until August 17, when health problems forced him to relinquish field command. From November 12, 1864, through the end of the war he commanded a brigade in the District of the Etowah. On March 13, 1865, he was brevetted brigadier general in the regular army for his performance at Ruff's Station, Georgia and major general in the regular army for his war service. He was brevetted major general of volunteers on May 31, 1865. He was promoted to colonel of the Ninth Infantry on July 30, 1865, and he was mustered out of the volunteer service on January 15, 1866. He remained in the regular army, serving at various posts on the frontier, until his retirement on August 20, 1882. He lived in Washington, D.C. until his death there six years later. He was buried in Section 1 at Arlington National Cemetery. The inscription on his grave marker correctly indicates the highest substantive and brevet grades King attained in the regular army, but there is no inscription concerning his service in the volunteers during the Civil War.[4]

WLADIMIR BONAWENTURA KRZYZANOWSKI

Born: July 8, 1824
Died: January 31, 1887

General Krzyzanowski was born in Raznova, Prussia.[1] After participating in the Polish revolt in Prussia in 1846, he fled to the United States. He lived in New York City, where he worked as a civil engineer and became a naturalized U. S. citizen. With the start of the Civil War he raised four companies, comprised of fellow Polish immigrants, and then merged them with six companies of German immigrants to form the 58th New York Infantry. He was named colonel of the regiment on October 22, 1861. The regiment, known as "The Polish Legion," spent the winter of 1861 – 1862 in the defenses at Washington, D.C. In early April 1862 the regiment was sent to the Shenandoah Valley and Krzyzanowski led the regiment during the Battle of Cross Keys on June 8, 1862.[2]

Several weeks later, on June 26, Krzyzanowski was given command of a brigade in the newly formed Army of Virginia. He ably led his brigade in the Second Manassas Campaign. On August 30, 1862, during fighting at Manassas, his horse was shot. When Krzyzanowski fell to the ground, he landed on his head. Although stunned by his fall, he remained in command of his brigade throughout the remainder of the campaign. With the reorganization of the Army of the Potomac after Second Manassas, he was given command of an Eleventh Corps brigade on September 12, 1862. The corps was assigned to the Washington, D.C. defenses and was not present during the fighting at South Mountain or Antietam later in September. On November 29, 1862, he was appointed brigadier general of volunteers, but the Senate failed to act on his nomination before the current congressional session ended on March 4, 1863. By operation of law the appointment expired without confirmation. He then reverted back to his grade of colonel, but he retained command of his Eleventh Corps brigade. He was not reappointed brigadier general of volunteers.[3]

Krzyzanowski led his brigade at the Battle of Chancellorsville in May 1863. The Eleventh Corps was routed during the Confederate flank attack of May 2, however, Krzyzanowski's brigade fought fairly well that evening. On July 1, 1863, during the first day of battle at Gettysburg, his horse was shot from under him and Krzyzanowski was injured when the horse fell on Krzyzanowski's left chest. He was unconscious for a while and he had trouble breathing, but he refused to leave the field or yield command of his brigade. For the rest of his life he was bothered by asthma. In September 1863 two divisions of the Eleventh Corps were sent to Chattanooga to reinforce the Army of the Cumberland. Krzyzanowski went west with his brigade and led the brigade in the fighting at Chattanooga in November 1863. That proved to be the last time that he led troops in combat in the war. In April 1864 the Eleventh and Twelfth Corps were consolidated, creating the 20th Corps, and Krzyzanowski lost command of his brigade through seniority. From April to July 1864 he commanded the post at Bridgeport, Alabama, where there was an important railroad crossing of the Tennessee River. From July 1864 to January 1865 he commanded a brigade in the defenses of the Nashville – Chattanooga Railroad in Tennessee. He commanded the post at Stevenson, Alabama from March 1865 through the end of the war. He was brevetted brigadier general of volunteers on March 2, 1865.[4]

After he was mustered out of the volunteer service on October 1, 1865, Krzyzanowski worked for the Internal Revenue Service in the west and south. He was a special customs inspector in Panama from 1878 to 1882 and he was a Treasury Department agent assigned to the customs house in New York City from 1883 until his death in that city four years later. He was originally buried at Green-Wood Cemetery in Brooklyn, but in 1937 his remains were reinterred in Section 1 at Arlington National Cemetery. The inscription on his grave marker implies that he was commissioned a substantive brigadier general of volunteers, whereas Krzyzanowski only attained that grade by brevet, two years after the Senate failed to confirm his nomination as a substantive brigadier general of volunteers.[5]

JOHN SANFORD MASON

Born: August 21, 1824
Died: November 29, 1897

General Mason was born in Steubenville, Ohio. He graduated from West Point in 1847, ranked ninth out of 38. He was immediately sent to Mexico as a second lieutenant in the Third Artillery and was engaged in garrison duties at Tampico. He then served at various posts on the frontier and in the east, performing routine garrison duties. He was promoted to first lieutenant on September 7, 1850, and he served as regimental quartermaster from June 27, 1854, to June 1, 1858. When the Civil War began he was stationed in the Pacific Northwest at Fort Vancouver, Washington Territory. He was named assistant adjutant general for the Department of the Pacific on May 2, 1861, and twelve days later he was promoted to captain in the regular army.[1]

That summer Mason returned to the east and on October 3, 1861, he was named colonel of the Fourth Ohio Infantry, which was on duty in western Virginia. He led the regiment in the engagements at Winchester and Port Republic during the 1862 Shenandoah Valley Campaign. The regiment was sent to the peninsula after the Peninsula Campaign had ended and then to Alexandria, Virginia. The regiment helped cover the Army of Virginia's retreat from the Second Manassas battlefield on September 1, 1862. The regiment was present at the Battle of Antietam but not engaged, however, Mason was brevetted major in the regular army on September 17, 1862, for his performance at Antietam. On November 29, 1862, he was appointed brigadier general of volunteers. His regiment was engaged at the Battle of Fredericksburg on December 13, 1862, and Mason took command of his brigade during that battle when the brigade commander, Brig. Gen. Nathan Kimball, was wounded. Mason was brevetted lieutenant colonel in the regular army on December 13, 1862, for his performance at Fredericksburg. The Senate confirmed his nomination on March 9, 1863, and his commission as brigadier general of volunteers ranked from November 29, 1862.[2]

In June 1862 Mason began to experience health problems, particularly diarrhea and bronchitis, and by early 1863 he was no longer able to command troops in the field. He was sent to Ohio, where he commanded the District of Ohio briefly in early April 1863, and then from April 14 to October 1863 he was involved with recruiting duties at

Columbus, Ohio. Next he was sent to California, where he served as assistant provost marshal general in San Francisco from November 17, 1863, until March 10, 1865. He was promoted to major in the regular army on October 14, 1864. He commanded the District of Arizona from March 7, 1865, through the end of the war. On March 13, 1865, he was brevetted colonel and brigadier general in the regular army. He was mustered out of the volunteer service on April 30, 1866, but he remained in the regular army.[3]

During the next twenty-two years Mason served at a number of posts on the frontier, as well as in Ohio and Washington, D.C. He was promoted to lieutenant colonel on December 11, 1873, and colonel of the Ninth Infantry on April 2, 1883. He retired from the army on August 21, 1888, having reached the mandatory retirement age of sixty-four. He lived in Washington, D.C. until his death there nine years later. He was buried in Section 1 at Arlington National Cemetery. The inscription on his grave marker correctly indicates that Mason was brevetted brigadier general in the regular army, but there is no inscription concerning his service in the volunteers during the Civil War.[4]

JAMES WINNING McMILLAN

Born: April 28, 1825
Died: March 9, 1903

General McMillan was born in Clark County, Kentucky. After moving to Illinois he served in the Mexican War, first as a sergeant in the Fourth Illinois Infantry from June 20 to October 13, 1846, and later as a private in the Third Battalion Louisiana Infantry from April 29, 1848, until his discharge on July 13, 1848. He then moved to Indiana, where he worked as a businessman until the beginning of the Civil War.[1]

On July 24, 1861, McMillan was named colonel of the 21st Indiana Infantry. Seven days later the regiment was sent to Baltimore, Maryland, where it performed garrison duties until February 1862. Next the regiment sailed to Ship Island, Mississippi, as a part of Maj. Gen. Benjamin F. Butler's New Orleans Expedition. After the capture of New Orleans the regiment was sent to Baton Rouge. On June 10, 1862, during an engagement near Baton Rouge, McMillan was wounded in the left arm and hand, as well as the abdomen, but he did not have to leave the field. The ball in his abdomen ended up near his spine and was never removed. The regiment remained in the Department of the Gulf throughout the remainder of 1862 and all of 1863, having its designation changed in February 1863 to the First Indiana Heavy Artillery. On March 4, 1863, he was appointed brigadier general of volunteers. The Senate confirmed his nomination on March 9, 1863, and his commission ranked from November 29, 1862.[2]

On August 15, 1863, McMillan was given command of a 19th Corps brigade. From that date until July 5, 1864, he commanded several different brigades and divisions in the 19th Corps in the Department of the Gulf. He ably led his commands in fighting at Mansfield, Pleasant Hill, and Cane River Crossing during the 1864 Red River Campaign. In July 1864 the 19th Corps was sent to Virginia, where it became a part of the Army of the Shenandoah. McMillan ably led his brigade at the Battle of Winchester on September 19, 1864, where he was hit in the head by a shell fragment but was unharmed. He was in command of his division on October 19, 1864, during the Battle of Cedar Creek. His division was driven from its camps by the unexpected Confederate assault, but soon McMillan was able to reform his men. The division presented a bold front, the Confederates did not advance any further, and other Union units behind McMillan's division were able to reform and regroup. The subsequent Union counterattack drove the enemy from the field, resulting in a victory for the Union army. McMillan was brevetted major general of volunteers on March 5, 1865. He remained in command of a division in the Army of the Shenandoah until April 1865 when he was placed in command of a division in West Virginia. On May 15, 1865, he resigned from the army.[3]

McMillan moved to Kansas after the war. In the 1870s he was appointed to the pension review board in Washington, D.C. He worked for the board until his death in Washington, D.C. many years later. He was buried in Section 3 at Arlington National Cemetery.[4]

MONTGOMERY CUNNINGHAM MEIGS

Born: May 3, 1816
Died: January 2, 1892

General Meigs was born in Augusta, Georgia. His family moved to Philadelphia when he was a child. After briefly attending the University of Pennsylvania he entered West Point in 1832. He graduated in 1836, ranked fifth out of 49. Initially assigned to the artillery, he was assigned to the Corps of Engineers on August 1, 1837. He spent the pre-Civil War years engaged in numerous engineering projects for the army, such as making navigational improvements to the Mississippi River and constructing Fort Jefferson in Florida. In the 1850s he was in charge of several important engineering projects in and around Washington, D.C. He designed and supervised the construction of the Cabin John Bridge, which carried the capital's main water supply as well as vehicular traffic. He was in charge of the construction of the Washington or Potomac Aqueduct. And he supervised the addition of the House and Senate wings to the United States Capitol building and the beginning of the construction of the capitol dome. He was promoted to first lieutenant on July 1, 1838, and captain on March 3, 1853. At the beginning of the Civil War he was an engineer in the Department of Florida, an assignment he had requested in order to ease the discomfort of rheumatism.[1]

On May 14, 1861, Meigs was promoted to colonel of the newly formed Eleventh Infantry. He contended that his engineering experience and talents could be put to better use than assigning him to field command. His argument had merit and eventually the powers that be realized it. On June 12, 1861, he was appointed brigadier general in the regular army. The Senate confirmed his nomination on August 5, 1861, and his commission ranked from May 15, 1861. Meigs was also named quartermaster general of the army. Now his organizational abilities and experience could be put to good use in handling the awesome task of supervising the acquisition and disbursement of all the supplies and equipment necessary to prosecute the war. Although he was gruff, egotistical, and opinionated, and he could be a difficult man to work with, he nevertheless performed his duties admirably throughout the war. No Federal army commander could ever complain that he was unable to perform his duties because his army lacked sufficient supplies, clothing, or equipment. Although there were instances where contracts were given to incompetent or dishonest contractors, particularly early in the war, these were isolated incidents that do not impugn the integrity or efficiency of Meigs. On July 5, 1864, he was brevetted major general in the regular army. He even briefly commanded a division of emergency troops that manned the Washington, D.C. defenses when Confederate forces threatened to attack the capital city in July 1864.[2]

Meigs continued to serve as quartermaster general of the army until his retirement on February 6, 1882. After the war he designed the Old Pension Building in Washington, D.C., he served as a regent of the Smithsonian Institution, and he was an early member of the National Academy of Sciences. He died in Washington, D.C. ten years after his retirement from the army. Although he was a native Southerner, Meigs viewed secession as treason and Confederate soldiers and officers as traitors. Before the war he had served under Robert E. Lee, and during the war he grew to despise that successful Confederate army commander. He came up with a way to exact revenge on Lee. It was his idea that the Custis-Lee property at Arlington be converted into a national military cemetery. This ensured that Lee would never return to his estate. Fittingly, Meigs was buried at the cemetery he had helped establish. He was buried in Section 1 at Arlington National Cemetery.[3]

NELSON APPLETON MILES

Born: August 8, 1839
Died: May 15, 1925

General Miles was born on a farm near Westminster, Massachusetts. He attended a local academy, but at the age of seventeen decided to move to Boston, where he could receive a better education. He worked there as a store clerk, he attended night classes, and he received private military instruction from a former French Army officer. On September 9, 1861, he was named first lieutenant in the 22nd Massachusetts Infantry. The next month the regiment was sent to Washington, D.C., where it spent the winter of 1861 – 1862 manning that city's defenses. Miles served on the staff of Brig. Gen. Oliver O. Howard during the early stages of the 1862 Peninsula Campaign. On May 31, 1862, he was named lieutenant colonel of the 61st New York Infantry and the next day he was slightly wounded in the foot during fighting at Fair Oaks. He saw action throughout the remainder of the Peninsula Campaign. At Antietam on September 17, 1862, command of the regiment devolved on Miles when its commander was seriously wounded. Miles was promoted to colonel of the regiment on September 30, 1862.[1]

Miles led his regiment in the fighting at Fredericksburg on December 13, 1862. He was wounded when a ball entered in the front of his throat and exited near his left ear. His division commander, Brig. Gen. Winfield S. Hancock, reported that Miles "conducted himself in the most admirable and chivalrous manner." Miles had to leave the field and he was not able to return to his regiment until February 1863. On May 3, 1863, during fighting near Chancellorsville, he was wounded yet again. This time a ball bounced off of his metal belt plate, entered his abdomen, and broke his pelvis. His lower body was temporarily paralyzed. He ended up in a Washington, D.C. hospital, where the ball and bone fragments were removed. He was not present at Gettysburg, but on July 4, 1863, he was given command of a Second Corps brigade. He gallantly led his brigade the next spring at The Wilderness and Spotsylvania, earning him an appointment as brigadier general of volunteers. The Senate confirmed his nomination on May 13, 1864, and his commission ranked from May 12, 1864. The next month he was slightly wounded in the neck during fighting at Petersburg. On July 29, 1864, he was given command of his division, which he ably led through the end of the war. He was brevetted major general of volunteers on August 25, 1864, for his performance at Reams's Station near Petersburg. On October 21, 1865, he was appointed a substantive major general of volunteers. The Senate confirmed his nomination on February 23, 1866, and his commission ranked from October 21, 1865.[2]

On July 28, 1866, Miles was named colonel of the 40th Infantry, and on September 1, 1866, he was mustered out of the volunteer service. On March 2, 1867, he was brevetted brigadier general in the regular army for his performance at Chancellorsville and major general in the regular army for his performance at Spotsylvania. He achieved considerable success fighting hostile Indians in the west. He was promoted to brigadier general on December 15, 1880, and major general on April 5, 1890. Two years later he was awarded the Medal of Honor for Chancellorsville, where he was severely wounded "while holding with his command an advanced position against repeated assaults by a strong force of the enemy." On October 5, 1895, he succeeded Lt. Gen. John M. Schofield as general-in-chief of the army. He commanded the army during the Spanish-American War, was promoted to lieutenant general on June 6, 1900, and retired on August 8, 1903, having reached the mandatory retirement age of sixty-four. He spent his remaining twenty-two years writing his memoirs and other military volumes. He died while attending the circus in Washington, D.C. and was buried inside a mausoleum in Section 3 at Arlington National Cemetery. The marker on the mausoleum merely lists his name, with no inscription concerning either his service in the volunteers during the Civil War or his service in the regular army after the war. Also, there is no notation or marker at his grave site concerning the Medal of Honor.[3]

JOHN FRANKLIN MILLER

Born: November 21, 1831
Died: March 8, 1886

General Miller was born in South Bend, Indiana. He graduated from New York Law School in 1852 and returned to South Bend to practice law. A year later he moved to Napa, California, where he spent two years practicing law and serving as county treasurer. In 1855 he moved back to South Bend and once again practiced law there. In 1861 he was elected to the Indiana senate, but he soon resigned his seat in order to serve in the Civil War.[1]

On August 27, 1861, Miller was named colonel of the 29th Indiana Infantry. The regiment was sent to Kentucky in October 1861 and was later assigned to the Army of the Ohio. Although the regiment fought at Shiloh on April 7, 1862, Miller was evidently not present, for the regiment was commanded that day by its lieutenant colonel. In July 1862 Miller was placed in command of the post at Nashville, Tennessee, and in late August 1862 he was given command of a light brigade of infantry and cavalry to operate against Confederate cavalry threatening Nashville. On September 14, 1862, he was given command of a brigade in the Army of the Ohio. He ably led a 14th Corps brigade in the Army of the Cumberland during the fighting at Stones River, receiving a minor wound in the neck on December 31, 1862. In the summer of 1863 he ably led his brigade in the Tullahoma Campaign until June 25, when he was wounded and lost his right eye during an engagement at Liberty Gap, Tennessee. His division commander, Brig. Gen. Richard W. Johnson, reported that Miller "moved his brigade forward in handsome style, but was soon seriously wounded while gallantly leading his men forward." Miller spent the next several months in Nashville recuperating from his wound. By November 1863 he was able to serve on a military commission. On January 5, 1864, he was nominated brigadier general of volunteers. The Senate confirmed his nomination on April 7, 1864, and his commission ranked from January 5, 1864.[2]

In June 1864 Miller was again placed in command of the post at Nashville. He held this command for the remainder of the war. During the Battle of Nashville on December 15 – 16, 1864, he commanded the garrison forces that manned the exterior lines protecting Nashville, while the Union army attacked and defeated the Army of Tennessee.

He was brevetted major general of volunteers on March 13, 1865, for his performance during the Battle of Nashville. He resigned from the army on September 25, 1865, and moved back to California, where he worked for four years as the collector for the port of San Francisco. During the 1870s he served as president of the Alaska Commercial Fur Company. In 1880 he was elected to the United States Senate and he died in office in Washington, D.C. six years later. He was originally buried at Laurel Hill Cemetery in San Francisco, however, in 1913 his remains were reinterred in Section 2 at Arlington National Cemetery.[3]

ROBERT BYINGTON MITCHELL

Born: April 4, 1823
Died: January 26, 1882

General Mitchell was born in Mansfield, Ohio. He practiced law in Mansfield before and after the Mexican War. During that war he served as a first lieutenant in the Second Ohio Infantry from September 4, 1847, until he was mustered out on July 26, 1848. In 1855 he was elected mayor of Mount Gilead, Ohio, but one year later he moved to Kansas Territory. Although he was a Democrat, he strongly supported the Free State cause in Kansas. He was a member of the territorial legislature and a delegate to the Leavenworth constitutional convention. He also served as treasurer of the territory and as a delegate to the 1860 Democratic National Convention.[1]

From May 2 to June 30, 1861, Mitchell served as a brigadier general and adjutant general in the Kansas militia, and on May 23, 1861, he was named colonel of the Second Kansas Infantry. On August 10, 1861, he led his three-month regiment at the Battle of Wilson's Creek, during which he was severely wounded in the hip and groin. It took a long time for him to sufficiently recover from his wounds to be able to return to the field. In the meantime, on March 28, 1862, he was nominated brigadier general of volunteers. The Senate confirmed his nomination on April 8, 1862, and his commission ranked from April 8, 1862. Finally on April 24, 1862, he was able to take command of a brigade in the Army of the Mississippi. He led that brigade until August 12, 1862, when he was given command of a division in that army. On September 29, 1862, he was placed in command of a division in the Army of the Ohio, which he led during the Battle of Perryville a month later. In late 1862 he was given command of the post at Nashville, Tennessee and was not present during the fighting at Stones River.[2]

In March 1863 Mitchell was placed in command of a cavalry division in the Department of the Cumberland, which he led that summer during the Tullahoma Campaign. In September 1863 he was named chief of cavalry for the Army of the Cumberland and he served as such during the Chickamauga Campaign. In early 1863 he had been stricken with typhoid or some other type of fever, and he continued to have complications from his wounds. By early November 1863 he was no longer able to command in the field. He was sent to Washington, D.C., where he served on several courts-martial. From February 28, 1864, until March 28, 1865, he commanded the District of Nebraska Territory, and from the latter date through the end of the war he commanded the District of Northern Kansas. He was mustered out of the volunteer service on January 15, 1866. Later that year he became governor of the New Mexico Territory. He resigned the governorship on August 16, 1869, and moved back to Kansas. He moved to Washington, D.C. in 1872 and died there ten years later. He was buried in Section 2 at Arlington National Cemetery.[3]

BRIG. GENL. ROBT. B. MITCHELL.
BORN IN OHIO, 1823.
DIED AT WASHINGTON, D.C. 1882.
CITIZEN, SOLDIER AND PATRIOT.

AN OHIO OFFICER
IN MEXICAN WAR, 1847-48.
COL. 2ND KANS. INFTY.
MAY 23, 1861.
BRIG. GENL. OF VOLS.
APRIL 8, 1862.
APPOINTED GOVERNOR OF
NEW MEXICO, 1866.

JOSEPH ANTHONY MOWER

Born: August 22, 1827
Died: January 6, 1870

General Mower was born in Woodstock, Vermont. His family moved to Lowell, Massachusetts when he was six years old. He attended the Norwich Academy and worked as a carpenter before the Mexican War. During that war he saw no combat, serving as a private with the army engineers from March 29, 1847, until his discharge on July 25, 1848. Seven years later, on June 18, 1855, he was directly commissioned in the army as a second lieutenant in the First Infantry. He was promoted to first lieutenant on March 13, 1857.[1]

On September 9, 1861, Mower was promoted to captain in the regular army and on May 3, 1862, he was named colonel of the Eleventh Missouri (Union) Infantry. He was brevetted major in the regular army on May 9, 1862, for his performance during fighting at Farmington, Mississippi. On August 9, 1862, he was given command of a brigade in the Army of the Mississippi. He ably led his brigade at the Battle of Iuka, being brevetted lieutenant colonel in the regular army on September 19, 1862, for his performance at that battle. Less than a month later, on October 4, 1862, during the Battle of Corinth his men were receiving fire from their left rear. Mistakenly thinking that it was friendly fire, Mower rode in that direction to stop it. Soon Mower found himself within enemy lines, he was slightly wounded in the back of his neck when he tried to escape, and he was captured. When the Confederates hastily retreated from the field later that day, Mower was able to escape.[2]

Mower commanded a 16th Corps brigade from December 18, 1862, until he was placed in command of a 15th Corps brigade on April 3, 1863. On January 19, 1863, he was nominated brigadier general of volunteers. The Senate confirmed his nomination on March 13, 1863, and his commission ranked from November 29, 1862. He ably led his brigade during the Vicksburg Campaign and was brevetted colonel in the regular army on May 14, 1863, for his performance during fighting at Jackson, Mississippi. In the spring of 1864 he commanded two 16th Corps divisions in the Red River Campaign. During that failed campaign he was conspicuous for his bravery in the assault against Fort De Russy on March 14, 1864, and in his rearguard action at Yellow Bayou on May 18, 1864. He led a 16th Corps division at the Battle of Tupelo on July 14, 1864. On August 12, 1864, he was appointed major general of volunteers. He ably led a 17th Corps division during the March to the Sea and in the Carolinas Campaign. The Senate confirmed his nomination on February 14, 1865, and his commission as major general of volunteers ranked from August 12, 1864. From April 2, 1865, through the end of the war he commanded the 20th Corps. On March 13, 1865, he was brevetted brigadier general in the regular army for his performance at Fort De Russy and major general in the regular army for his performance in crossing the Salkehatchie River. By the end of the war he had amassed an enviable record as a regimental, brigade, and division commander and had earned his nickname of "Fighting Joe."[3]

On February 1, 1866, Mower was mustered out of the volunteer service, but he remained in the regular army. He was promoted to colonel of the 39th Infantry on July 28, 1866, and he was given command of the 25th Infantry on March 15, 1869. Ten months later he died in New Orleans of pneumonia. He was buried in Section 2 at Arlington National Cemetery. The inscription on his grave marker correctly indicates that Mower was brevetted major general in the regular army, but there is no inscription concerning his service in the volunteers during the Civil War.[4]

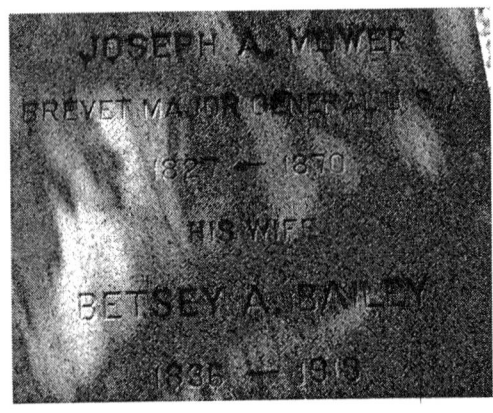

EDWARD OTHO CRESAP ORD

Born: October 18, 1818
Died: July 22, 1883

General Ord was born in Cumberland, Maryland. His family moved to Washington, D.C. when he was one year old. He graduated from West Point in 1839, ranked 17th out of 31. Immediately afterwards he was sent to Florida, where he saw action in the Second Seminole War. He was promoted to first lieutenant on July 1, 1841. During the Mexican War he was stationed in California. Between the Mexican War and the Civil War he mainly served at posts in the Pacific Northwest, and on September 7, 1850, he was promoted to captain. He was stationed in the east in the autumn of 1859 and was a member of the force that defeated John Brown's raiders at Harpers Ferry. At the start of the Civil War he was in California. He was sent back to the east and on September 14, 1861, he was appointed brigadier general of volunteers.[1]

Between October 5, 1861, and March 13, 1862, Ord commanded a brigade that was manning the defenses at Washington, D.C. The Senate confirmed his nomination on January 23, 1862, and his commission as brigadier general of volunteers ranked from September 14, 1861. He was promoted to major in the regular army on November 21, 1861. He was brevetted lieutenant colonel in the regular army on December 20, 1861, for his performance in leading the Union forces to victory in a small engagement at Dranesville, Virginia. From March 13 to April 4, 1862, he commanded a First Corps brigade in the Army of the Potomac and from the latter date until May 16, 1862, he commanded a brigade in the Department of the Rappahannock. On April 28, 1862, he was nominated major general of volunteers. The Senate confirmed his nomination on May 2, 1862, and his commission ranked from May 2, 1862. From May 16 until June 10, 1862, he commanded a division in the Department of the Rappahannock. He was then sent to the Western Theater of the war and given command of a division in the Army of the Tennessee. He was brevetted colonel in the regular army on September 19, 1862, for his performance at Iuka, although he was never actually involved in the fighting there. He commanded the District of Jackson from September 24 until October 5, 1862, when he was wounded in the ankle during fighting at Davis Bridge along the Hatchie River near Corinth, Mississippi. It took a long time for the wound to heal, although he was able to serve on the Buell Commission between November 1862 and March 1863.[2]

By the summer of 1863 Ord was able to return to the field. On June 19, 1863, he replaced Maj. Gen. John A. McClernand as commander of the 13th Corps in the Army of the Tennessee, and he led that corps for the remainder of the siege at Vicksburg. In September 1863 the 13th Corps was sent to Louisiana and assigned to the Department of the Gulf. Ord contracted a fever the next month, he went back north to recuperate, and he was not able to return to his command until early January 1864. In the summer of 1864 he was sent back east and on July 21 he took command of the 18th Corps in the Army of the James. He ably led his corps in the successful assault against Fort Harrison, near Richmond, Virginia on September 29, 1864, until he was severely wounded in the right thigh. On January 8, 1865, he was given command of the Army of the James, which he led through the end of the war. On March 13, 1865, he was brevetted brigadier general in the regular army for his performance at the Hatchie River and major general in the regular army for his performance at Fort Harrison.[3]

On December 11, 1865, Ord was promoted to lieutenant colonel in the regular army and he was promoted to brigadier general in the regular army on July 26, 1866. He was mustered out of the volunteer service on September 1, 1866. He commanded various military districts and departments until he retired from the army on December 6, 1880. He was placed on the retirement list as a major general on January 28, 1881. He then worked as a construction engineer for Mexican railroads. He was stricken with yellow fever while on a boat going from Vera Cruz to New York, and he died less than a week later in Havana, Cuba. He was originally buried at Oak Hill Cemetery in Washington, D.C., but in 1900 his remains were reinterred in Section 2 at Arlington National Cemetery. The inscription on his grave marker correctly indicates that Ord was placed on the retired list as a major general in the regular army, but there is no inscription concerning his service in the volunteers during the Civil War.[4]

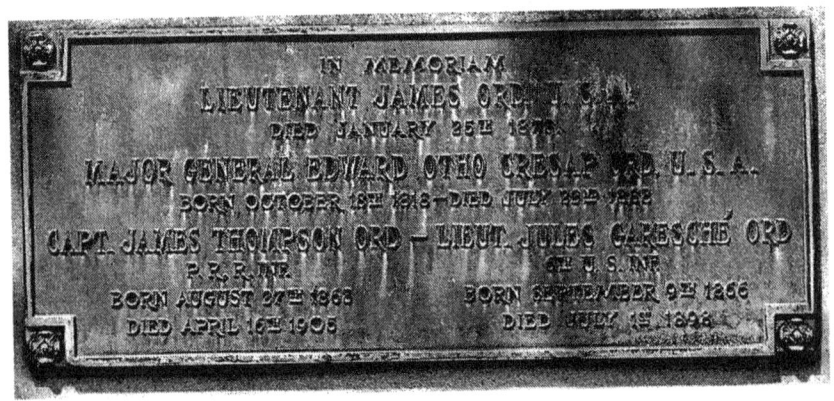

THOMAS OGDEN OSBORN

Born: August 11, 1832
Died: March 27, 1904

General Osborn was born in Jersey, Ohio. He graduated from Ohio University in 1854. He moved to Crawfordsville, Indiana, where he studied law in the office of future Civil War Union major general and *Ben Hur* author Lewis Wallace. In 1858 Osborn moved to Chicago, Illinois, where he practiced law until the beginning of the Civil War. During the summer of 1861 he helped raise the 39th Illinois Infantry, which was organized in Chicago and called "The Yates Phalanx" as an honor to the governor, Richard Yates. Osborn was named lieutenant colonel of the regiment on October 11, 1861. Later that month the regiment was sent to western Maryland, where it was busy for the next few months protecting the Baltimore & Ohio Railroad.[1]

On January 1, 1862, Osborn was promoted to colonel of the regiment, and two days later the regiment was engaged in a skirmish at Bath, (West) Virginia. In March 1862 the regiment was assigned to Maj. Gen. Nathaniel Banks' forces in the Shenandoah Valley. The regiment was present but not engaged at the Battle of Kernstown on March 23, 1862. In May 1862 the regiment was sent to Fredericksburg and in early July it was sent to the peninsula after the Peninsula Campaign had ended. In September 1862 the regiment was sent to Suffolk, Virginia, where it fought in several minor engagements. On January 2, 1863, Osborn was given command of an 18th Corps brigade that was stationed on the North Carolina coast and on March 26, 1863, he was given command of a different brigade stationed on the South Carolina coast. On April 16, 1863, he reverted back to command of his regiment, which was stationed at Folly Island near Charleston, South Carolina. In July 1863 he led his regiment in several unsuccessful assaults against nearby Fort Wagner on Morris Island. Osborn was slightly wounded during one of these assaults. After a siege of several months, the Confederates abandoned the fort on September 7, after which Osborn commanded a Tenth Corps brigade at Morris Island between September 19 and October 12, 1863. Then Osborn again reverted back to command of his regiment, which was stationed at Folly Island from October to December 1863 and at Hilton Head from December 1863 until April 1864. The regiment was sent to southeastern Virginia in April 1864 and assigned to the Army of the James.[2]

On May 14, 1864, Osborn was seriously wounded while leading his regiment in an attack against Drewry's Bluff near Richmond. A ball struck his right elbow, shattering the bone and making his right arm useless. While he was recuperating from his wound he campaigned for President Abraham Lincoln's reelection in Illinois, Indiana, and Michigan. Osborn was finally able to return to the field in December 1864. He ably led a 24th Corps brigade from December 8, 1864, through the end of the war. On March 10, 1865, he was brevetted brigadier general of volunteers for his performance at Richmond and Petersburg. He was conspicuous in leading his brigade in the successful assaults against the Confederate line at Petersburg on April 2, 1865 and he was brevetted major general of volunteers to rank from that date. Finally his excellent performance in the war was rewarded when, on May 1, 1865, he was appointed a substantive brigadier general of volunteers. He resigned from the army on September 28, 1865, and resumed his law practice in Chicago. The Senate confirmed his nomination on February 23, 1866, and his commission as a substantive brigadier general of volunteers ranked from May 1, 1865.[3]

Osborn served as county treasurer from 1867 to 1869. Fittingly, he served on the board of the National Home for Disabled Volunteers. He served as United States Minister to Argentina from 1874 to 1885, during which time he was able to negotiate a peaceful settlement of a boundary dispute between Argentina and Chile. Between 1885 and 1890 he lived in South America, where he was involved in several railroad construction projects. In 1890 he returned to Chicago and retired. He died in Washington, D.C. fourteen years later and was buried in Section 1 at Arlington National Cemetery. His grave site is marked with a simple government marker, on which his last name is misspelled "Osbourne." The inscription on his grave marker implies that Osborn was a substantive major general in the regular army, whereas he was never in the regular army and was brevetted major general of volunteers.[4]

HALBERT ELEAZER PAINE

Born: February 4, 1826
Died: April 14, 1905

General Paine was born in Chardon, Ohio. He graduated from Western Reserve University in 1845. After briefly teaching school in Mississippi he moved back to Ohio to study law. In 1848 he opened a law office in Cleveland, but nine years later he moved to Milwaukee, Wisconsin, where he became a law partner with future Civil War Union major general Carl Schurz. Paine and Schurz were both staunch abolitionists.[1]

On July 2, 1861, Paine was named colonel of the Fourth Wisconsin Cavalry. In late July the regiment was sent to Baltimore, Maryland, where it performed railroad guard duty until February 1862. In March 1862 the regiment sailed to Ship Island, Mississippi, as a part of Maj. Gen. Benjamin F. Butler's New Orleans Expedition. The regiment participated in the subsequent operations against the two Confederate forts guarding the entrance to the Mississippi River and the occupation of New Orleans. In May 1862 the regiment was sent to Baton Rouge. During his time in Louisiana Paine acted on his abolitionist views by refusing to return fugitive slaves to their owners. He was given orders by Butler to burn Baton Rouge when Union forces evacuated that city in August 1862, but he refused to obey those orders. Paine was placed in command of a brigade in the Department of the Gulf in August 1862 and on January 3, 1863, he was placed in command of a 19th Corps brigade in that department. On January 19, 1863, he was nominated brigadier general of volunteers. The Senate confirmed his nomination on March 13, 1863, and his commission ranked from March 13, 1863. He commanded his brigade until May 2, 1863, when he was given command of a 19th Corps division. On June 14, 1863, during an assault against the Confederate position at Port Hudson, Louisiana, he received three serious wounds to his left leg, his left side, and his left shoulder. After lying on the field all that day under a hot sun, he was finally taken to a field hospital. His left leg was amputated and he went home to recuperate. Later he used an artificial limb.[2]

By September 1863 Paine was able to serve on a military commission in Washington, D.C. Later he served on various boards, commissions, and courts-martial. In July 1864, when Confederate forces were threatening to attack the Washington, D.C. defenses, Paine was given command of Union infantry manning the lines between Forts

Stevens and Totten. He briefly served as commander of the District of Illinois from August 12 to September 30, 1864. He was brevetted major general of volunteers on March 13, 1865, for his performance at Port Hudson. He resigned from the army on May 15, 1865.[3]

Paine served three terms in the United States House of Representatives from March 1865 until March 1871. He was a moderate member of the Radical Republicans. During his third term he served as chairman of the committee on elections, which was involved in questions concerning the seating of representatives from the South. He chose to not run for a fourth term and instead opened a law practice in the nation's capital. In March 1877 his former law partner, Carl Schurz, became Secretary of the Interior, and in 1878 Schurz arranged to have Paine appointed Commissioner of Patents. Paine instituted reforms, such as the use of typewriters by office clerks and the use of drawn plans rather than scaled working models. He resigned in 1880 and resumed his law practice in Washington, D.C. In 1888 he published *A Treatise on the Law of Elections to Public Office*, which remains a highly regarded book on the subject. Paine died in Washington, D.C. and was buried in Section 3 at Arlington National Cemetery.[4]

INNIS NEWTON PALMER

Born: March 30, 1824
Died: September 10, 1900

General Palmer was born in Buffalo, New York. He graduated from West Point in 1846, ranked 38th out of 59. He served gallantly in the mounted rifles during the Mexican War, being promoted to second lieutenant on July 20, 1847. He was brevetted first lieutenant on August 20, 1847, for his performance at both Contreras and Churubusco and captain on September 13, 1847, for his performance at Chapultepec. He was slightly wounded during the latter battle. Between the Mexican War and the Civil War he performed routine garrison duties on the western frontier. He served as regimental adjutant from May 1, 1850, until July 1, 1854. He was promoted to first lieutenant on January 27, 1853, and captain in the Second Cavalry on March 3, 1855.[1]

On April 25, 1861, Palmer was promoted to major in the regular army. During the First Manassas Campaign he commanded a battalion of regular cavalry and he was brevetted lieutenant colonel in the regular army on July 21, 1861, for his performance at First Manassas. In August 1861 he was given command of the cavalry in the Army of the Potomac. On September 28, 1861, he was appointed brigadier general of volunteers. He was given command of a brigade of infantry in the Army of the Potomac in December 1861 and in March 1862 the brigade was assigned to the Fourth Corps. The Senate confirmed his nomination on March 17, 1862, and his commission as a brigadier general of volunteers ranked from September 23, 1861. In May 1862 he ably led his brigade during the fighting at Williamsburg and Fair Oaks during the early stages of the Peninsula Campaign. On June 7, 1862, he was placed in command of a different Fourth Corps brigade, which he ably led during the ensuing Seven Days Campaign. Palmer spent the remainder of 1862 away from the battlefield, organizing new volunteer regiments in Delaware and New Jersey, and managing the draft rendezvous in Philadelphia.[2]

In December 1862 Palmer was sent to North Carolina, where he served for the rest of the war. From January 2, 1863, until March 1, 1865, he commanded at various times an 18th Corps division, the Department of North Carolina, the 18th Corps, the defenses at New Bern, the Subdistrict of New Bern, and the District of North Carolina. He was promoted to lieutenant colonel in the regular army on September 23, 1863. On March 1,

1865, he was given command of a division in the District of Beaufort, and he ably led his command during the fighting at Kinston, North Carolina from March 8 – 10, 1865. On March 13, 1865, he was brevetted colonel and brigadier general in the regular army, as well as major general of volunteers. He commanded the District of Beaufort from March 18, 1865, through the end of the war.[3]

Palmer was mustered out of the volunteer service on January 15, 1866, but he remained in the regular army, being promoted to colonel of the Second Cavalry on June 9, 1868. He spent the next eight years serving on the frontier, mainly in present-day Nebraska and Wyoming. In August 1876 he was forced to go on an extended sick leave. Finally his health problems forced him to resign from the army on March 29, 1879. He lived in and near Washington, D.C. for the next twenty-one years. He died in Chevy Chase, Maryland and was buried in Section 1 at Arlington National Cemetery. The inscription on his grave marker correctly indicates that Palmer was brevetted brigadier general in the regular army, but there is no inscription concerning his service in the volunteers during the Civil War.[4]

GABRIEL RENE PAUL

Born: March 22, 1813
Died: May 5, 1886

General Paul was born in St. Louis, Missouri. He graduated from West Point in 1834, ranked 18th out of 36. He was promoted to second lieutenant on December 4, 1834. He saw action in Florida during the Second Seminole War and was promoted to first lieutenant on October 26, 1836. Prior to the Mexican War he performed routine garrison duty on the frontier and was promoted to captain on April 19, 1846. During the Mexican War he was slightly wounded on April 18, 1847, at Cerro Gordo and he gallantly stormed the enemy defenses at Chapultepec five months later. He was brevetted major on September 13, 1847, for his performance at Chapultepec. After the war he again served at various posts on the western frontier.[1]

At the start of the Civil War Paul was in Albuquerque, where he was serving as acting inspector general of the Department of New Mexico. On April 22, 1861, he was promoted to major in the regular army and on December 9, 1861, he was named colonel of the Fourth New Mexico Infantry. In early 1862 he was in command of the Union forces at Fort Union, as well as the District of Southern New Mexico. He led a column in fighting at Peralta, New Mexico Territory on April 15, 1862, and was promoted to lieutenant colonel in the regular army on April 25, 1862. He was mustered out of the volunteer service on May 31, 1862, the same day that his regiment was mustered out, leaving Paul without an assignment. Soon his wife went to Washington, D.C. She met with Abraham Lincoln on August 23, 1862, and urged the president to appoint her husband a brigadier general of volunteers. On September 5, 1862, Lincoln appointed Paul brigadier general of volunteers. Paul was given command of a First Corps brigade on October 14, 1862. He was not present with his brigade during the fighting at Fredericksburg on December 13, 1862. The Senate failed to act on his nomination before the current congressional session ended on March 4, 1863. By operation of law the appointment expired without confirmation.[2]

Paul was reappointed brigadier general of volunteers on April 18, 1863. He led his brigade during the Chancellorsville Campaign the next month, although it was not involved in any combat. On June 17, 1863, he was placed in command of a different First

Corps brigade, which he ably led during the first day of fighting at Gettysburg on July 1, 1863. His brigade was repelling an enemy assault against its position on the northern end of Seminary Ridge near Oak Hill when Paul was severely wounded in the head by a gunshot. The ball entered behind the right eye and came out through his left eye, rendering him blind for the remainder of his life. His sense of smell and hearing were permanently impaired, and he suffered severe pains in his head and epilepsy for the rest of his life. The Senate finally confirmed his nomination on April 1, 1864, and his commission as brigadier general of volunteers ranked from April 18, 1863. He was promoted to colonel in the regular army on September 13, 1864.[3]

Unable to command forces in the field, Paul retired from the army on February 16, 1865. He was brevetted brigadier general in the regular army on February 23, 1865, for his performance at Gettysburg. On July 28, 1866, he was placed on the retired list as a brigadier general. He was mustered out of the volunteer service on September 1, 1866. He died at his home in Washington, D.C. twenty years later and was buried in Section 1 at Arlington National Cemetery. The inscription on his grave marker correctly indicates that Paul was placed on the retired list as a brigadier general in the regular army, but there is no inscription concerning his service in the volunteers during the Civil War.[4]

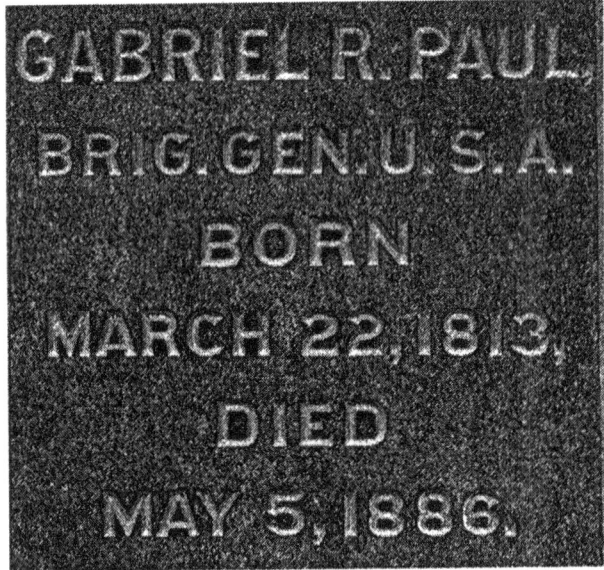

WILLIAM HENRY PENROSE

Born: March 10, 1832
Died: August 29, 1903

General Penrose was born in Sackets Harbor, New York. His father was an officer in the United States army. William attended Dickinson College (Pennsylvania) for two years, and then he moved to Michigan, where he worked as a civil and mechanical engineer until the beginning of the Civil War. He was directly commissioned in the regular army on April 13, 1861, as a second lieutenant in the Third Infantry. A month later, on May 14, 1861, he was promoted to first lieutenant. In May 1862 the regiment was assigned to the Fifth Corps in the Army of the Potomac. Penrose and his regiment saw action during the Seven Days Campaign at Gaines' Mill, White Oak Swamp, and Malvern Hill. In August 1862 the regiment was engaged in the fighting at Second Manassas. Penrose was not with his regiment during the Antietam Campaign of September 1862. He had contracted a fever immediately after the fighting at Manassas, he was sent to Washington, D.C. to recuperate, and then he was assigned as an instructor of new regiments until November 1862. He was with his regiment during the fighting at Fredericksburg in December 1862, although the regiment was only lightly engaged. Between March 1 and April 18, 1863, he was regimental adjutant.[1]

On April 18, 1863, Penrose was named colonel of the 15th New Jersey Infantry, which was assigned to the Sixth Corps. He ably led his regiment in the fighting at Fredericksburg during the Chancellorsville Campaign of May 1863. He was brevetted captain in the regular army on May 3, 1863, for his performance at Fredericksburg. He and his regiment saw little action during the Gettysburg Campaign, however, he was brevetted major in the regular army on July 2, 1863, for his performance at Gettysburg. On September 11, 1863, he was promoted to captain in the regular army. At the beginning of the 1864 Overland Campaign he ably led his regiment in the fighting at The Wilderness and Spotsylvania. He was brevetted lieutenant colonel in the regular army on May 5, 1864, for his performance at The Wilderness. On May 9, 1864, he succeeded to command of his Sixth Corps brigade, which he ably led until July 8, 1864. After briefly returning to command of his regiment, he again commanded his brigade from August 6, 1864, until he was severely wounded in the right arm during the Battle of Cedar Creek on October 19,

1864. He was brevetted colonel in the regular army and brigadier general of volunteers on October 19, 1864, for his performance at Cedar Creek.[2]

Penrose was finally able to return to the field and resume command of his brigade on February 26, 1865. He ably led his brigade through the end of the war. He was slightly wounded in the hip on April 2, 1865, during the assault against the Confederate line at Petersburg. He was brevetted brigadier general in the regular army on April 9, 1865. His excellent performance during the war was finally rewarded when, on June 27, 1865, he was appointed a substantive brigadier general of volunteers. The Senate confirmed his nomination on February 23, 1866, and his commission ranked from June 27, 1865. He was mustered out of the volunteer service on January 15, 1866, but he remained in the regular army as a captain in the Third Infantry. He was promoted to major on May 31, 1883, lieutenant colonel on August 21, 1888, and colonel of the 20th Infantry on November 28, 1893. On September 15, 1894, he became colonel of the 16th Infantry and on March 10, 1896, he retired from the army, having reached the mandatory retirement age of sixty-four. He lived in Salt Lake City, Utah until his death there seven years later. He was buried in Section 3 at Arlington National Cemetery. The inscription on his grave marker correctly indicates the highest substantive and brevet grades Penrose attained in the regular army, but there is no inscription concerning his service in the volunteers during the Civil War.[3]

THOMAS GAMBLE PITCHER

Born: October 23, 1824
Died: October 19, 1895

General Pitcher was born in Rockport, Indiana.[1] He graduated from West Point in 1845, ranked 40th out of 41. He was assigned to the Fifth Infantry and was sent to Texas. He saw action during the Mexican War, being promoted to second lieutenant in the Eighth Infantry on September 21, 1846, and brevetted first lieutenant on August 20, 1847, for his performance at Contreras and Churubusco. After the war he served at various posts on the frontier. From October 2, 1848, until July 1, 1849, he served as regimental quartermaster. He was promoted to first lieutenant on June 26, 1849. He served as regimental adjutant from July 1, 1849, until July 1, 1854, and as regimental quartermaster from the latter date until March 5, 1857. On October 19, 1858, he was promoted to captain.[2]

At the start of the Civil War Pitcher and his regiment were stationed at Fort Bliss, near El Paso, Texas. Pitcher was the depot commissary. In June 1862 he was given command of a battalion of regulars from the Eighth and Twelfth Infantry that was assigned to the Army of Virginia. He ably led his battalion in skirmishing at Cedar Mountain, Virginia on August 9, 1862, until he was severely wounded in the right knee joint. In his after action report Brig. Gen. Christopher C. Augur, Pitcher's division commander, stated that "great credit is due [to Pitcher] for his skillful and effective management of his battalions of skirmishers, which…were of so serious an annoyance to the enemy." Augur went on to recommend that Pitcher be promoted. Pitcher was brevetted major in the regular army on August 9, 1862, for his performance at Cedar Mountain. On March 4, 1863, he was nominated brigadier general of volunteers. The Senate confirmed his nomination on March 10, 1863, and his commission ranked from November 29, 1862.[3]

Pitcher's wound was slow to mend and for a while he had to use crutches in order to move about. Accordingly he was unable to return to the field, but in May 1863 he was sent to Vermont as an assistant provost marshal general. He was promoted to major in the regular army on September 19, 1863. In October 1864 he was sent to Indiana, where he served as an assistant provost marshal through the end of the war. He was brevetted lieutenant colonel, colonel, and brigadier general in the regular army on March 13, 1865. On April 30, 1866, he was mustered out of the volunteer service, but he remained in the regular army, being promoted to colonel of the 44th Infantry on July 28, 1866. He served as superintendent of West Point from August 28, 1866, until September 1, 1871. This would seem to be quite an extraordinary thing, considering his very low class rank and his limited combat experience, but it might have been a convenient means of finding a meaningful assignment for a colonel (and academy graduate) who was unfit for duty on the frontier. After leaving his position of superintendent in 1871 he was named governor of the Soldiers' Home in Washington, D.C., a post he held until 1878. In February 1878 a retirement board found that Pitcher was incapacitated due to immobility or fixation of his right knee joint. This prompted his retirement from the army on June 28, 1878. He died seventeen years later at the post hospital at Fort Bayard, New Mexico Territory and was buried in Section 3 at Arlington National Cemetery. The inscription on his grave marker implies that Pitcher was a substantive brigadier general in the regular army, whereas he had been a substantive brigadier general of volunteers and brevetted brigadier general in the regular army.[4]

JOSEPH BENNETT PLUMMER

Born: November 15, 1816
Died: August 9, 1862

General Plummer was born in Barre, Massachusetts.[1] He taught school for a while before entering West Point in 1837. He graduated in 1841, ranked 22nd out of 52. Prior to the Mexican War he served in the First Infantry in Florida and on the frontier. From August 1846 to June 1847 he was on sick leave. He served as regimental quartermaster from January 1, 1848, until March 1, 1852, and was promoted to first lieutenant on March 15, 1848. He was on an extended sick leave from August 1851 until April 1854, although he was promoted to captain on May 1, 1852. Between October 1860 and January 1861 he was yet again on sick leave. At the start of the Civil War he was stationed in St. Louis, Missouri.[2]

Plummer ably led a battalion of three companies of the First Infantry during the Battle of Wilson's Creek on August 10, 1861, until he was wounded in the right hip. On September 25, 1861, he was named colonel of the Eleventh Missouri (Union) Infantry, which was stationed at Cape Girardeau, Missouri until February 1862. Plummer commanded the Union forces at Cape Girardeau from September 1861 until February 1862. On October 21, 1861, he ably led a column in fighting at Fredericktown, Missouri. On February 21, 1862, he was nominated brigadier general of volunteers. Four days later he was given command of a brigade in the Army of the Mississippi, which he led until March 4, 1862, when he was placed in command of a division in that army. The Senate confirmed his nomination on March 7, 1862, and his commission as brigadier general of volunteers ranked from October 22, 1861. He ably led his division during the siege and capture of New Madrid, Missouri in March 1862 and the siege and capture of Island No. 10 in early April 1862. On April 25, 1862, he was promoted to major in the regular army and the next day he was given command of a brigade in the Army of the Mississippi, which he led during the advance to Corinth, Mississippi.[3]

In early May 1862 Plummer was sick and in early August 1862 he was in Baltimore to see a physician. He was still experiencing problems from his Wilson's Creek wound and he was diagnosed as suffering liver and gastric problems caused by his constant exposure to the elements and camp life. He ignored the advice of his doctors and immediately returned to his command at Corinth, but within a few days of his return there he suddenly died. It is possible that he had contracted malaria and died of liver failure. Certainly his previous bouts with illnesses that had necessitated so many sick leaves before the Civil War suggests that he had a weak constitution and was susceptible to disease. It is not known where he was originally buried, but he was ultimately buried in Section 1 at Arlington National Cemetery. The inscription on his grave marker implies that Plummer was a brigadier general in the regular army, whereas he was a brigadier general of volunteers and a major in the regular army.[4]

ORLANDO METCALFE POE

Born: March 7, 1832
Died: October 2, 1895

General Poe was born in Navarre, Ohio. He graduated from West Point in 1856, ranked sixth out of 49. Based on his class ranking, he was assigned to the prestigious Corps of Topographical Engineers. He spent the next four and a half years engaged in surveying work along the northern lakes and was promoted to second lieutenant on October 7, 1856, and first lieutenant on July 1, 1860. In May 1861 he was assigned as a topographical engineer to the Department of the Ohio, serving in Ohio and western Virginia under Maj. Gen. George B. McClellan. When McClellan became the commander of the Army of the Potomac later that summer, Poe went with him to Washington, D.C. as a topographical engineer.[1]

On September 16, 1861, Poe was named colonel of the Second Michigan Infantry. The regiment spent the winter of 1861 – 1862 manning the defenses at Washington, D.C. In March 1862 the regiment was assigned to the Third Corps and in May 1862 it saw action at Williamsburg and Seven Pines during the early stages of the Peninsula Campaign. On May 31, 1862, during fighting at Seven Pines the horse Poe was riding was killed and Poe suffered severe bruises when the horse fell on him. This injury, in conjunction with a fever Poe had contracted the previous month, compelled him to go home on sick leave. Accordingly he missed the fighting during the ensuing Seven Days Campaign. When he returned to the field in early August 1862 Poe was given command of a Third Corps brigade, which he led during the Second Manassas Campaign later that month. His brigade was left behind in the Washington, D.C. defenses during the Antietam Campaign of September 1862. He was appointed brigadier general of volunteers on November 29, 1862, and based on his appointment he was given command of a Ninth Corps brigade on November 31, 1862. He led his brigade during the Fredericksburg Campaign the next month, although his command saw little action during the fighting of December 13, 1862. On March 3, 1863, he was promoted to captain in the regular army.[2]

The Senate failed to act on Poe's nomination as brigadier general of volunteers before the current congressional session ended on March 4, 1863. By operation of law the appointment expired without confirmation. Poe was not reappointed brigadier general of volunteers and he reverted back to a captain of engineers in the regular army. On April 11, 1863, he was named chief engineer for the 23rd Corps, which, as a part of the Army of the Ohio, was stationed in Tennessee. Poe was mainly involved in preparing the defenses at Knoxville, Tennessee, and in late 1863 Union forces manning those defenses withstood an assault by Confederate forces. In the spring of 1864 he was named chief engineer of the Military Division of the Mississippi and in that capacity he ably assisted Maj. Gen. William T. Sherman in the latter's Atlanta Campaign, the March to the Sea, and the Carolinas Campaign. Poe was brevetted major in the regular army on July 6, 1864, for his performance at Knoxville, lieutenant colonel in the regular on September 1, 1864, for his performance in the Atlanta Campaign, colonel in the regular army on December 21, 1864, for his performance at Savannah, and brigadier general in the regular army on March 13, 1865, for his performance in the Carolinas Campaign.[3]

Poe remained in the regular army after the war, serving in the Corps of Engineers and later on the lighthouse board. He was promoted to major on March 7, 1867. On July 1, 1873, he was promoted to colonel of staff and as such he served as an aide-de-camp to army commander William T. Sherman until the latter's retirement on February 8, 1884. Poe was promoted to lieutenant colonel on June 30, 1882, and colonel on July 23, 1888. He retired from the army on February 8, 1894. On September 18, 1895, Poe fell and bruised his left leg while inspecting a lighthouse in Michigan. The leg became infected, the infection quickly spread, and he died less than a month later in Detroit, Michigan. He was buried in Section 1 at Arlington National Cemetery. The inscription on his grave marker correctly indicates the highest substantive and brevet grades Poe attained in the regular army, but there is no inscription concerning his service in the volunteers during the Civil War.[4]

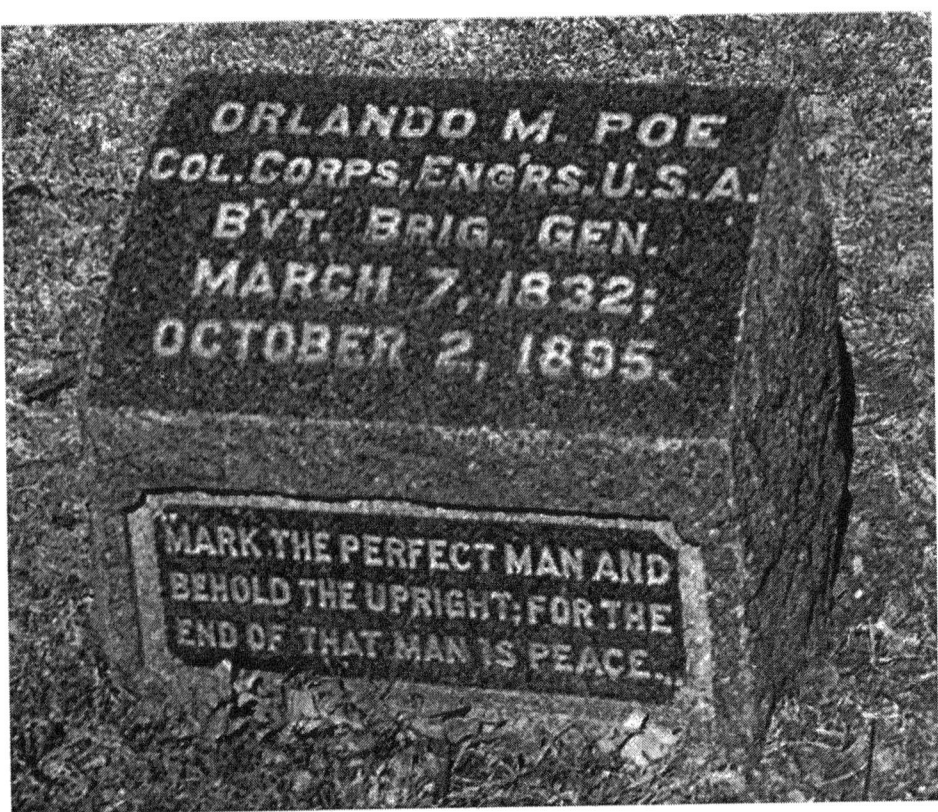

GREEN BERRY RAUM

Born: December 3, 1829
Died: December 18, 1909

General Raum was born in Golconda, Illinois. His father was an officer in the War of 1812 and the Black Hawk War, as well as a local politician and court clerk. In his youth Green made three flatboat trips down the Mississippi River to New Orleans. In 1853 he began to practice law in Illinois. He moved to Kansas Territory in 1856, but the next year he returned to Illinois and opened a law practice in Harrisburg, Illinois. He attended the 1860 Democratic National Convention as an alternate delegate. Although he supported Stephen A. Douglas for president in the election that autumn, he supported the war effort when the Civil War began.[1]

On September 28, 1861, Raum was named major of the 56th Illinois Infantry. The regiment was finally mustered into the Federal service on February 27, 1862, and it was immediately sent to Paducah, Kentucky, where it engaged in garrison duties until late April 1862. At that time the regiment was assigned to the Army of the Mississippi and it participated in the advance to Corinth, Mississippi in May 1862. On June 26, 1862, Raum was promoted to lieutenant colonel and on August 31, 1862, he became colonel of his regiment. He ably led his regiment in the fighting at Corinth on October 4, 1862, where his men retook a captured Union battery. In January 1863 the regiment was assigned to the 17th Corps in the Army of the Tennessee. Raum ably led his regiment during the army's advance to Vicksburg in the spring of 1863, seeing action on May 16 at Champion Hill and the next day at Big Black River, as well as the two assaults against the Vicksburg defenses on May 19 and 22. On June 10, 1863, Raum was given command of his brigade, which he ably led during the remainder of the siege of Vicksburg. He commanded a 17th Corps brigade during the Chattanooga Campaign, until he was severely wounded in the left thigh on November 25, 1863, during the fighting at Missionary Ridge. His sciatic nerve was damaged and he spent the next two months at home recuperating from his wound.[2]

On February 10, 1864, Raum was given command of a 15th Corps brigade, which he ably led during the Atlanta Campaign and the March to the Sea. He was brevetted brigadier general of volunteers on September 19, 1864. In late January 1865 ongoing problems regarding his wound compelled him to take sick leave. For the rest of his life his leg was weak and painful, and he had numbness in his leg. While he was convalescing he was nominated a substantive brigadier general of volunteers on February 14, 1865. The Senate confirmed his nomination on February 23, 1865, and his commission ranked from February 15, 1865. Finally in the spring of 1865 he was able to resume field command, and on April 2, 1865, he was placed in command of a brigade in the Shenandoah Valley, which he led until he resigned from the army on May 6, 1865.[3]

Raum led an active life after the war. He created and was the first president of the Cairo and Vincennes Railroad. Now aligned with the Radical Republicans, he served one term in the United States House of Representatives from 1867 to 1869. He served as United States Commissioner of Internal Revenue from 1876 to 1883. Between 1883 and 1889 he practiced law in Washington, D.C. and from 1889 until 1893 he served as United States Pension Commissioner. Although his tenure as pension commissioner was marred with allegations of corruption, no charges were ever filed against Raum. In 1893 he moved to Chicago, Illinois, where he practiced law. He died in Chicago sixteen years later and was buried in Section 2 at Arlington National Cemetery.[4]

JOHN AARON RAWLINS

Born: February 13, 1831
Died: September 6, 1869

General Rawlins was born in Galena, Illinois. In 1854 he began to practice law in Galena and in 1857 he became the city attorney. He was involved in local politics and he served as an elector for Stephen A. Douglas in the 1860 presidential election. With the start of the Civil War, Rawlins, who strongly supported the war effort, made numerous speeches to rally local support for the war. His efforts caught the attention of another Galena resident, Ulysses S. Grant. When Grant became a brigadier general of volunteers in the summer of 1861, Rawlins agreed to serve as Grant's aide-de-camp.[1]

For the remainder of his life Rawlins' career was inextricably associated with Grant. He proved to be an invaluable friend, staff officer, and adviser to Grant, and as Grant became more and more successful in the war, Rawlins was rewarded with promotions. On August 30, 1861, Rawlins was named captain and assistant adjutant general on Grant's staff, and on May 14, 1862, he was promoted to major. He served on Grant's staff as chief of staff and assistant adjutant general of the Army of the Tennessee from October 16, 1862, until October 16, 1863. On November 1, 1862, he was promoted to lieutenant colonel. On August 11, 1863, he was appointed brigadier general of volunteers. He served on Grant's staff as chief of staff of the Military Division of the Mississippi from October 16, 1863, until March 29, 1864. The Senate confirmed his nomination on April 1, 1864, and his commission as brigadier general of volunteers ranked from August 11, 1863. When Grant was promoted to lieutenant general and named general-in-chief of the Union armies in the spring of 1864, Rawlins became Grant's chief of staff for general headquarters in the field. He was brevetted major general of volunteers on February 24, 1865, and was mustered out of the volunteer service on March 3, 1865. That same day he was nominated a substantive brigadier general in the regular army and he was named chief of staff of the Union army. The Senate confirmed his nomination six days later, and his commission ranked from March 3, 1865. On April 9, 1865, he was brevetted major general in the regular army.[2]

Rawlins contracted bronchitis in November 1863 and he experienced other health problems during 1864. In 1865 Rawlins learned that he was suffering from tuberculosis, the same disease that had killed his wife four years earlier. Despite his deteriorating health, Rawlins continued to serve as army chief of staff for the next four years. His doctors advised him to spend time out west, so he traveled on the high plains along the proposed route of the Union Pacific Railroad and he explored parts of Idaho Territory, but his health did not improve. Rawlins, Wyoming is named for him. On March 12, 1869, Rawlins resigned from the army in order to assume his new duties as President Grant's Secretary of War. Unfortunately Rawlins died in Washington, D.C. from tuberculosis barely six months later. He was buried in Section 2 at Arlington National Cemetery. The inscription on his grave marker does not clearly indicate that Rawlins was a major general by brevet only in both the regular army and the volunteers.[3]

JOSEPH JONES REYNOLDS

Born: January 4, 1822
Died: February 25, 1899

General Reynolds was born in Flemingsburg, Kentucky. In 1836 his family moved to Lafayette, Indiana. After attending Wabash College in Crawfordsville, Indiana for a year he entered West Point in 1839. He graduated in 1843, ranked tenth out of 39. During the next three years he performed routine garrison duties on the frontier and in Texas, being promoted to second lieutenant on May 11, 1846. Then he taught at West Point from 1846 to 1854, and afterwards he again served on the frontier. He resigned from the army on February 28, 1857, in order to assume his new duties as a professor of mechanics and engineering at Washington University in St. Louis, Missouri. At the beginning of the Civil War he was working in Lafayette, Indiana as a wholesale grocer, in partnership with his brother.[1]

On April 23, 1861, Reynolds was named colonel of the Tenth Indiana Militia and on May 10, 1861, he was named brigadier general of Indiana militia. On June 14, 1861, he was appointed brigadier general of volunteers. He was given command of a brigade in the Department of the Ohio in July 1861. The Senate confirmed his nomination on August 3, 1861, and his commission ranked from May 17, 1861. He commanded the Union column that won a minor victory at Cheat Mountain, (West) Virginia in September 1861. He resigned from the army on January 23, 1862, in order to return to Lafayette and settle the estate of his brother and business partner. While he was away from the army Reynolds helped organize and train Indiana recruits. By the autumn of 1862 he was ready to return to field command. On September 17, 1862, he was again appointed brigadier general of volunteers and on November 29, 1862, he was appointed major general of volunteers. The latter appointment is puzzling, considering his limited combat experience as of November 1862.[2]

On December 11, 1862, Reynolds was given command of a division in the Army of the Cumberland. His division was not present during the fighting at Stones River later that month, instead being engaged in guarding the Louisville & Nashville Railroad against Confederate cavalry. On March 9, 1863, the Senate confirmed his nomination as major general of volunteers and two days later the Senate confirmed his nomination as brigadier general of volunteers. Both commissions ranked from the dates of appointment. He commanded a 14th Corps division during the Battle of Chickamauga in September 1863 and on October 10, 1863, he was named chief of staff for the Army of the Cumberland, a position he held during the fighting at Chattanooga in November 1863. From January 6 to June 16, 1864, he commanded the Union defenses at New Orleans and he commanded the 19th Corps in the Department of the Gulf from July 7 to November 7, 1864. He commanded the Department of Arkansas from December 22, 1864, through the end of the war.[3]

On July 28, 1866, Reynolds was promoted to colonel in the regular army and on September 1, 1866, he was mustered out of the volunteer service. He remained in the regular army, commanding forces in Texas and Louisiana. On March 2, 1867, he was brevetted brigadier general in the regular army for his performance at Chickamauga and major general in the regular army for his performance at Chattanooga. In 1871 he briefly served in the United States Senate, until the election results were overturned. In March 1876 he led an expedition that captured a Sioux village along the Powder River, however, he inexplicably retreated without pursuing the hostile Indian warriors. A court-martial was held and Reynolds retired from the army on June 25, 1877, exactly one year after some of those Sioux warriors participated in the Battle of the Little Bighorn. Reynolds lived in Washington, D.C. until his death there more than twenty years later. He was buried in Section 1 at Arlington National Cemetery. The inscription on his grave marker does not clearly indicate that he was a major general in the regular army by brevet only, and there is no inscription concerning his service in the volunteers during the Civil War.[4]

AMERICUS VESPUCIUS RICE

Born: November 18, 1835
Died: April 4, 1904

General Rice was born in Perryville, Ohio. After attending Antioch College in Yellow Springs, Ohio for a while, he entered Union College in Schenectady, New York and graduated from there in 1860. At the start of the Civil War he was studying law. He quickly enlisted in the 21st Ohio Infantry, a three-month regiment, and was named captain on April 27, 1861. The regiment saw no combat, mainly being assigned to garrison duties along the Ohio River and in western Virginia, and it was mustered out on August 12, 1861.[1]

Soon Rice enlisted in the 57th Ohio Infantry and was named captain on September 2, 1861. In February 1862 the regiment was sent to Paducah, Kentucky and Rice was named lieutenant colonel of the regiment on February 8, 1862. The next month the regiment was assigned to the Army of the Tennessee and Rice commanded the regiment during the fighting at Shiloh on April 6 – 7, 1862. Col. Jesse Hildebrand, Rice's brigade commander, stated in his after action report that Rice "rendered efficient service" and that he "behaved with bravery, and exhibited much skill in the movement of the regiment." Rice ably led his regiment during the advance to Corinth, Mississippi in May 1862, during the fighting at Chickasaw Bluffs, Mississippi in late December 1862, and during the capture of Fort Hindman at Arkansas Post in January 1863. He ably led his regiment throughout the early stages of the Vicksburg Campaign until he was severely wounded in the leg and abdomen during one of the major Union assaults against the Confederate defenses at Vicksburg on May 22, 1863. He was promoted to colonel of his regiment on May 24, 1863. He went home on sick leave and was unable to return to the field until February 1864.[2]

Rice led his regiment during the early stages of the advance from Chattanooga towards Atlanta in the spring of 1864. On June 27, 1864, he received three wounds almost simultaneously while bravely leading his regiment in the assault against the Confederate defenses at Kennesaw Mountain, Georgia. He suffered a slight laceration on the forehead, several bones near the left ankle were broken, and his right thighbone was shattered. His right leg was amputated and he was away from the army, recuperating from his wounds, until late June 1865. In the meantime on May 31, 1865, he was appointed a substantive brigadier general of volunteers, which was a rather extraordinary thing, considering the fact that the war was over and he had only commanded a regiment throughout the war. When he was able to resume field command in late June he was given command of a 15th Corps brigade. He was mustered out of the volunteer service on January 15, 1866. The Senate finally confirmed his nomination on February 23, 1866, and his commission as a brigadier general of volunteers ranked from May 31, 1865.[3]

After the war Rice worked as a banker in Ottawa, Ohio and he served as a delegate to the 1872 Democratic National Convention. He served in the United States House of Representatives from 1875 to 1879. He chose to not run for reelection after his second term and returned to Ottawa, where he engaged in business. He also worked as a state pension agent. In 1898 he moved to Washington, D.C., where he worked as a purchasing agent for the United States Census Bureau. He died in the nation's capital six years later and was buried in Section 3 at Arlington National Cemetery.[4]

JAMES BREWERTON RICKETTS

Born: June 21, 1817
Died: September 22, 1887

General Ricketts was born in New York, New York. He graduated from West Point in 1839, ranked 16th out of 31. Assigned to the First Artillery, he was promoted to first lieutenant on April 21, 1846. He participated in the battles of Monterey and Buena Vista during the Mexican War, but he was not awarded any brevets. Between the Mexican War and Civil War he was engaged in garrison duties at various posts. He was regimental quartermaster from June 15, 1849, until August 3, 1852. On the latter date he was promoted to captain.[1]

On July 21, 1861, Ricketts commanded a battery at the Battle of First Manassas. During that battle he was wounded four times in the head and legs. Captured by the Confederates, he was sent to a prison in Richmond, Virginia. His wife was permitted to come to Richmond and take care of him while he was imprisoned. He was brevetted lieutenant colonel in the regular army on July 21, 1861, for his performance at First Manassas. In January 1862 he was exchanged for Capt. Julius A. de Lagnel and on March 27, 1862, while still recuperating from his wounds, he was nominated brigadier general of volunteers. The Senate confirmed his nomination on April 28, 1862, and his commission ranked from July 21, 1861. In May 1862 he was able to return to the field and was given command of a brigade and later a division in the Department of the Rappahannock. On June 26, 1862, he was placed in command of a division in the newly formed Army of Virginia. He led his division in the fighting at Cedar Mountain and Second Manassas. With the reorganization of the Army of the Potomac after the latter battle, Ricketts was given command of a First Corps division, which he led at Antietam on September 17, 1862. During that battle two horses he was riding were killed and Ricketts suffered injuries when the second of these horses fell on him. He would not be able to return to field command until the spring of 1864.[2]

During 1863 Ricketts served on several commissions and courts-martial, including the celebrated court-martial of Maj. Gen. Fitz John Porter. On June 1, 1863, he was promoted to major in the regular army. He ably led a Sixth Corps division during the Overland Campaign in the spring of 1864, being brevetted colonel in the regular army on

June 3, 1864, for his performance at Cold Harbor. In July 1864 his division was sent to the Washington, D.C. area to oppose Confederate forces threatening the nation's capital. He ably led his division in the fighting at Monocacy, Maryland on July 9, 1864, which delayed the Confederate advance towards Washington, D.C. and helped save the capital. He then ably led his division during the 1864 Shenandoah Valley Campaign. On October 19, 1864, during the Battle of Cedar Creek, he was severely wounded in the right shoulder while temporarily commanding the Sixth Corps. He was brevetted major general of volunteers on August 1, 1864, for his performance at Monocacy and the Shenandoah Valley. On March 13, 1865, he was brevetted brigadier general in the regular army for his performance at Cedar Creek and major general in the regular army for his war service. In April 1865 he was able to return to command of his division, which he led through the end of the war.[3]

Ricketts was mustered out of the volunteer service on April 30, 1866. He tried to remain in the regular army, although he was suffering considerable pain in his right shoulder and arm from his Cedar Creek wound. Eight months later, on January 3, 1867, complications from his wound compelled him to retire from the army and he was placed on the retired list as a major general. He continued to serve on courts-martial until 1869. He lived in Washington, D.C. until his death there eighteen years later. He was buried in Section 1 at Arlington National Cemetery. The inscription on his grave marker correctly indicates that Ricketts was placed on the retired list as a major general in the regular army, but there is no inscription concerning his service in the volunteers during the Civil War.[4]

WILLIAM STARKE ROSECRANS

Born: September 6, 1819
Died: March 11, 1898

General Rosecrans was born on a farm in Delaware County, Ohio. He graduated from West Point in 1842, ranked fifth out of 56. Assigned to the prestigious Engineer Corps, he saw no action during the Mexican War. He was promoted to second lieutenant on April 3, 1843, and first lieutenant on March 3, 1853. On April 1, 1854, he resigned from the army. For the next seven years he worked as an architect, civil engineer, petroleum refiner, and president of two different coal companies. In 1859 he was severely burned when an oil lamp exploded near his head.[1]

In April 1861 Rosecrans became an aide-de-camp on the staff of Maj. Gen. George B. McClellan as well as a colonel in the Ohio militia. On June 14, 1861, he was appointed a substantive brigadier general in the regular army. Between May and July 1861 he commanded a brigade under McClellan in the Department of the Ohio. On July 11, 1861, Rosecrans led the successful Union forces in fighting at Rich Mountain, (West) Virginia. He succeeded McClellan as commander of the Department of the Ohio on July 23, 1861. The Senate confirmed his nomination on August 3, 1861, and Rosecrans' commission as a brigadier general in the regular army ranked from May 16, 1861. He commanded the victorious Union forces at Carnifex Ferry, (West) Virginia on September 10, 1861. On September 19, 1861, he was placed in command of the Department of Western Virginia, which he commanded until March 11, 1862. Then Rosecrans was sent to the Western Theater, where he would achieve great success and suffer great misfortune.[2]

Rosecrans commanded a wing of the Army of the Mississippi during the advance to Corinth in May 1862. On June 26, 1862, he was given command of that army, and he successfully led his army in fighting at both Iuka on September 19, 1862, and Corinth on October 3 – 4, 1862. He was given command of the Army of the Cumberland on October 24, 1862, and the next day he was appointed major general of volunteers. He led his army to victory at the Battle of Stones River (December 31, 1862 – January 3, 1863). The Senate confirmed his nomination on March 10, 1863, and his commission as major general of volunteers ranked from March 21, 1862. In June 1863 he maneuvered the Confederate forces out of Middle Tennessee during the Tullahoma Campaign. His streak of battlefield successes ended abruptly on September 20, 1863, during the second day of fighting at Chickamauga, when Confederate forces exploited a gap in Rosecrans' line and routed more than half of the army (including Rosecrans himself) from the field. His army was then besieged at Chattanooga and Rosecrans was unable to find a way to either end the siege or open up a reliable supply line for his starving army. He was removed from command of his army on October 19, 1863. On January 22, 1864, he was placed in command of the Department of the Missouri, which he commanded until December 2, 1864. He spent the remainder of the war awaiting orders that never came. On March 13, 1865, he was brevetted major general in the regular army for his performance at Stones River. He was mustered out of the volunteer service on January 15, 1866, and he resigned from the army on March 28, 1867.[3]

Rosecrans served as United States minister to Mexico from 1868 to 1869 and then he moved to California, where he worked as a rancher, railroad construction engineer, and mine operator. He served two terms in the United States House of Representatives, from 1881 until 1885. From 1885 until 1893 he served as registrar of the United States Treasury Department. He then retired to his ranch at Redondo Beach, California, where he died five years later. He was originally buried at Rosedale Cemetery in Los Angeles, California, but on May 17, 1902, his remains were reinterred in Section 3 at Arlington National Cemetery. The inscription on his grave marker does not clearly indicate that Rosecrans was a major general in the regular army by brevet only and a major general of volunteers.[4]

LOVELL HARRISON ROUSSEAU

Born: August 4, 1818
Died: January 7, 1869

General Rousseau was born near Stanford, Kentucky. His father died of cholera when Lovell was fifteen. This prompted Lovell to cease his education in local schools and begin to work as a laborer on the construction of a turnpike. Later he moved to Lexington, Kentucky, in order to study law. In 1840 he moved to Bloomfield, Indiana, where he practiced law. He was elected to the Indiana legislature as a Whig in 1844. On June 22, 1846, he enlisted as a captain in the Second Indiana Infantry. He saw action at Buena Vista during the Mexican War and mustered out of the army on June 23, 1847. After serving in the Indiana senate from 1847 to 1849, he moved to Louisville, Kentucky, where he became a successful criminal lawyer. He was elected to the Kentucky senate in 1860, but he resigned his seat in 1861 in order to recruit volunteers to fight for the Union.[1]

On September 9, 1861, Rousseau was named colonel of the Third Kentucky (Union) Infantry. His efforts to keep Kentucky in the Union were rewarded when, on October 1, 1861, he was appointed brigadier general of volunteers. Between October 5, 1861, and July 11, 1862, he commanded several different brigades, first in the Department of the Cumberland and then in the Army of the Ohio. The Senate confirmed his nomination on March 7, 1862, and his commission as brigadier general of volunteers ranked from October 1, 1861. He ably led his brigade in fighting at Shiloh on April 7, 1862. On July 11, 1862, he was given command of a division in the Army of the Ohio, which he ably led during the Battle of Perryville on October 8, 1862. On October 22, 1862, he was appointed major general of volunteers. Between October 24, 1862, and November 10, 1863, he commanded several different divisions in the Army of the Cumberland. He ably led his division during the fighting at Stones River (December 31, 1862 – January 3, 1863). The Senate confirmed his nomination on March 9, 1863, and his commission as major general of volunteers ranked from October 8, 1862. He ably led his division during the Tullahoma Campaign in June 1863. He was not present during the Battle of Chickamauga in September 1863. On November 10, 1863, he was placed in command of the District of Nashville and on May 30, 1864, he was given command of the District of Tennessee. In July 1864 he led a successful cavalry raid in northern Alabama, wherein railroads and vital supplies were destroyed with minimal losses to his forces. On February 28, 1865, he was placed in command of the District of Middle Tennessee, which he commanded through the end of the war.[2]

Rousseau had been elected to the United States House of Representatives, and so he resigned from the army on November 30, 1865, in order to take his seat in Congress. Elected as a Radical Republican, he soon became a moderate. Unfortunately one day after a heated debate he lost his temper and caned a Radical representative from Iowa. Rousseau was censured by the House and forced to resign on July 21, 1866. He was soon reelected and held his seat from December 3, 1866, until March 3, 1867. During his service in the House he had supported the policies of President Andrew Johnson. That support was rewarded when Johnson sent Rousseau to Alaska to formally receive Alaska from Russia. Johnson also nominated Rousseau for several promotions in the regular army. On March 28, 1867, Rousseau was commissioned brigadier general and brevet major general in the regular army. He commanded the Department of the Columbia from April 29, 1867, until April 4, 1868, and the Department of Louisiana from July 28, 1868, until his death in New Orleans the next January. He was buried in Section 2 at Arlington National Cemetery. The inscription on his grave marker correctly indicates the highest substantive and brevet grades Rousseau attained in the regular army, but there is no inscription concerning his service in the volunteers during the Civil War. Rousseau shares the same headstone with his son-in-law, Brig. Gen. Louis D. Watkins.[3]

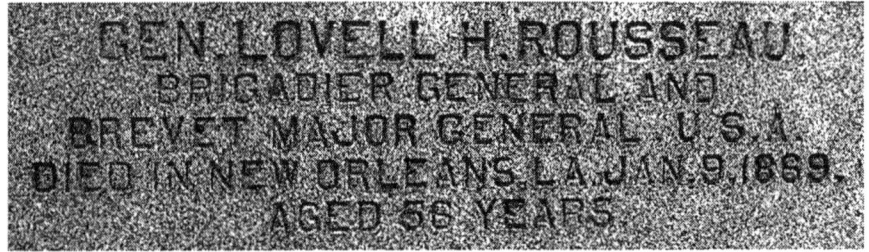

DANIEL HENRY RUCKER

Born: April 28, 1812
Died: January 6, 1910

General Rucker was born in Belleville, New Jersey. On October 13, 1837, he was directly commissioned in the army as a second lieutenant in the First Dragoons. He served at various posts on the frontier and was promoted to first lieutenant on October 8, 1844, and captain on February 7, 1847. He saw action during the Mexican War, being brevetted major on February 23, 1847, for his performance at Buena Vista. On August 23, 1849, he was named an assistant quartermaster and he spent the next thirty-three years in the Quartermaster Department.[1]

On April 29, 1861, Rucker was named chief quartermaster of the Department of Washington, D.C. He held this position through the end of the war, making him one of the few Union officers to command the same post throughout the entire war. He was promoted to major of staff in the regular army on August 3, 1861. On September 28, 1861, he was promoted to colonel of staff in the regular army and was named an aide-de-camp. He ably assisted his chief, Brig. Gen. and Quartermaster General Montgomery C. Meigs, by smoothly operating the huge quartermaster depot in Washington, D.C. Rucker greatly aided the successful prosecution of the war, by working tirelessly behind the scenes to keep the armies operating in Virginia properly supplied. In his annual report of the operations of the Quartermaster's Department, dated November 3, 1864, Meigs praised Rucker's management of the Washington, D.C. depot, noting that its "operations have been conducted with dispatch, order, and regularity, and the large force of men employed about the depot have been governed in such manner that discontent and disorder have been prevented." Rucker's efforts were rewarded when, on May 23, 1863, he was appointed brigadier general of volunteers. The Senate finally confirmed his nomination on May 7, 1864, and his commission ranked from May 23, 1863. Then on July 5, 1864, he was brevetted lieutenant colonel, colonel, and brigadier general in the regular army. And on March 13, 1865, he was brevetted major general of volunteers and major general in the regular army.[2]

With the reorganization of the army after the war, Rucker was promoted to colonel of staff and named assistant quartermaster general on July 28, 1866. He was mustered out of the volunteer service on September 1, 1866. As assistant quartermaster general he continued to serve under Quartermaster General Montgomery C. Meigs until Meigs retired in February 1882. On February 13, 1882, Rucker was promoted to brigadier general and named quartermaster general of the army. He retired from the army ten days later and lived in Washington, D.C. for the next 28 years. He died in Washington, D.C. at the age of ninety-seven and was buried in Section 1 at Arlington National Cemetery. His son-in-law was Maj. Gen. Philip H. Sheridan. The inscription on his grave marker correctly indicates the highest substantive grade Rucker attained in the regular army, but there is no inscription concerning his service in the volunteers during the Civil War.[3]

RUFUS SAXTON

Born: October 19, 1824
Died: February 23, 1908

General Saxton was born in Greenfield, Massachusetts. He attended the Deerfield Academy and then worked as a farmer. He graduated from West Point in 1849, ranked 18th out of 43. During the next twelve years he served in Florida against the Seminoles, performed routine garrison duties at various posts on the frontier, participated in the Northern Pacific Railroad survey, served as an instructor of artillery tactics at West Point, and served on coastal surveys in the East. He was promoted to second lieutenant on September 12, 1850, and first lieutenant on March 2, 1855. He also patented a self-registering thermometer used for deep-sea soundings.[1]

At the start of the Civil War Saxton was in command of an artillery detachment at the St. Louis arsenal. On May 10, 1861, he assisted Capt. Nathaniel Lyon in the capture of pro-secessionist forces at Camp Jackson in St. Louis. Three days later Saxton was promoted to captain of staff in the regular army and was named assistant quartermaster under Lyon. That summer he briefly served as assistant quartermaster in the Department of the Ohio under Maj. Gen. George B. McClellan. From September 9, 1861, until March 15, 1862, he served as assistant quartermaster of the Port Royal Expedition in South Carolina. On March 25, 1862, he was nominated brigadier general of volunteers. The Senate confirmed his nomination on April 15, 1862, and his commission ranked from April 15, 1862. In late May 1862 he was placed in command of the post at Harpers Ferry, which was then threatened by the advancing Confederate forces under Maj. Gen. Thomas J. Jackson. Saxton's forces repulsed several enemy attacks and maintained possession of Harpers Ferry. Secretary of War Edwin M. Stanton sent Saxton a message congratulating him for his "able and gallant defense" of Harpers Ferry.[2]

In the summer of 1862 Saxton was sent to South Carolina, where he was the independent military governor of the coastal islands off South Carolina and Georgia. He commanded the Tenth Corps stationed at Beaufort, South Carolina from February 19, 1863, until April 17, 1864. From April 25, 1864, through the end of the war he commanded several different military districts in the Department of the South. His major task during his three years in South Carolina was to recruit former slaves from that area, train them as Union soldiers, and organize them into units. He performed this task admirably, winning the confidence and respect of his recruits, and raising combat ready black regiments. On January 12, 1865, he was brevetted major general of volunteers. He also served as assistant inspector general for the Department of the South from January 23, 1865, through the end of the war. On March 13, 1865, he was brevetted major, lieutenant colonel, and colonel in the regular army. He was brevetted brigadier general in the regular army on April 9, 1865. He was mustered out of the volunteer service on January 15, 1866.[3]

With the reorganization of the army after the war, Saxton was promoted to major of staff in the Quartermaster Department on July 29, 1866. For the next twenty-two years he served in that department at various posts. On June 6, 1872, he was promoted to lieutenant colonel of staff and named deputy quartermaster. On March 10, 1882, he was promoted to colonel of staff and named assistant quartermaster. He retired from the army on October 19, 1888, and moved to Washington, D.C. In 1893 he was awarded the Medal of Honor for his "distinguished gallantry and good conduct in the defense" of Harpers Ferry on May 26 – 30, 1862. On April 23, 1904, he was placed on the retired list of the army as a brigadier general. He died in Washington, D.C. four years later and was buried in Section 1 at Arlington National Cemetery.[4]

JOHN McALLISTER SCHOFIELD

Born: September 29, 1831
Died: March 4, 1906

General Schofield was born in Gerry, New York. His family moved to Freeport, Illinois in 1843. Schofield was sixteen years old when in 1847 he took a job in Wisconsin as a surveyor and the next year he began to work as a teacher in Wisconsin. He graduated from West Point in 1853, ranked seventh out of 52. Assigned to the artillery, he was sent to Florida, where he saw action against the Seminoles. He was promoted to second lieutenant on August 31, 1853, and first lieutenant on March 3, 1855. In 1855 he became ill with fever (malaria, or typhoid, or yellow fever) and was sent back north to recuperate. He stayed at the home of future Confederate Lt. Gen. Ambrose P. Hill in Culpeper, Virginia, until he had recovered from his illness. Soon he became an instructor of philosophy at West Point. In 1860 he took a leave of absence from the army to assume his duties as a professor of physics at Washington University in St. Louis, Missouri. He held that position when the Civil War began.[1]

On April 26, 1861, Schofield was named major of the First Missouri (Union) Infantry, a three-month regiment organized in St. Louis. He was promoted to captain in the regular army on May 14, 1861. On June 10, 1861, his regiment was reorganized as a three-year regiment and Schofield was again named major of the regiment (which soon became the First Missouri Light Artillery). He also served as an aide-de-camp for Brig. Gen. Nathaniel Lyon in Missouri during the first months of the war, and on July 2, 1861, Schofield became Lyon's chief of staff and an assistant adjutant general in Lyon's Army of the West. He served as such until Lyon's death at the Battle of Wilson's Creek on August 10, 1861. On November 21, 1861, Schofield was appointed brigadier general of volunteers. He commanded the District of St. Louis from November 21, 1861, until April 10, 1862. On November 26, 1861, he was also named brigadier general in the Missouri militia and was given command of all Missouri militia forces. The Senate confirmed his nomination on February 3, 1862, and his commission as brigadier general of volunteers ranked from November 21, 1861. He commanded the District of Missouri from June 1 until September 26, 1862, during which time his major task was to subdue Confederate guerilla activities in Missouri and Kansas. He briefly commanded the Army of Southwest

Missouri in early October 1862 and on October 8, 1862, he was named major general of Missouri militia. On October 12, 1862, he was given command of the Army of the Frontier. His army won a strategic victory at the Battle of Prairie Grove in northwestern Arkansas on December 7, 1862, although Schofield was not present during the fighting. Several weeks earlier he had gone to St. Louis to recuperate from typhoid.[2]

On November 29, 1862, Schofield was appointed major general of volunteers, but the Senate failed to act on his nomination before the current congressional session ended on March 4, 1863. By operation of law the appointment expired without confirmation. A few senators who were unhappy with Schofield's actions while in command in Missouri held up the nomination in committee. Schofield briefly commanded a 14th Corps division in the Army of the Cumberland between April 17 and May 10, 1863, but he was soon returned to administrative positions. He was reappointed major general of volunteers on May 12, 1863. He commanded the Department of the Missouri from May 13, 1863, until January 22, 1864, and then he commanded the Department of the Ohio from January 28 to November 8, 1864. Schofield had been seeking a change of assignment to field command and finally in early 1864 his requests were granted. In addition to commanding the Department of the Ohio, he was placed in command of the Army of the Ohio. He commanded the Army of the Ohio, which then only consisted of two divisions of the 23rd Corps, from February 9, 1864, through the end of the war. His small army was one of three Union armies that participated in the 1864 Atlanta Campaign, and he ably led his command in many engagements during that campaign. The Senate finally confirmed his nomination on May 18, 1864, and his commission as major general of volunteers ranked from November 29, 1862. On the night of May 25, 1864, near Cassville, Georgia, he was slightly injured when his horse fell, but two days later he returned to command in the field. After the capture of Atlanta Schofield was sent to Tennessee to assist in opposing an invasion of that state by the Army of Tennessee. He now commanded the 23rd Corps and two divisions of the Fourth Corps. Although initially outmaneuvered at Spring Hill, he successfully repulsed the Confederate assaults at the Battle of Franklin on November 30, 1864. Schofield also participated in the successful attacks against the Confederate forces at Nashville on December 15 – 16, 1864. In January and February 1865 the Army of the Ohio was transported by railroad and boats to eastern North Carolina, where Schofield assisted Maj. Gen. William T. Sherman during the final military activities in North Carolina in the spring of 1865. On February 25, 1865, Schofield was nominated brigadier general in the regular army. The Senate confirmed his nomination on March 3, 1865, and his commission ranked from November 30, 1864. On March 13, 1865, he was brevetted major general in the regular army for his performance at Franklin.[3]

Schofield had a very active career in the army after the war. In 1865 he was secretly sent to France to negotiate the removal of French troops from Mexico. After his return to the United States in 1866 he held several administrative military posts before he was mustered out of the volunteer service on September 1, 1866. Remaining in the regular army, he was placed in command of a military district. He served as Secretary of War at the end of the Andrew Johnson administration from May 28, 1868, until March 11, 1869. On March 4, 1869, he was promoted to major general. Between 1869 and 1876 he again held several administrative posts, commanding various military districts and departments. During his tenure as commander of the Department of the Pacific in the early 1870s he recommended that a naval base be established at Pearl Harbor, Hawaii. He served as superintendent at West Point from September 1, 1876, until June 21, 1881. He served as president of the board that in 1879 recommended the reversal of Maj. Gen. Fitz John Porter's 1863 dismissal from the army. On August 14, 1888, Schofield succeeded Lt. Gen. Philip H. Sheridan as general-in-chief of the army and he commanded the army for the next seven years. Schofield set the precedent of an army general-in-chief operating under the authority and orders of the Secretary of War. In 1892 he was awarded the Medal of Honor for being "conspicuously gallant in leading a regiment in a successful charge against the enemy" at Wilson's Creek. He was promoted to lieutenant general on February 5, 1895. He retired from the army on September 29, 1895, having reached the mandatory retirement age of sixty-four. After his retirement from the army in 1895 he moved to Florida and two years later his memoirs were published. During the Spanish-American War of 1898 he served as President William McKinley's personal military advisor. Schofield died in St. Augustine, Florida and was buried in Section 2 at Arlington National Cemetery. The inscription on his grave marker correctly indicates the highest substantive grade Schofield attained in the regular army, but there is no inscription concerning his service in the volunteers during the Civil War. Also, there is no notation or marker at his grave site concerning the Medal of Honor.[4]

PHILIP HENRY SHERIDAN

Born: March 6, 1831
Died: August 5, 1888

General Sheridan was born in Albany, New York.[1] Shortly after his birth his parents, who were Irish immigrants, moved to Somerset, Ohio. After clerking in a local store for several years he received an appointment to West Point in 1848 after the original appointee failed the entrance examination. In September 1851 a quarrel with fellow cadet (and future Union Civil War brigadier general) William R. Terrill led to Sheridan threatening Terrill with a bayonet and hitting Terrill after Terrill reported the bayonet incident. Sheridan was suspended for one year, and so he graduated in 1853, ranked 34th out of 52. He spent the next eight years performing routine garrison duties at various frontier posts and was promoted to second lieutenant on November 22, 1854. On March 28, 1857, he was slightly wounded on the bridge of his nose during a fight with Yakima Indians at Middle Cascade, Oregon Territory. He was promoted to first lieutenant on March 1, 1861.[2]

On May 14, 1861, Sheridan was promoted to captain in the regular army, but he was not ordered to leave his post in Oregon Territory until early September 1861. He arrived in New York in November 1861 and then immediately went to St. Louis to join his regiment, the Thirteenth U. S. Infantry. At first Sheridan did not receive a field assignment. Instead he was named president of a board in St. Louis that audited claims against the government. On December 25, 1861, he was named assistant quartermaster for the Army of the Southwest. He held that position until April 26, 1862, when he was named assistant quartermaster of the Army of the Mississippi. Sheridan had been seeking a field command, and finally on May 25, 1862, he was named colonel of the Second Michigan Cavalry. Soon he was given command of a small brigade, consisting of two regiments of cavalry. A superior force of Confederate cavalry attacked Sheridan's brigade at Booneville, Mississippi on July 1, 1862. Characteristically he chose to attack rather than retreat, although he had received permission to withdraw. He struck the enemy's rear and routed the Confederates from the field. His aggressiveness was rewarded when, on July 14, 1862, he was nominated brigadier general of volunteers.[3]

Sheridan was given command of an infantry division in the Army of the Ohio on September 4, 1862. He ably led his division during the Battle of Perryville on October 8, 1862. On October 24, 1862, he was again named commander of his division in the newly designated Army of the Cumberland. On December 31, 1862, during the first day of fighting at Stones River, his division fought stubbornly, slowing down the successful Confederate assault against the Union right. Sheridan's stand helped save the Union army at Stones River. His performance at Stones River led to his nomination as major general of volunteers on March 7, 1863, despite the fact that the Senate had not yet acted on his nomination as a brigadier general of volunteers. The Senate confirmed both of his nominations on March 10, 1863. His commission as brigadier general of volunteers ranked from July 1, 1862, and his commission as major general of volunteers ranked from December 31, 1862. He led his division during the Tullahoma Campaign in June 1863, but at Chickamauga on September 20, 1863, his division, along with most of the Union forces in the center and on the right of the line, was routed from the field. Although he was not to blame for this defeat, Sheridan failed to take any actions to either stop the rout or reinforce the Union forces still fighting on the field. He redeemed himself on November 25, 1863, when his division led the Union charge up Missionary Ridge at Chattanooga, which resulted in the retreat of the enemy army from the field. This was the first time Sheridan had served under Maj. Gen. Ulysses S. Grant, and Grant was impressed with Sheridan's performance.[4]

Grant was promoted to lieutenant general and was named general-in-chief of the Union army in early March 1864. He decided that Sheridan's aggressive style of warfare was sorely needed in the Army of the Potomac, and so on April 4, 1864, Sheridan became the commander of that army's cavalry corps. His performance as cavalry chief during the Overland Campaign was mediocre. His cavalry did a poor job of screening the Union army in the Wilderness. The Richmond and Trevilian raids were largely unsuccessful, although Maj. Gen. Jeb Stuart, the legendary Confederate cavalry leader, was mortally wounded in a clash with Sheridan's cavalry at Yellow Tavern on May 11, 1864. Grant, however, remained impressed with Sheridan's aggressiveness and Grant still had confidence in Sheridan. In early August 1864 Confederate forces that had threatened Washington, D.C. the previous month were now occupying the northern part of the Shenandoah Valley. Grant wanted those enemy forces driven from the northern Shenandoah Valley. On August 7, 1864, Sheridan was given command of the newly created Middle Military Division and the Army of the Shenandoah, and in September and October 1864 he won three battles that finally drove the Confederates out of the northern Shenandoah Valley. The last of these battles occurred at Cedar Creek on October 19, 1864. The Confederates launched a surprise attack against Sheridan's army that morning, at a time when Sheridan was not on the field. The Union army was defeated but not completely driven from the field. Sheridan arrived on the field that afternoon, he personally rallied his forces, and his rejuvenated army attacked and routed the enemy from the field. Under orders from Grant, Sheridan's men then laid waste to much of the northern Shenandoah Valley, thereby eliminating it as a source of food and provisions for the Confederates. Sheridan was appointed brigadier general in the regular army on September 20, 1864, and major general in the regular army on November 14, 1864. The Senate confirmed both nominations on January 13, 1865. His commission as brigadier general in the regular army ranked from September 20, 1864, and his commission as major general in the regular army ranked from November 8, 1864. He was mustered out of the volunteer service on November 8, 1864. On March 26, 1865, Sheridan was given command of all the Union cavalry operating against Richmond, and his command was instrumental in the capture of Petersburg and the successful pursuit of the Confederate army to Appomattox Courthouse in early April 1865.[5]

In May 1865 Sheridan was sent to Texas with a large army as a show of force to persuade the French to withdraw their forces from Mexico. Then he held various administrative military positions, being promoted to lieutenant general on March 4, 1869. He went to Europe in the early 1870s as an observer during the Franco-Prussian War. Upon his return to the United States he again held several administrative military posts and was involved in planning military operations against the hostile Plains Indians. On November 1, 1883, he succeeded Gen. William T. Sherman as general-in-chief of the army, and he held that position until his death five years later. On June 1, 1888, he was promoted to full General (four stars). He died in Nonquitt, Massachusetts two months later, and was buried in Section 2 at Arlington National Cemetery. His father-in-law was Brig. Gen. Daniel H. Rucker. Sheridan's grave marker merely has a bas-relief of his face and the basic inscription "SHERIDAN." There is no inscription on his impressive grave marker concerning his military record or his service in the volunteers during the Civil War.[6]

DANIEL EDGAR SICKLES

Born: October 20, 1819
Died: May 3, 1914

General Sickles was born in New York, New York. He attended New York University and then studied law, but his real interest was politics. Aligned with the Tammany Hall Democratic faction in New York City, he became corporation counsel of the city. Later he served as secretary to the United States legation in London. Next he served in the New York legislature, and from 1857 to 1861 he served in the United States House of Representatives. On February 27, 1859, he shot and killed his wife's lover, who happened to be the son of Francis Scott Key, on a Washington, D.C. street near the White House. Several months later he was acquitted of murder, based on the defense of temporary insanity. He furthered the scandal by then forgiving and taking back his wife.[1]

Sickles supported the war and he quickly raised an entire brigade from New York City, called "The Excelsior Brigade." On June 29, 1861, he was named colonel of the 70th New York Infantry, one of the regiments in that brigade. Eager to encourage Democratic support of the war and thankful for Sickles' efforts in raising a brigade, President Abraham Lincoln appointed Sickles brigadier general of volunteers on September 3, 1861. On October 3, 1861, Sickles was given command of the Excelsior Brigade. The Senate rejected his nomination on March 17, 1862, but Lincoln renominated Sickles on April 25, 1862. The Senate confirmed his renomination on May 12, 1862, and his commission as a brigadier general of volunteers ranked from September 3, 1861. In May 1862 the Excelsior Brigade was assigned to the Third Corps in the Army of the Potomac. Sickles ably led his brigade during the Peninsula Campaign. Although he was not with his brigade during the Battle of Second Manassas, in the reorganization of the Army of the Potomac after that battle, Sickles was advanced to command of a Third Corps division. The Third Corps saw no action during the Antietam Campaign of September 1862, as it was manning the defenses at Washington, D.C., and the corps saw little action during the Fredericksburg Campaign of December 1862. Nevertheless, on January 16, 1863, Sickles was nominated major general of volunteers and on February 5, 1863, he was given command of the Third Corps. The Senate confirmed his nomination on March 9, 1863, and his commission ranked from November 29, 1862. His political connections had carried him far up the chain of command in the Army of the Potomac.[2]

Sickles ably led his corps in the fighting at Chancellorsville in May 1863. During the second day of fighting at Gettysburg on July 2, 1863, the Third Corps was located on the left end of the Union line. Unhappy with the position assigned to his corps, Sickles moved his two divisions to an advanced position. His orders did not clearly authorize such an advance and now his corps was separated from the remainder of the Union army. The Confederates attacked his exposed corps that afternoon, the Third Corps was pushed back after suffering heavy losses, and numerous reinforcements were needed to stabilize the Union left flank at Sickles' original position. During the fighting that afternoon Sickles' right leg was shattered by a cannon ball. The leg was later amputated, Sickles' career as a field commander was over, and his actions at Gettysburg created controversy that continues to this day.[3]

After the war Sickles remained in the army. He commanded several military departments in the South between November 1865 and November 1866. He was named colonel of the 42nd Infantry on July 28, 1866, and on March 2, 1867, he was brevetted brigadier general in the regular army for his performance at Fredericksburg and major general in the regular army for his performance at Gettysburg. He was finally mustered out of the volunteer service on January 1, 1868, and he retired from the army on April 14, 1869, being placed on the retired list as a major general. He served as United States minister to Spain from 1869 to 1873 and he served in the United States House of Representatives from 1893 to 1895. He was awarded the Medal of Honor in 1897 for his "conspicuous gallantry" and for "continuing to encourage his troops after being himself severely wounded" at Gettysburg. He was largely responsible for the creation of the national military park at Gettysburg. He died in New York City at the age of ninety-four and was buried in Section 3 at Arlington National Cemetery. The inscription on his grave marker correctly indicates that Sickles was placed on the retired list as a major general in the regular army, but there is no inscription concerning his service in the volunteers during the Civil War.[4]

GREEN CLAY SMITH

Born: July 4, 1826
Died: June 29, 1895

General Smith was born in Richmond, Kentucky.[1] He graduated from Transylvania University in Lexington, Kentucky in 1844. He served in the Mexican War as a second lieutenant in the First Kentucky Infantry from June 9, 1846, until he was mustered out on June 8, 1847. In 1853 he graduated from the Lexington Law School, and then he practiced law with his father, who was a powerful Kentucky politician. Smith was elected to the Kentucky legislature as a Republican in 1860.[2]

The record is murky concerning Smith's military record during the first year of the Civil War. It is possible that he enlisted in an unknown regiment as a private and that at some point he was a major in the Third Kentucky (Union) Cavalry. It is certain that on March 15, 1862, he was named colonel of the Fourth Kentucky (Union) Cavalry. On May 5, 1862, during a fight with Confederate cavalry at Lebanon, Tennessee he was wounded in the right leg, resulting in a broken kneecap. While recuperating from his wound he was nominated brigadier general of volunteers on June 9, 1862. The Senate confirmed his nomination two days later and his commission ranked from June 11, 1862. Finally in July 1862 he was able to return to the field, being assigned to Lexington, Kentucky. In mid-July 1862 Smith was sent from Lexington to engage Confederate cavalry raiding in that area. There was an inconclusive clash near Paris, Kentucky on July 19, but Smith failed to stop the raid or block the enemy's escape back into Tennessee. Smith's immediate commander, Brig. Gen. Jeremiah T. Boyle, criticized Smith for his perceived shortcomings. Boyle stated that Smith "ought to have taken" the Confederates and that "with such officers as...General Smith I cannot hope to accomplish much." Despite these comments Smith commanded a division in the Army of Kentucky for a week in early October 1862, and then he commanded a brigade in that division from October 1862 until January 1863.[3]

In the spring of 1863 Smith commanded a cavalry brigade stationed near Franklin, Tennessee. He led his brigade during an expedition from Franklin to Columbia, Tennessee in early March 1863 that only resulted in some minor skirmishing. But on March 25, 1863, his command successfully drove Confederate cavalry from Brentwood, Tennessee. Maj. Gen. William S. Rosecrans praised Smith and his men for their "spirit and gallantry" in this action and he stated that they showed themselves "worthy of the cause in which they combat." On April 10, 1863, Smith again performed well in fighting near Franklin, Tennessee. Next he served as provost marshal in Kentucky from August 28 to December 1, 1863. He had been elected to the United States House of Representatives in the autumn of 1862 and so he resigned from the army on December 1, 1863, in order to take his seat in Congress. On March 13, 1865, he was brevetted major general of volunteers.[4]

Smith served in Congress until July 13, 1866, when he resigned his seat to assume his new duties as governor of Montana Territory. He resigned the post of territorial governor on April 9, 1869, in order to return to Kentucky and become a minister at a Baptist church in Frankfort, Kentucky. He spent the remainder of his life in the ministry. A member of the temperance movement, he was the presidential candidate of the National Prohibition Party in 1876, although he only received 9,522 votes in that election. He had moved to Washington, D.C. and from 1890 until his death in the nation's capital five years later he served as minister of the Metropolitan Baptist Church in Washington, D.C. He was buried in Section 1 at Arlington National Cemetery.[5]

MORGAN LEWIS SMITH

Born: March 8, 1821
Died: December 29, 1874

General Smith was born in Mexico, New York.[1] In the early 1840s he moved to New Albany, Indiana, where he taught school for several years. On July 19, 1845, he enlisted in the United States Army as a private, under the alias Martin L. Sanford. During the next few years he advanced to corporal, sergeant, and drill instructor. He was discharged from the army on July 19, 1850, and moved to Missouri. For the next eleven years he worked as a river boatman on the Ohio and Mississippi Rivers.[2]

During the summer of 1861 Smith recruited and organized the Eighth Missouri (Union) Infantry in St. Louis. On July 4, 1861, Smith was named the regiment's colonel. The regiment was first sent to Cape Girardeau, Missouri in August 1861 and the next month it was stationed at Paducah, Kentucky. On February 1, 1862, Smith was given command of a brigade that later that month participated in the capture of Fort Donelson, Tennessee. On February 17, 1862, he was placed in command of a brigade in the Army of the Tennessee and he ably led his brigade in the second day of fighting at Shiloh on April 7, 1862. On April 26, 1862, he was nominated brigadier general of volunteers. The Senate confirmed his nomination on July 16, 1862, and his commission ranked from July 16, 1862. On October 26, 1862, he was given command of a Thirteenth Corps brigade and on November 12, 1862, he was placed in command of a Thirteenth Corps division. He ably led his division in the fighting at Chickasaw Bluff, Mississippi in late December 1862, until he was severely wounded in the hip on December 28. The surgeons were unable to remove the bullet and for the next ten months Smith was disabled.[3]

Finally in the autumn of 1863 Smith was able to return to the field and on October 6, 1863, he was given command of a Fifteenth Corps division in the Army of the Tennessee. He ably led his division in the fighting at Chattanooga in November 1863 and throughout the major engagements of the 1864 Atlanta Campaign. On August 4, 1864, Smith had to go on sick leave because of complications relating to his hip wound. His left leg had become partially paralyzed, his left foot and ankle had become almost useless, and he suffered intense pain. He was assigned to command of the post at Vicksburg on August 5, 1864, although he was not able to actually assume his duties until November 1864. He held this position through the end of the war. He resigned from the army on July 12, 1865. Probably because he resigned without waiting to be mustered out of the volunteer service, he did not receive the usual brevet promotion to major general of volunteers.[4]

After leaving the army Smith moved to Washington, D.C. and in 1866 he was appointed United States consul general in Honolulu. He served in Hawaii until 1868 and then returned to Washington, D.C. There he engaged in business for the next six years, representing claimants against the federal government, bidding on mail routes, and working with a building association. He died in Jersey City, New Jersey while on a business trip and was buried in Section 3 at Arlington National Cemetery. His younger brother was Union Maj. Gen. Giles A. Smith.[5]

WILLIAM FARRAR SMITH

Born: February 17, 1824
Died: February 28, 1903

General Smith was born in St. Albans, Vermont. He graduated from West Point in 1845, ranked fourth out of 41. While at the academy he was given the nickname "Baldy." Based on his class rank he was assigned to the prestigious Topographical Engineers. During the next sixteen years he was engaged in numerous surveying and engineering projects, he taught mathematics at West Point, and he served on the lighthouse board both as a member and as secretary. While on duty in Florida in 1855 he contracted malaria and for the rest of his life he suffered from weakness, chills, and fevers. He was promoted to second lieutenant on July 14, 1849, first lieutenant on March 3, 1853, and captain on July 1, 1859.[1]

On July 16, 1861, Smith was named colonel of the Third Vermont Infantry. Although the regiment did not participate in the First Manassas Campaign, Smith served as an aide to Brig. Gen. Irvin McDowell, the Union army commander. On August 13, 1861, Smith was appointed brigadier general of volunteers. From August to October 1861 he commanded a brigade in the Army of the Potomac and on October 3, 1861, he was given command of a division that was later assigned to the Fourth Corps in that army. He led his division in the early actions of the 1862 Peninsula Campaign at Yorktown, Lee's Mill, and Williamsburg. On April 16, 1862, at Lee's Mill his horse stepped into a hole while galloping and Smith was slightly injured when he was thrown from the horse. He was given command of a Sixth Corps division on May 18, 1862, and he ably led his division during the fighting of the Seven Days Campaign. He was brevetted lieutenant colonel in the regular army on June 28, 1862, for his performance at White Oak Swamp. The Senate confirmed his nomination on July 7, 1862, and his commission as brigadier general of volunteers ranked from August 13, 1861. He ably led his division during the Antietam Campaign and was brevetted colonel in the regular army on September 17, 1862, for his performance at Antietam.[2]

Smith was named commander of the Sixth Corps on November 16, 1862, and he led the corps in the fighting at Fredericksburg the next month. After that disastrous battle he criticized his army commander, Maj. Gen. Ambrose E. Burnside. On July 25, 1862, Smith had been appointed major general of volunteers. He was not nominated until

December 23, 1862, and because of his criticisms of Burnside, the Senate failed to act on his nomination before the current congressional session ended on March 4, 1863. By operation of law the appointment expired without confirmation. He commanded the Ninth Corps from February 5 to March 8, 1863, and he was promoted to major in the regular army on March 3, 1863. Next he commanded a division in the Department of the Susquehanna from June 17 to August 3, 1863, and a division in the Department of West Virginia from August 3 to September 5, 1863. He was sent to Chattanooga in early October 1863, where as chief engineer he was greatly responsible for opening up the supply line that saved the besieged Union army there. This won him the admiration of Maj. Gen. Ulysses S. Grant and it enabled President Abraham Lincoln to reappoint Smith major general of volunteers on March 24, 1864. The Senate confirmed his nomination the next day and his commission ranked from March 9, 1864.[3]

Grant became the general-in-chief of the Union army in March 1864 and on May 2, 1864, he gave Smith command of the 18th Corps in the Army of the James. Smith's lackluster performance at Cold Harbor and Petersburg in June 1864 and his continuing criticisms of his superiors led to his removal from corps command in July 1864. From December 1864 through the end of the war he served as an assistant inspector general in western Mississippi. On March 13, 1865, he was brevetted brigadier general in the regular army for his performance at Chattanooga and major general in the regular army for his war service. He resigned from the volunteer service on November 4, 1865, and from the regular army on March 21, 1867.[4]

Smith had become president of the International Telegraph Company in 1864 and he held that position until 1873. He served as Police Commissioner of New York City from 1875 until 1881. Then he worked as a civil engineer and he wrote several books about his war experiences. He died in Philadelphia, Pennsylvania and was buried in Section 1 at Arlington National Cemetery. The inscription on his grave marker correctly indicates the highest grade Smith attained by brevet in the regular army, but there is no inscription concerning his service in the volunteers during the Civil War.[5]

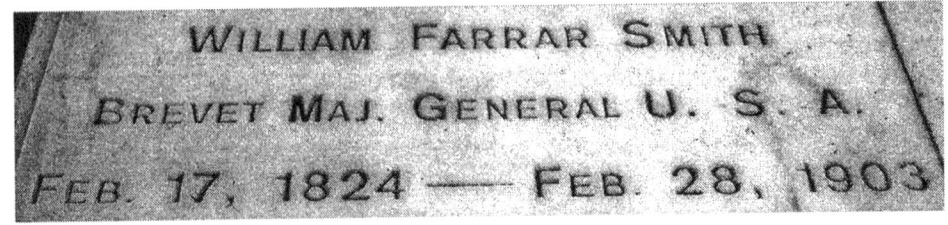

JULIUS STAHEL

Born: November 5, 1825
Died: December 4, 1912

General Stahel was born in Szeged, Hungary. His original full name was Julius Gyula Stahel-Szamvald. He enlisted in the Austrian army as a private and advanced to lieutenant. He sided with the revolutionary Lajos Kossuth during the Hungarian Revolution of 1848. When the revolution failed, Stahel was forced to flee to Berlin and London. He worked as a teacher from 1849 until he moved to New York City in the late 1850s. There he worked as a journalist for a German language newspaper.[1]

In April 1861 Stahel helped recruit the Eighth New York Infantry in New York City. The regiment was known as "The First German Rifles" and Stahel was named lieutenant colonel of the regiment on April 23, 1861. Stahel commanded the regiment at the Battle of First Manassas. The regiment was in reserve during the battle, but it helped cover the retreat of the Union army back to Washington, D.C. Stahel was named colonel of the regiment on August 11, 1861. On November 12, 1861, he was appointed brigadier general of volunteers and he was immediately given command of a brigade in the Army of the Potomac. On April 1, 1862, he was placed in command of a brigade in the Mountain Department. He led his brigade in the fighting at Cross Keys on June 8, 1862, during the Shenandoah Valley Campaign. He was given command of a brigade in the newly formed Army of Virginia on June 26, 1862. On July 16, 1862, the Senate confirmed his nomination and his commission as a brigadier general of volunteers ranked from November 12, 1861. On August 30, 1862, during the fighting at Second Manassas, he succeeded to command of his division when its commander was wounded. With the reorganization of the Army of the Potomac after the latter battle, Stahel was given command of an Eleventh Corps division. The corps did not participate in the Antietam or Fredericksburg Campaigns.[2]

On March 14, 1863, Stahel was nominated major general of volunteers, although his limited combat experience did not justify such a promotion. It is assumed that the promotion was based on the fact that Stahel was a German speaking officer and the promotion would likely encourage support of the war by German immigrants. The Senate confirmed his nomination that same day and his commission ranked from March 14, 1863.

On March 21, 1863, Stahel was given command of the cavalry stationed in the defenses at Washington, D.C. He briefly commanded a cavalry division in the Army of the Potomac in June 1863, but he did not participate in the fighting at Gettysburg. From July 2, 1863, until March 14, 1864, he commanded the cavalry in the Department of the Susquehanna. On March 14, 1864, he was placed in command of the cavalry in the Department of West Virginia and on April 26, 1864, he was given command of a cavalry division in that department. He led his division during the fighting at New Market on May 15, 1864. On June 5, 1864, during the Battle of Piedmont he was wounded in the shoulder. Problems with the wound forced him to turn over command of his division four days later. He then served on several courts-martial before resigning from the army on February 8, 1865.[3]

From 1866 to 1869 Stahel served as United States consul in Yokohama, Japan, and then he worked as a mining engineer. He served as United States consul in Japan from 1877 to 1884 and as United States consul general in Shanghai, China from 1884 to 1885. He then worked as an executive for the Equitable Insurance Company of New York. In 1893 he was awarded the Medal of Honor for leading "his division into action until he was severely wounded" at Piedmont. He died in New York City and was buried in Section 2 at Arlington National Cemetery.[4]

CHARLES JOHN STOLBRAND

Born: May 11, 1821
Died: February 3, 1894

General Stolbrand was born near Kristianstad, Sweden. His full baptismal name was Charles John Meuller Stohlbrand, but in the United States army records the middle name "Meuller" was dropped and his last name was spelled "Stolbrand." He graduated from the Swedish Military Academy and became a cadet with the Royal Vendes Artillery in Sweden. Several years later, during the Danish – Prussian War of 1848 – 1850 he participated in the Schleswig – Holstein campaign, wherein a Prussian invasion of Denmark was thwarted. After that war he immigrated to the United States. He lived in Chicago, Illinois and became a leader in the Scandinavian immigrant community there.[1]

In the early days of the Civil War Stolbrand raised an artillery company, consisting of local Scandinavian immigrants. Unfortunately the company could not be accepted into the Federal service, because Illinois had already fulfilled its quota. Undeterred, he raised another artillery company which became a part of the Second Illinois Light Artillery, and on October 5, 1861, he was named a captain in the battery. On December 3, 1861, he was promoted to major in the battery. He participated in the New Madrid – Island No. 10 Campaign of March - April 1862. On March 31, 1862, during an engagement at Union City, Missouri, he was slightly injured when he fell from his horse, but he remained with his battery on the field. Then in May 1862 he participated in the advance to Corinth, Mississippi. Later that year he was assigned to command of the artillery posted at Jackson, Tennessee. In December 1862 he was named commander of the artillery assigned to Maj. Gen. John A. Logan's Seventeenth Corps division in the Army of the Tennessee. Stolbrand ably led his artillery during the Vicksburg Campaign of 1863. In his after action report Logan praised Stolbrand for his performance in that campaign as his divisional artillery chief.[2]

In December 1863 Logan became the commander of the Fifteenth Corps, and soon Stolbrand was named chief of artillery for the corps. He commanded the corps artillery during the early stages of the 1864 Atlanta Campaign, until he was captured by Confederate cavalry near Kingston, Georgia on May 19, 1864. In noting Stolbrand's capture in his after action report, Logan described his artillery chief as "a gallant and untiring officer." Stolbrand was sent to the prison camp at Andersonville, Georgia, but he escaped in October 1864 and was soon reinstated as chief of artillery for the Fifteenth Corps. He led his command during the March to the Sea. In January 1865 Stolbrand's army commander, Maj. Gen. William T. Sherman, learned that Stolbrand was contemplating resigning from the volunteer service. Stolbrand was frustrated because he had not received any promotions since being named major in December 1861. Sherman sent Stolbrand to Washington, D.C. to personally deliver to the president some papers. Stolbrand did not realize it, but one of the papers was a message from Sherman to Abraham Lincoln wherein Sherman strongly recommended that Stolbrand be promoted to brigadier general of volunteers. Lincoln quickly acted on the recommendation and on February 18, 1865, Stolbrand was nominated brigadier general of volunteers. The Senate confirmed his nomination on March 3, 1865, and his commission ranked from February 18, 1865. On April 28, 1865, he was given command of a Seventeenth Corps brigade in the Carolinas, which he led through the end of the war. He was mustered out of the volunteer service on January 15, 1866.[3]

Stolbrand lived in South Carolina for the rest of his life. He served as secretary of the state constitutional convention in 1868, as a delegate to the 1868 Republican National Convention, as a presidential elector for Ulysses S. Grant in 1868, as superintendent of the state penitentiary, and as superintendent of the Federal buildings in Charleston. He also spent time working with steam engineering projects and inventing various mechanical and industrial devices. He died in Charleston and was buried in Section 3 at Arlington National Cemetery. His grave site is marked with a simple government marker.[4]

SAMUEL DAVIS STURGIS

Born: June 11, 1822
Died: September 28, 1889

General Sturgis was born in Shippensburg, Pennsylvania. He graduated from West Point in 1846, ranked 32nd out of 59. During the Mexican War he served in the dragoons and was promoted to second lieutenant on February 16, 1847. He was captured on February 20, 1847, while performing a reconnaissance near Buena Vista, but was exchanged eight days later. After the war he served on the frontier and was involved in numerous engagements with hostile Indians. He served as regimental quartermaster from April 1, 1851, until March 1, 1852, and was promoted to first lieutenant on July 15, 1853, and captain in the First Cavalry on March 3, 1855.[1]

In April 1861 Sturgis was in command of Fort Smith, Arkansas with two companies of cavalry. Soon state forces cut off supplies to the fort, making the post untenable, and Sturgis learned that armed state militia would shortly arrive. So on April 23 he safely evacuated his men and most of the government property under his care. On May 3, 1861, he was promoted to major in the regular army. He was given command of a brigade in the Army of the West on July 24, 1861, and during the fighting at Wilson's Creek on August 10, 1861, command of the army devolved on him when its commander, Brig. Gen. Nathaniel Lyon, was killed. Later that day Sturgis decided to withdraw his army from that field, based on a shortage of ammunition and his troops being exhausted, but his decision to withdraw has often been criticized. He was brevetted lieutenant colonel in the regular army on August 10, 1861, for his performance at Wilson's Creek. He commanded a brigade in the Western Army between September and October 1861 and he served briefly as chief of staff for the Western Department in November 1861. On January 29, 1862, he was nominated brigadier general of volunteers. The Senate confirmed his nomination on March 5, 1862, and his commission ranked from August 10, 1861. He commanded the District of Kansas from April 10 to May 5, 1862.[2]

Next Sturgis was sent to Washington, D.C. to command a brigade in the defenses there. On June 18, 1862, he was given command of the Reserve Corps and eight days later his corps became a part of the newly created Army of Virginia. Only one of his brigades saw action at Second Manassas. He was brevetted colonel in the regular army on August 29, 1862, for his performance at Second Manassas. With the reorganization of the Army of the Potomac after that battle, Sturgis was placed in command of a Ninth Corps division. He led his division in the fighting at South Mountain and Antietam in September 1862 and at Fredericksburg in December 1862. In March 1863 the Ninth Corps was sent to the Department of the Ohio, and Sturgis remained in command of his division until May 1863. After briefly commanding the District of Central Kentucky in June 1863 and a division in the 23rd Corps between June and July 1863, he was given command of the cavalry in the Army of the Ohio on July 10, 1863. He was promoted to lieutenant colonel in the regular army on October 27, 1863. In June 1864 he was given command of an expeditionary force which was soon routed by Confederate cavalry on June 10, 1864, at the Battle of Brice's Cross Roads, Mississippi. A board of investigation looked into the defeat and although the board made no findings, Sturgis spent the remainder of the war awaiting orders that never came. On March 13, 1865, he was brevetted brigadier general in the regular army for his performance at South Mountain and major general in the regular army for his performance at Fredericksburg.[3]

Sturgis was mustered out of the volunteer service on August 24, 1865, but he remained in the regular army. He served on the frontier and was involved in several campaigns against hostile Indians. On May 6, 1869, he was promoted to colonel of the Seventh Cavalry, although he was not present with his regiment during its famous fight at the Little Bighorn in June 1876. He retired from the army on June 11, 1886, having reached the mandatory retirement age of sixty-four. He died three years later in St. Paul, Minnesota and was buried in Section 2 at Arlington National Cemetery. The inscription on his grave marker correctly indicates the highest substantive and brevet grades Sturgis attained in the regular army, but there is no inscription concerning his service in the volunteers during the Civil War.[4]

WAGER SWAYNE

Born: November 10, 1834
Died: December 18, 1902

General Swayne was born in Columbus, Ohio. Before his birth his parents had moved from Virginia, a slave state, to Ohio, a free territory, because they were opposed to the institution of slavery. Wager graduated from Yale University in 1856 and three years later he graduated from Cincinnati Law School. He then began to practice law in Columbus with his father.[1]

On August 31, 1861, Swayne was named major of the 43rd Ohio Infantry and on December 14, 1861, he was advanced to lieutenant colonel of the regiment. The regiment left Ohio in late February 1862 and went to Missouri, where it was attached to a brigade in the Army of the Mississippi. From March to April 1862 the regiment participated in the New Madrid – Island No. 10 Campaign and May 1862 it participated in the advance to Corinth, Mississippi. The regiment saw action at both the Battle of Iuka on September 19, 1862, and the Battle of Corinth on October 3 – 4, 1862. During the latter battle command of the regiment devolved on Swayne when the regiment's colonel was mortally wounded. The regiment was shaken by the loss of its leader, but Swayne quickly rallied his men and they participated in the repulse of the Confederate attack. His brigade commander, Col. John W. Fuller, praised Swayne in his after action report, stating the Swayne assumed "command under the most trying circumstances" and that he "soon restored order in his regiment, and fought it with the utmost gallantry." On October 18, 1862, Swayne was promoted to colonel of the regiment. For the next nineteen months the regiment was mainly engaged in garrison duties in western Tennessee and it participated in several expeditions in northern Mississippi and northern Alabama.[2]

The regiment, which had been attached to the Sixteenth Corps in the Army of the Tennessee in late 1862, saw considerable action during the 1864 Atlanta Campaign. Swayne briefly commanded a Sixteenth Corps brigade in September 1864 and then he commanded a Seventeenth Corps brigade from September 23 to November 1, 1864. He returned to command of his regiment during the March to the Sea. On February 2, 1865, at River's Bridge along the Salkehatchie River in South Carolina he was so severely wounded in the right leg by a piece of shell that the leg had to be amputated. On February 5, 1865, he was brevetted brigadier general of volunteers and on March 8, 1865, he was nominated a substantive brigadier general of volunteers. The Senate confirmed his nomination two days later and his commission ranked from March 8, 1865. On October 31, 1865, he was brevetted major general of volunteers, and on March 31, 1866, he was nominated a substantive major general of volunteers. The Senate confirmed his nomination on April 26, 1866, and his commission ranked from June 20, 1865. On July 28, 1866, Swayne was named colonel of the 45th Infantry and on March 2, 1867, he was brevetted brigadier general in the regular army for his performance at River's Bridge and major general in the regular army for his war service. Although Swayne had a good military record, his promotions after the war and his being named colonel in the regular army were likely motivated by the fact that his father, Noah Swayne, was now a United States Supreme Court justice.[3]

Swayne was mustered out of the volunteer service on September 1, 1867, and on July 1, 1870, he retired from the army. Soon he was practicing law in Toledo, Ohio. In 1881 he moved to New York City, where he was a successful corporate lawyer. In 1893 he was awarded the Medal of Honor for "conspicuous gallantry in restoring order at a critical moment and leading his regiment in a charge" at Corinth. He died in New York City nine years later and was buried in Section 3 at Arlington National Cemetery. There is no notation or marker at his grave site concerning the Medal of Honor.[4]

STEWART VAN VLIET

Born: July 21, 1815
Died: March 28, 1901

General Van Vliet was born in Ferrisburg, Vermont. He graduated from West Point in 1840, ranked ninth out of 42. He was assigned to the artillery and was promoted to first lieutenant on November 19, 1843. Between March 28 and June 7, 1847, he served as regimental quartermaster, and on June 4, 1847, he was promoted to captain of staff and named assistant quartermaster general. During the Mexican War he was present at the engagements at Monterrey and Vera Cruz. After the war he was sent to the frontier, where he spent much of his time dealing with the construction of various army posts along the Oregon Trail.[1]

At the start of the Civil War Van Vliet was stationed at Fort Leavenworth, Kansas. On August 3, 1861, he was promoted to major of staff in the regular army and on August 20, 1861, he was named chief quartermaster of the Army of the Potomac. He ably carried out those duties during the early stages of the 1862 Peninsula Campaign, until a dispute between himself and Navy Flag Officer Louis M. Goldsborough erupted in late June 1862. Van Vliet sent a message to Goldsborough in which he meant to request the cooperation of the navy, but Goldsborough read the message as an "order" from an army officer to a naval officer. In a subsequent message from Goldsborough to the secretary of the navy, the irate Goldsborough mentioned "the ignorance or impertinence" of Van Vliet and he stated that Van Vliet's message had an "exceptionable tone and address." On July 10, 1862, Van Vliet was relieved from his duties as chief quartermaster of the Army of the Potomac, at his own request. It is not known if the flap with Goldsborough motivated that request, but the timing of Stewart's request would suggest such a connection. Maj. Rufus Ingalls replaced Van Vliet as chief quartermaster of the Army of the Potomac.[2]

On September 23, 1861, Van Vliet had been appointed brigadier general of volunteers, but the Senate failed to act on his nomination before the current congressional session ended on July 17, 1862. By operation of law the appointment expired without confirmation. It is also unknown if the flap with Goldsborough caused the Senate to take no action on Van Vliet's nomination. Van Vliet spent the remainder of the war in New York City as quartermaster for the Department of the East, working tirelessly to provide supplies and transportation for the various armies in his department. He was brevetted lieutenant colonel, colonel, and brigadier general in the regular army on October 28, 1864. On November 23, 1865, he was again appointed brigadier general of volunteers and on February 23, 1866, the Senate confirmed his nomination. His commission ranked from March 13, 1865. He was brevetted major general of volunteers and major general in the regular army on March 13, 1865.[3]

With the reorganization of the army after the war, Van Vliet was promoted to lieutenant colonel of staff on July 29, 1866, and he was named deputy quartermaster general as of that same date. He was mustered out of the volunteer service on September 1, 1866. He served as the chief quartermaster for several different military departments and divisions, and on June 6, 1872, he was promoted to colonel of staff and named assistant quartermaster general. Between 1875 and 1881 he served as inspector of the Quartermaster Department. He retired from the army on January 22, 1881, and lived in Washington, D.C. until his death there twenty years later. He was buried in Section 2 at Arlington National Cemetery. All that remains of his private grave marker is the base. The inscription on his simple government grave marker does not clearly indicate that Van Vliet was a major general in the regular army by brevet only and there is no inscription concerning his service in the volunteers during the Civil War.[4]

LOUIS DOUGLASS WATKINS

Born: November 29, 1833
Died: March 29, 1868

General Watkins was born near Tallahassee, Florida.[1] When he was young his family moved to Washington, D.C. Little is known about his early life, other than the fact that in the 1850s he became active in a local militia unit called "The National Rifles." At the start of the Civil War that militia company took an anti-Union position and Watkins resigned from the company. On April 12, 1861, he enlisted as a private in the Third Battalion of the District of Columbia Infantry, but soon he was mustered out of that outfit. On May 14, 1861, he was commissioned first lieutenant in the regular army and assigned to the 14th Infantry. He was transferred to the Second Cavalry on June 22, 1861, and then to the Fifth Cavalry on August 3, 1861. He ably served with the Fifth Cavalry during the early stages of the Peninsula Campaign, until he was severely wounded and trampled on by several horses on June 27, 1862, near Woodbury's Bridge on the Chickahominy River. He was promoted to captain in the regular army on July 17, 1862.[2]

In July 1862 Watkins was sent to Kentucky, where he served as an aide-de-camp on the staff of Brig. Gen. Andrew J. Smith. In December 1862 Watkins was named chief of cavalry for the Army of Kentucky. He temporarily served on the staff of Brig. Gen. Samuel P. Carter during the latter's successful expedition into East Tennessee in late December 1862. Watkins was brevetted major in the regular army on January 8, 1863, for his performance in the East Tennessee campaign. On February 1, 1863, he was named colonel of the Sixth Kentucky (Union) Cavalry. Watkins ably led his regiment in numerous skirmishes and minor engagements in middle Tennessee during the next several months. He was brevetted lieutenant colonel in the regular army on March 5, 1863, for his performance in one of these fights at Thompson's Station.[3]

On July 8, 1863, Watkins was given command of a cavalry brigade in the Army of the Cumberland. He ably led his brigade during the Chickamauga Campaign of September 1863 and the Chattanooga Campaign of November 1863. During the Atlanta Campaign of 1864 his cavalry brigade was employed in guarding the Union railroad supply line. On June 24, 1864, Watkins bravely led his men in the successful defense of La Fayette, Georgia against a superior force of enemy cavalry. He was brevetted brigadier general of volunteers and colonel in the regular army on June 24, 1864, for his performance at La Fayette. Watkins commanded a cavalry brigade during the Tennessee Campaign of November – December 1864. On March 13, 1865, he was brevetted brigadier general in the regular army for his performance at Resaca, Georgia. He commanded the Union forces at Louisville, Kentucky from March 24, 1865, through the end of the war. His excellent performance during the war was finally rewarded when on September 25, 1865, he was appointed a substantive brigadier general of volunteers. The Senate confirmed his nomination on February 23, 1866, and his commission ranked from September 25, 1865.[4]

With the reorganization of the army after the war, Watkins was promoted to lieutenant colonel in the regular army on July 28, 1866. He was mustered out of the volunteer service on September 1, 1866. In January 1867 his regiment, the Twentieth Infantry, was assigned to Louisiana. Watkins died in New Orleans the next year. He was originally buried at the Girod Street Cemetery in New Orleans, but later his remains were reinterred in Section 2 at Arlington National Cemetery. The inscription on his grave marker does not clearly indicate that he was a brigadier general of volunteers and a brevet brigadier general in the regular army. He shares the same headstone with his father-in-law, Maj. Gen. Lovell H. Rousseau.[5]

JOSEPH RODMAN WEST

Born: September 19, 1822
Died: October 31, 1898

General West was born in New Orleans, Louisiana. When he was an infant his family moved to Philadelphia, Pennsylvania. After receiving his early education in private schools he attended the University of Pennsylvania from 1836 to 1837. In 1841 he moved back to New Orleans and worked as a journalist. He served during the Mexican War as a captain in the Maryland and District of Columbia Volunteers from July 25, 1847, until he was mustered out on August 10, 1848. In 1849 he moved to California and later he became the owner of the *Price Current*, a San Francisco newspaper.[1]

On August 5, 1861, West was named lieutenant colonel of the First California Infantry. The regiment was stationed in Oakland and Los Angeles in the autumn of 1861. In the spring of 1862 the regiment became a component of "The California Column." The column left southern California on April 13, 1862, and West commanded the advance guard that captured Tucson, Arizona Territory on May 20, 1862. On June 1, 1862, he was named colonel of his regiment. West led his regiment during the second phase of the expedition. West's component of the column left Tucson on July 20, 1862, marched through the desert, and arrived at La Mesilla on the Rio Grande River on August 15, 1862. This important expedition solidified the Union's hold on Arizona and New Mexico Territories. The commander of the column, Brig. Gen. James H. Carleton, praised West in his after action report, stating that "The amount of labor performed by Col. Joseph R. West, the second in command, was immense and of the greatest practical importance. Much of our success was dependent on his energy, perseverance, cheerfulness, and high soldierly qualities." Carleton recommended that West be promoted to brigadier general of volunteers.[2]

On September 5, 1862, West was given command of the District of Arizona and he held that administrative position until January 29, 1864. His two major tasks were to secure the territory from Confederate invasion and to deal with various bands of hostile Indians. On October 25, 1862, he was appointed brigadier general of volunteers. The Senate confirmed his nomination on March 13, 1863, and his commission ranked from October 25, 1862. In the spring of 1864 West was sent to Arkansas and he briefly commanded a Seventh Corps division stationed there from April 25 to June 16, 1864. In both May and August 1864 he was largely unsuccessful in trying to stop or defeat Confederate cavalry raids in Arkansas. On September 15, 1864, he was given command of a cavalry division in the Department of Arkansas, and in November and December 1864 he participated in several minor expeditions in Arkansas. From April 1865 through the end of the war he commanded cavalry in the Military Division of West Mississippi. He was brevetted major general of volunteers on January 4, 1866, and was mustered out of the volunteer service that same day.[3]

After leaving the army West returned to New Orleans, where he became a deputy United States marshal. Between 1867 and 1871 he served as an auditor for customs in New Orleans. He served one term in the United States Senate as a Republican, from March 4, 1871, until March 3, 1877. He did not seek reelection, but he continued to reside in Washington, D.C. after his term ended. Between 1882 and 1885 he served as a member of the board of commissioners of the District of Columbia. He died in Washington, D.C. and was buried in Section 1 at Arlington National Cemetery.[4]

FRANK WHEATON

Born: May 8, 1833
Died: June 18, 1903

General Wheaton was born in Providence, Rhode Island. He briefly attended Brown University, but in 1850 he moved to California, where he spent five years working as a surveyor for the Mexican – American Boundary Commission. Then on March 3, 1855, he was directly commissioned in the army as a first lieutenant in the First Cavalry. During the next six years he served on the frontier and was involved in several engagements with hostile Indians. He was promoted to captain on March 1, 1861.[1]

On July 10, 1861, Wheaton was named lieutenant colonel of the Second Rhode Island Infantry. During the Battle of First Manassas on July 21, 1861, command of the regiment devolved on him when the regiment's colonel was mortally wounded. Wheaton ably led his regiment for the remainder of the battle and was promoted to colonel on July 21, 1861. His brigade commander, Col. Ambrose E. Burnside, praised Wheaton in his after action report by "attesting to the admirable conduct" of Wheaton during that disastrous battle. In March 1862 the regiment was placed in the Fourth Corps of the Army of the Potomac. Wheaton ably led his regiment during the fighting at Williamsburg and Fair Oaks during the 1862 Peninsula Campaign. Wheaton and his regiment were not involved in the subsequent Second Manassas and Antietam Campaigns. On November 29, 1862, he was appointed brigadier general of volunteers. His regiment participated in the Fredericksburg Campaign of December 1862, although it saw little combat. On December 15, 1862, he was given command of a Sixth Corps brigade. The Senate confirmed his nomination on March 9, 1863, and his commission as a brigadier general of volunteers ranked from November 29, 1862.[2]

In the spring of 1863 Wheaton ably led his brigade during the Chancellorsville Campaign. He temporarily commanded his division during the fighting at Gettysburg in July 1863, although his division saw little fighting there. He was promoted to major in the regular army on November 5, 1863. With the reorganization of the Army of the Potomac in the spring of 1864 he was given command of a different Sixth Corps brigade, which he ably led during the 1864 Overland Campaign. He was brevetted lieutenant colonel in the regular army on May 5, 1864, for his performance at The Wilderness. In July 1864 the

Sixth Corps was sent to Washington, D.C. to protect the capital from a Confederate attack and then in August 1864 the corps was sent to the Shenandoah Valley to drive out the remaining Confederate forces there. Wheaton led his brigade during the fighting at Winchester on September 19, 1864. Two days later he was placed in command of a Sixth Corps division, which he ably led during the remaining fighting in the Shenandoah that autumn. On October 19, 1864, he was brevetted colonel in the regular army for his performance at Cedar Creek and major general of volunteers for his performance in the 1864 Shenandoah Campaign. When the Sixth Corps rejoined the Army of the Potomac in December 1864 Wheaton retained command of his division. On March 13, 1865, he was brevetted brigadier general in the regular army for his performance at Petersburg and major general in the regular army for his war service. In April 1865 he ably led his division during the successful assaults at Petersburg and the pursuit of the Confederate army to Appomattox Courthouse.[3]

Wheaton was mustered out of the volunteer service on April 30, 1866, but he remained in the regular army for the next thirty-one years. With the reorganization of the army after the war he was promoted to lieutenant colonel of the 39th Infantry on July 28, 1866. He was transferred to the 21st Infantry on March 15, 1869, and in 1873 he led an expedition against the Modoc Indians in northern California. On December 15, 1874, he was promoted to colonel of the Second Infantry. He was promoted to brigadier general on April 18, 1892, and major general on April 2, 1897. He retired from the army on May 8, 1897, having reached the mandatory retirement age of sixty-four. He died in Washington, D.C. six years later and was buried in Section 1 at Arlington National Cemetery. His father-in-law was Gen. Samuel Cooper, the adjutant and inspector general of the Confederacy and the South's highest ranking officer.[4]

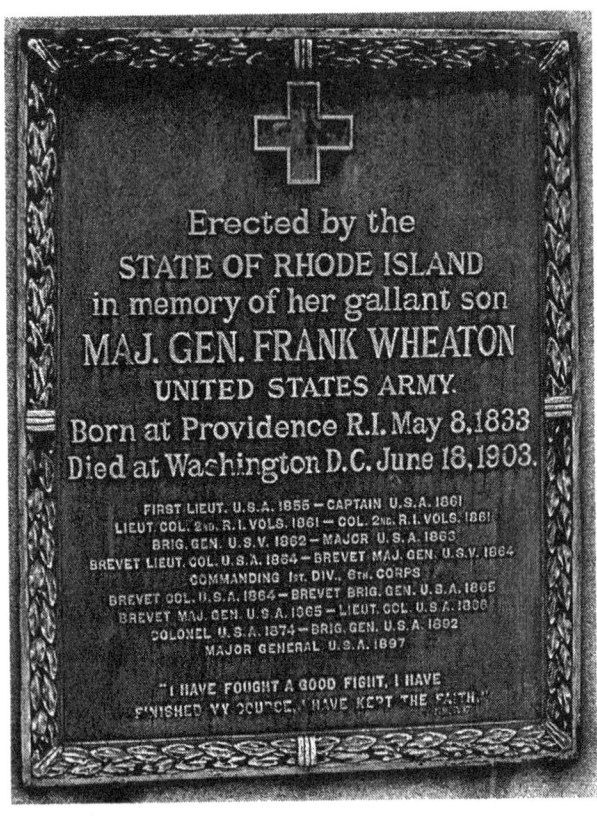

JOSEPH WHEELER

Born: September 10, 1836
Died: January 25, 1906

General Wheeler was born in Augusta, Georgia. He graduated from West Point in 1859, ranked 19th out of 22. Originally assigned to the First Dragoons, he was transferred to the Mounted Rifles on June 26, 1860. He served on the frontier and saw action against hostile Indians. He was promoted to second lieutenant on September 1, 1860. On April 22, 1861, he resigned his commission in order to accept his commission as a first lieutenant of artillery in the fledgling Confederate army.[1]

On September 4, 1861, Wheeler was named colonel of the 19th Alabama Infantry. He ably led his regiment during the fighting at Shiloh on April 6 – 7, 1862. In the late afternoon of the second day of that battle he was given command of a makeshift brigade that helped cover the Confederate retreat from the field. His division commander, Brig. Gen. Jones M. Withers, praised Wheeler in his after action report, stating that Wheeler "had proved himself worthy of all trust and confidence" and he called Wheeler "a gallant commander and an accomplished soldier." On September 14, 1862, Wheeler was given command of a cavalry brigade in the Army of Mississippi as that army advanced into Kentucky, and the next month he was named that army's chief of cavalry as the army retreated back to Tennessee. On October 30, 1862, he was nominated brigadier general. The Senate confirmed his nomination on April 22, 1863, and his commission ranked from October 30, 1862. He was slightly wounded on November 27, 1862, at La Vergne, Tennessee when a shell exploded near him. In December 1862 the Army of Mississippi was renamed the Army of Tennessee and Wheeler led the army's cavalry corps during the subsequent Stones River Campaign of December 1862 – January 1863. On January 23, 1863, he was nominated major general.[2]

Wheeler commanded the cavalry corps in the Army of Tennessee throughout 1863 and 1864. Although he capably handled his duties as cavalry chief, he never attained the status nor gained the reputation of Nathan B. Forrest as a cavalry raider or leader. In particular during the 1864 Atlanta Campaign his cavalry was never able to disrupt the Union army's supply lines and force the advancing Union army to retreat. He was slightly wounded in the foot during fighting at Ringgold, Georgia on November 27, 1863, during the army's retreat from Chattanooga. The Senate finally confirmed his nomination on February 4, 1864, and his commission as a major general ranked from January 20, 1863. At the end of the war he commanded cavalry in the Carolinas. Captured at Conyer's Station, Georgia on May 9, 1865, Wheeler was briefly imprisoned at Fort Delaware before being paroled on June 8, 1865.[3]

After the war Wheeler moved to New Orleans, where he worked as a merchant until 1868. He then moved to Alabama, where he worked as a planter and a lawyer in the town of Wheeler, which was named for him. He served in the United States House of Representatives from March 4, 1881, to June 3, 1882, then from January 15 to March 3, 1883, and finally from March 4, 1885, to April 20, 1900. During the Spanish – American War he served in Cuba as a major general of volunteers from May 4, 1898, until April 12, 1899. He was mustered out of the volunteer service on June 16, 1900, but he was named a brigadier general in the regular army on that same date. He retired from the army on September 10, 1900, having reached the mandatory retirement age of sixty-four. He died in Brooklyn, New York and was buried in Section 2 at Arlington National Cemetery.[4]

WILLIAM DENISON WHIPPLE

Born: August 2, 1826
Died: April 1, 1902

General Whipple was born in Nelson, New York. He graduated from West Point in 1851, ranked 31st out of 42. For the next ten years he performed routine garrison duties on the frontier, mainly in New Mexico Territory and Texas. He was promoted to second lieutenant on September 9, 1851, and first lieutenant on December 31, 1856. In February 1861 he was on duty as a quartermaster in Indianola, Texas when all army posts in Texas were unexpectedly surrendered to rebel forces. Whipple avoided capture and managed to make his way safely back east.[1]

On May 11, 1861, Whipple was brevetted captain of staff in the regular army and named assistant adjutant general. For the duration of the war he held numerous staff and administrative positions, and he proved to be an efficient and capable staff officer. He served on the staff of Brig. Gen. David Hunter during the First Manassas Campaign of July 1861. On August 3, 1861, Whipple was promoted to captain of staff in the regular army and on September 25, 1861, he was named Hunter's chief of staff for the Department of Virginia. On February 10, 1862, Whipple was promoted to lieutenant colonel of staff in the regular army and was named an aide-de-camp on the staff of Brig. Gen. John E. Wool. Whipple was promoted to major of staff in the regular army on July 17, 1862, and in September 1862 he was named assistant adjutant general for the Middle Department. On July 17, 1863, he was appointed brigadier general of volunteers.[2]

On November 12, 1863, Whipple was named chief of staff for the Department of the Cumberland. In early 1864 he became chief of staff for the Army of the Cumberland, and in that capacity he ably served Maj. Gen. George H. Thomas throughout the 1864 Atlanta Campaign and the Tennessee Campaign of November – December 1864. The Senate failed to act on his nomination as brigadier general of volunteers before the current congressional session ended on July 4, 1864. By operation of law the appointment expired without confirmation. He was reappointed brigadier general of volunteers on September 6, 1864, and on February 14, 1865, the Senate confirmed his nomination. His commission ranked from July 17, 1863. On March 13, 1865, he was brevetted lieutenant colonel in the regular army for his performance in the Atlanta Campaign, colonel in the regular army for his performance at Nashville, Tennessee, brigadier general in the regular army for his performance both in the Atlanta Campaign and at Nashville, and major general in the regular army for his war service.[3]

Whipple was mustered out of the volunteer service on January 15, 1866, but he remained in the regular army for the next twenty-four years, mostly serving as an assistant adjutant general in several different military departments and divisions. He also served as an aide-de-camp for general-in-chief William T. Sherman from January 1, 1873, until January 1, 1881. He was promoted to lieutenant colonel of staff on March 3, 1875, and colonel of staff on February 28, 1887. He retired from the army on August 2, 1890, having reached the mandatory retirement age of sixty-four. He died in New York City twelve years later and was buried in Section 1 at Arlington National Cemetery. The inscription on his grave marker correctly indicates the highest substantive and brevet grades Whipple attained in the regular army, but there is no inscription concerning his service in the volunteers during the Civil War.[4]

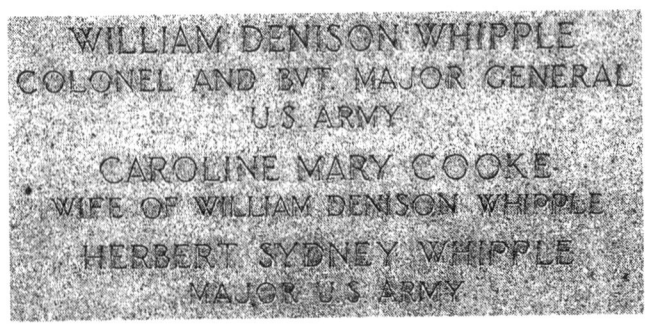

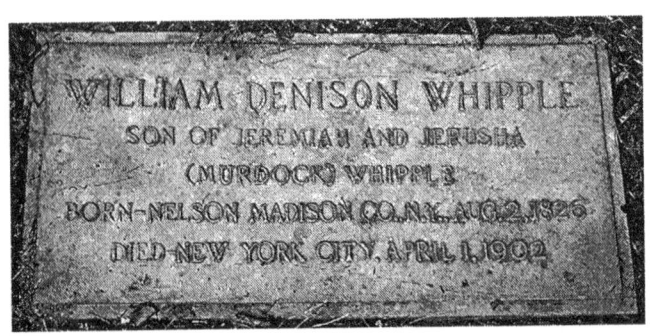

ORLANDO BOLIVAR WILLCOX

Born: April 16, 1823
Died: May 10, 1907

General Willcox was born in Detroit, Michigan.[1] He graduated from West Point in 1847, ranked eighth out of 38. He was sent to Mexico where he performed garrison duty at the end of the Mexican War. Then he performed routine garrison duties at various posts on the frontier, in Florida, and in Massachusetts. He was promoted to first lieutenant on April 30, 1850. On September 10, 1857, he resigned from the army in order to pursue a career in the law. He practiced law in Detroit and was a captain in the Michigan militia. He also wrote two novels under the pseudonym "Major Walter March."[2]

On May 1, 1861, Willcox was named colonel of the First Michigan Infantry. The next month he was given command of a brigade stationed at Washington, D.C. While commanding his brigade on July 21, 1861, at the Battle of First Manassas he was wounded in the right arm by a shell and then he was captured. He spent two weeks at a Confederate hospital at Manassas, and then he was sent to Richmond where he spent another six weeks in a hospital. Once he had recovered from his wound, he was confined in various prisons in Richmond, in Charleston and Columbia, South Carolina, and in Salisbury, North Carolina. For a time he was one of fourteen Union prisoners who were deemed hostages for fourteen captive Confederate sailors being threatened with execution for piracy. Eventually the Rebel captives were ruled prisoners of war and not pirates, thus freeing Willcox from his role as a hostage. Finally Willcox was exchanged and he was released on August 19, 1862. That same day he was appointed brigadier general of volunteers.[3]

With the reorganization of the Army of the Potomac after the Second Manassas Campaign, Willcox was given command of a Ninth Corps division on September 8, 1862. He ably led his division in the Antietam Campaign later that month. He temporarily commanded the Ninth Corps from October 8, 1862, until January 16, 1863. His corps saw little action during the Fredericksburg Campaign of December 1862. He returned to command of his division on February 7, 1863, and went with his command when the Ninth Corps was transferred to the Department of the Ohio in March 1863. The Senate confirmed his nomination on March 11, 1863, and his commission as brigadier general of volunteers ranked from July 21, 1861. Between March 1863 and April 1864 he commanded at various times his division, the Ninth Corps, and several different military districts. He commanded a Ninth Corps division during the 1864 Overland Campaign in Virginia. He was brevetted major general of volunteers on August 1, 1864, for his performance at the Rapidan River. During the siege at Petersburg he commanded at various times several different Ninth Corps divisions and the corps itself. Although he ably served as a division and corps commander throughout much of the war, the record contains no explanation as to why he did not receive an appointment as a substantive major general of volunteers.[4]

Willcox was mustered out of the volunteer service on January 15, 1866, and he briefly returned to his law practice in Detroit. With the reorganization of the army after the war, he was named colonel of the 29th Infantry on July 28, 1866, and he would serve in the army for the next twenty-one years. On March 2, 1867, he was brevetted brigadier general in the regular army for his performance at Spotsylvania and major general in the regular army for his performance at Petersburg. He served at San Francisco between 1869 and 1878, and then he commanded the Department of Arizona from 1878 to 1882. The town of Willcox, Arizona was named for him. On October 13, 1886, he was promoted to brigadier general and on April 16, 1887, he retired from the army, having reached the mandatory retirement age of sixty-four. He served as governor of the Soldiers' Home in Washington, D.C. from 1889 until 1892. In 1895 he was awarded the Medal of Honor based on the fact that he "led charges until wounded and taken prisoner" at First Manassas. In 1905 he moved to Coburg, Ontario, Canada, and he died there two years later. He was buried in Section 1 at Arlington National Cemetery.[5]

HORATIO GOUVERNEUR WRIGHT

Born: March 6, 1820
Died: July 2, 1899

General Wright was born in Clinton, Connecticut. He graduated from West Point in 1841, ranked second out of 52. Based on his class rank, he was assigned to the prestigious Corps of Engineers. After teaching engineering and French at West Point for a year, he spent the next nineteen years on various engineering assignments, mainly involving the construction of forts and the improvement of harbors. He was promoted to first lieutenant on February 28, 1848, and captain on July 1, 1855.[1]

In April 1861 Wright was at the Gosport Navy Yard in Norfolk, Virginia. He was to supervise the destruction of the valuable dry docks there, prior to the Union evacuation of Norfolk. On April 20, 1861, Wright was captured by Virginia state forces before he completed his mission, but he was released four days later. He served as an aide-de-camp and chief engineer on the staff of Brig. Gen. Samuel P. Heintzelman during the First Manassas Campaign of July 1861. Wright was promoted to major in the regular army on August 6, 1861. On September 14, 1861, he was appointed brigadier general of volunteers. Five days later he was given command of a brigade in the Port Royal Expedition and he acted as chief engineer during that expedition as well. The Senate confirmed his nomination on February 3, 1862, and his commission as a brigadier general of volunteers ranked from September 14, 1861. In April 1862 he was placed in command of a division in the Department of the South. He led his division on June 16, 1862, during the defeat at Secessionville, South Carolina, although he had urged his commander to refrain from attacking the Confederate defenses there. He commanded the Department of the Ohio from August 19, 1862, until March 25, 1863. On August 20, 1862, he was appointed major general of volunteers, probably because he had been named commander of a department. But in March 1863 his nomination was negated and the appointment was revoked, probably because he was no longer a department commander.[2]

On May 23, 1863, Wright was given command of a Sixth Corps division in the Army of the Potomac. He led his division during the Gettysburg Campaign of June – July 1863, although his division saw little action during the battle itself, and during several campaigns in Virginia later that year. He was brevetted lieutenant colonel in the regular army on November 8, 1863, for his performance at Rappahannock Station. He led his division during the first several days of the 1864 Overland Campaign, but on May 9, 1864, he became commander of the Sixth Corps upon the death of Maj. Gen. John Sedgwick at Spotsylvania. Wright ably led the corps through the end of the war. He was nominated major general of volunteers on May 10, 1864. The Senate confirmed his nomination two days later and his commission ranked from May 12, 1864. That same day he was slightly wounded in the thigh by a shell fragment, but he did not have to leave the field. He was brevetted colonel in the regular army on May 12, 1864, for his performance at Spotsylvania. In early July 1864 the Sixth Corps was sent to Washington, D.C. to defend the capital from a threatened Confederate assault. Wright was given command of the various Union forces manning the defenses at Washington, D.C. and the assault was repulsed. In early August 1864 the Sixth Corps was sent to the Shenandoah Valley, where it constituted a part of the Army of the Shenandoah. Wright ably led his corps that autumn in the fighting at Winchester, Fishers Hill, and Cedar Creek. During the latter battle on October 19, 1864, he was slightly wounded in the chin, but he remained on the field. On March 13, 1865, he was brevetted brigadier general in the regular army for his performance at Cold Harbor and major general in the regular army for his performance at Petersburg. In April 1865 he ably led the Sixth Corps in the successful assault at Petersburg and during the pursuit of the Confederate army to Appomattox Courthouse.[3]

On November 23, 1865, Wright was promoted to lieutenant colonel in the regular army and on September 1, 1866, he was mustered out of the volunteer service. He then worked on various engineering assignments for the army, such as completion of the Washington Monument, the construction of bridges and tunnels, and river and harbor improvements. He was promoted to colonel on March 4, 1879. On June 30, 1879, he was promoted to brigadier general and was named army chief of engineers. He retired from the army on March 6, 1884, having reached the mandatory retirement age of sixty-four. He died in Washington, D.C. fifteen years later and was buried in Section 2 at Arlington National Cemetery.[4]

MARCUS JOSEPH WRIGHT

Born: June 5, 1831
Died: December 27, 1922

General Wright was born in Purdy, Tennessee. After attending a local academy he studied law. Then he moved to Memphis, where he practiced law and worked as a court clerk. He was also active in the 154th Tennessee militia regiment, rising to the grade of lieutenant colonel in 1861. During the early stages of the Civil War the regiment was mustered into the Confederate army, being designated the 154th Senior Tennessee Infantry. On August 17, 1861, Wright was named lieutenant colonel of the regiment. He led his regiment during the minor engagement at Belmont, Missouri on November 7, 1861. On February 3, 1862, he was named military governor of Columbus, Kentucky, but that post had to be abandoned in early March 1862. He ably led his regiment during the Battle of Shiloh on April 6 – 7, 1862. He was slightly wounded in the leg on the first day of that battle, but he remained on the field. His division commander, Maj. Gen. Benjamin F. Cheatham, praised Wright in his after action report, calling Wright "an efficient and gallant officer." Wright briefly served on Cheatham's staff as an assistant adjutant general from June 10 to September 1, 1862. His regiment saw no action at Perryville on October 8, 1862.[1]

On December 20, 1862, Wright was nominated brigadier general. Beginning in January 1863 he was given command of several different brigades in the Army of Tennessee. The Senate confirmed his nomination on April 22, 1863, and his commission as a brigadier general ranked from December 13, 1862. He ably led his brigades during the fighting at Chickamauga in September 1863 and at Chattanooga in November 1863, but health problems after the latter battle forced him to relinquish field command for the remainder of the war. In March 1864 he was placed in command of the post at Atlanta, Georgia. He held that position until August 6, 1864, thereby seeing no combat during the Union advance south from Chattanooga to Atlanta in the spring and summer of 1864. He briefly commanded the post at Macon, Georgia, from August 6 to 23, 1864, and then he commanded the post at Augusta, Georgia from August 23 to December 14, 1864. On the latter date he was sent west to command reserves in the Military Division of the West. He commanded the District of Northern Mississippi and Western Tennessee from February 3,

1865, through the end of the war. He was paroled at Grenada, Mississippi on May 19, 1865, and pardoned on August 3, 1866.[2]

After the war Wright returned to Memphis, where he resumed his law practice and served as assistant purser at the United States Navy Yard. He also became the editor of the Columbia, Tennessee *Journal*. Then he moved to Washington, D.C., where he practiced law. In 1878 the United States War Department placed Wright in charge of collecting the voluminous Confederate war records for inclusion in the proposed publication of the official records of the Civil War. He worked on this mammoth project until his retirement in June 1917. Although some Confederate records were lost or destroyed during the course of the war, Wright was responsible for finding and saving a considerable amount of those precious records. Through his efforts the *Official Records* contains much of the Confederate war records. Wright also wrote an impressive number of magazine articles and books concerning military and historical topics. He died in Washington, D.C. and was buried at the base of the Confederate Monument in Section 16 at Arlington National Cemetery. His grave site is marked with a simple government marker.[3]

APPENDIX 1

Burials Listed By Section Numbers

A. SECTION 1

1. Christopher Columbus Augur (Page 3)
2. Romeyn Beck Ayres (Page 5)
3. Absalom Baird (Page 7)
4. William Worth Belknap (Page 11)
5. Stephen Gano Burbridge (Page 17)
6. Abner Doubleday (Page 35)
7. Alexander Brydie Dyer (Page 37)
8. John Edwards (Page 39)
9. George Washington Getty (Page 43)
10. Lawrence Pike Graham (Page 47)
11. William Alexander Hammond (Page 51)
12. William Selby Harney (Page 53)
13. Joseph Abel Haskin (Page 55)
14. John Porter Hatch (Page 57)
15. William Babcock Hazen (Page 59)
16. Charles Edward Hovey (Page 61)
17. Rufus Ingalls (Page 63)
18. Benjamin Franklin Kelley (Page 69)
19. John Haskell King (Page 71)
20. Wladimir Bonawentura Krzyzanowski (Page 73)
21. John Sanford Mason (Page 75)
22. Montgomery Cunningham Meigs (Page 79)
23. Thomas Ogden Osborn (Page 91)
24. Innis Newton Palmer (Page 95)
25. Gabriel Rene Paul (Page 97)
26. Joseph Bennett Plummer (Page 103)
27. Orlando Metcalfe Poe (Page 105)
28. Joseph Jones Reynolds (Page 111)
29. James Brewerton Ricketts (Page 115)
30. Daniel Henry Rucker (Page 121)
31. Rufus Saxton (Page 123)
32. Green Clay Smith (Page 133)
33. William Farrar Smith (Page 137)
34. Joseph Rodman West (Page 151)
35. Frank Wheaton (Page 153)
36. William Denison Whipple (Page 157)
37. Orlando Bolivar Willcox (Page 159)

B. Section 2

1. Alexander Sandor Asboth (Page 1)
2. Joseph Jackson Bartlett (Page 9)
3. Luther Prentice Bradley (Page 13)
4. John Rutter Brooke (Page 15)
5. William Wallace Burns (Page 19)
6. George Crook (Page 29)
7. John Wynn Davidson (Page 31)
8. Frederick Tracy Dent (Page 33)
9. John Gibbon (Page 45)
10. Walter Quintin Gresham (Page 49)
11. August Valentine Kautz (Page 65)
12. Philip Kearny (Page 67)
13. John Franklin Miller (Page 83)
14. Robert Byington Mitchell (Page 85)
15. Joseph Anthony Mower (Page 87)
16. Edward Otho Cresap Ord (Page 89)
17. Green Berry Raum (Page 107)
18. John Aaron Rawlins (Page 109)
19. Lovell Harrison Rousseau (Page 119)
20. John McAllister Schofield (Page 125)
21. Philip Henry Sheridan (Page 128)
22. Julius Stahel (Page 139)
23. Samuel Davis Sturgis (Page 143)
24. Stewart Van Vliet (Page 147)
25. Louis Douglass Watkins (Page 149)
26. Joseph Wheeler (Page 155)
27. Horatio Gouverneur Wright (Page 161)

C. Section 3

1. Cyrus Bussey (Page 21)
2. William Thomas Clark (Page 23)
3. Powell Clayton (Page 25)
4. James Winning McMillan (Page 77)
5. Nelson Appleton Miles (Page 81)
6. Halbert Eleazer Paine (Page 93)
7. William Henry Penrose (Page 99)
8. Thomas Gamble Pitcher (Page 101)
9. Americus Vespucius Rice (Page 113)
10. William Starke Rosecrans (Page 117)
11. Daniel Edgar Sickles (Page 131)
12. Morgan Lewis Smith (Page 135)
13. Charles John Stolbrand (Page 141)
14. Wager Swayne (Page 145)

D. Section 4

    1. Charles Ewing (Page 41)

E. Section 7

    1. Thomas Turpin Crittenden (Page 27)

F. Section 16

    1. Marcus Joseph Wright (Page 163)

APPENDIX 2

Union Brevet Generals Listed By Section Numbers

A. SECTION 1

1. Nathan Williams Brown
2. William Henry Browne
3. John Allen Campbell
4. Henry Capehart
5. Benjamin Cozzens Card
6. George Washington Clark
7. James Bolles Coit
8. Joseph Conrad
9. Charles Henry Crane
10. James Jackson Dana
11. George Brown Dandy
12. Nathan Augustus Monroe Dudley
13. William Wade Dudley
14. Arthur Henry Dutton
15. George Alexander Forsyth
16. John Hasset Gleason
17. John Irvin Gregg
18. Marcus LaRue Harrison
19. Charles Henry Hoyt
20. Dennis Thomas Kirby
21. John Randolph Lewis
22. Robert Macfeely
23. David Bell McKibbin
24. John Kemp Mizner
25. Eli Huston Murray
26. William Myers
27. Alvred Bayard Nettleton
28. James Oakes
29. Albert Ordway
30. Alexander James Perry
31. Carroll Hagadorn Potter
32. John Ramsey (Surname spelled "Ramsay" on grave marker)
33. Benjamin Piatt Runkle
34. Allan Rutherford
35. Charles Henry Smith
36. Oliver Lyman Spaulding
37. George Eliphaz Spencer
38. Nelson Bowman Sweitzer
39. Thomas Thompson Taylor

40. John Eaton Tourtellotte
41. Thomas MacCurdy Vincent
42. Duncan Stephen Walker
43. James Monroe Williams
44. John Seashoales Witcher
45. Henry Clay Wood

B. Section 2

1. Ira Corey Abbott
2. Orville Elias Babcock
3. Richard Napoleon Batchelder
4. Hiram Berdan
5. Horace Boughton
6. Henry Van Ness Boynton
7. Ezra Ayres Carman
8. Isaac Swartwood Catlin
9. Cecil Clay
10. Henry Clarke Corbin
11. John Coughlin
12. Joseph Dickinson
13. Thomas Duncan
14. John Eaton, Jr.
15. Charles Lane Fitzhugh
16. Samuel Lyle Glasgow
17. Guy Vernor Henry
18. Daniel Macauley
19. Clinton Dugald MacDougall
20. James Douglass McBride
21. Martin Thomas McMahon
22. Lewis Merrill
23. Eugene Beauharnais Payne
24. Louis Henry Pelouze
25. Samuel Woodson Price
26. Charles Greene Sawtelle
27. Joseph Sewall Smith
28. Ellis Spear
29. Roy Stone
30. Eliphalet Whittlesey
31. Robert Williams
32. Thomas Wilson

C. Section 3

1. Harrison Allen
2. John Walker Barriger
3. Edward Griffin Beckwith
4. James Biddle
5. Thomas Jefferson Brady
6. Van Hartness Bukey
7. Hugh Cameron
8. Charles Candy
9. Milton Cogswell
10. John Thomas Deweese
11. Richard Coulter Drum
12. William Henry Enochs
13. Llewellyn Garrish Estes
14. William Baker Kinsey
15. Marshall Independence Ludington
16. George Washington Mindil
17. George Henry Nye
18. Thomas Ellwood Rose
19. George David Ruggles
20. Ira Spaulding
21. Jacob Hale Sypher
22. William Cooper Talley
23. Jonathan Tarbell
24. Augustus Gabriel Tassin
25. Edward Washburn Whitaker
26. Samuel Baldwin Marks Young

D. Section 7

1. Elwell Stephen Otis

E. Section 26

1. James Smith

ENDNOTES

ABBREVIATIONS

The following abbreviations are used in the notes for these frequently cited sources.

ANC   James Edward Peters, *Arlington National Cemetery: Shrine to America's Heroes* (Kensington, Maryland: Woodbine House, 1986)

CWD   Mark M. Boatner III, *The Civil War Dictionary* (New York: David McKay Company, Inc., 1959)

CWG   James Spencer, compiler, *Civil War Generals: Categorical Listings and Biographical Directory* (New York: Greenwood Press, 1986)

CWHC   John H. Eicher and David J. Eicher, *Civil War High Commands* (Stanford, CA: Stanford University Press, 2001)

CWR   Frederick H. Dyer, *A Compendium of the War of the Rebellion* (Des Moines: The Dyer Publishing Company, 1908; reprint, Dayton, Ohio: Morningside, 1979)

GG   Larry Tagg, *The Generals of Gettysburg: The Leaders of America's Greatest Battle* (Campbell, CA: Savas Publishing Company, 1998)

GIB   Ezra J. Warner, *Generals in Blue: Lives of the Union Commanders* (Baton Rouge, LA: Louisiana State University Press, 1964)

GIG   Ezra J. Warner, *Generals in Gray: Lives of the Confederate Commanders* (Baton Rouge, LA: Louisiana State University Press, 1959)

HTIE   Patricia L. Faust, editor, *Historical Times Illustrated Encyclopedia of the Civil War* (New York: Harper & Row, 1986)

MHCG   Jack D. Welsh, *Medical Histories of Confederate Generals* (Kent, OH: The Kent State University Press, 1995)

MHUG   Jack D. Welsh, *Medical Histories of Union Generals* (Kent, OH: The Kent State University Press, 1996)

OR   United States War Department, *The War of the Rebellion: A Compilation of the Official Records of the Union and Confederate Armies*, 70 vols. In 128 parts (Washington, D.C.: U.S. Government Printing Office, 1880 - 1901) All references are to Series 1, unless otherwise noted.

Introduction

1. Information concerning the history of Arlington National Cemetery was obtained from the following two sources: *ANC*, pp. 1 – 37; John V. Hinkel, *Arlington: Monument to Heroes* (Englewood Cliffs, NJ: Prentice – Hall, Inc., 1970), pp. 8 – 24.

Alexander Sandor Asboth

1. *GIB*, p. 11; *MHUG*, p. 7; *CWD*, p. 27; *CWHC*, p. 108.

2. *GIB*, p. 11; *MHUG*, p. 7; *CWD*, pp. 27 – 28; *CWHC*, pp. 108, 717.

3. *GIB*, p. 11; *MHUG*, pp. 7 - 8; *CWD*, p. 28; *CWHC*, pp. 108 - 109.

4. *GIB*, pp. 11 – 12; *MHUG*, p. 8; *CWD*, p. 28; *CWHC*, pp. 109, 710; Phil Arnold, editor, *Grave Matters*, "Welcome Home, General!," Vol. 5, No. 1 (Summer 1995), p. 8.

Christopher Columbus Augur

1. *GIB*, p. 12; *MHUG*, p. 9; *CWD*, p. 34; *CWHC*, pp. 109, 717; *HTIE*, p. 30.

2. *GIB*, p. 12; *MHUG*, p. 9; *CWD*, p. 34; *CWHC*, pp. 109, 717; *HTIE*, p. 30.

3. *GIB*, p. 12; *MHUG*, p. 9; *CWD*, p. 34; *CWHC*, pp. 109, 702, 706, 731; *HTIE*, p. 30.

4. *GIB*, p. 12; *MHUG*, p. 9; *CWD*, pp. 34 – 35; *CWHC*, p. 109; *HTIE*, p. 30.

Romeyn Beck Ayres

1. *GIB*, pp. 13 – 14; *MHUG*, p. 11; *CWD*, p. 36; *CWHC*, p. 110; *HTIE*, p. 32; *GG*, pp. 91 – 92.

2. *GIB*, p. 14; *MHUG*, p. 11; *CWD*, p. 36; *CWHC*, pp. 110, 718; *HTIE*, p. 32; *GG*, p. 92; *OR*, vol. 2, pp. 368 – 369, 372 – 373; *OR*, vol. 11, part 1, pp. 367, 373 – 374; *OR*, vol. 19, part 1, pp. 377, 401, 403, 411; *OR*, vol. 21, pp. 188, 524.

3. *GIB*, p. 14; *MHUG*, p. 11; *CWD*, p. 36; *CWHC*, pp. 110 – 111, 706, 710, 732; *HTIE*, p. 32; *GG*, pp. 92 - 93.

4. *GIB*, p. 14; *MHUG*, pp. 11 – 12; *CWD*, p. 36; *CWHC*, p. 111; *HTIE*, p. 32; *GG*, p. 93.

Absalom Baird

1. *GIB*, p. 15; *MHUG*, p. 13; *CWD*, p. 38; *CWHC*, p. 112; *HTIE*, p. 33.

2. *GIB*, p. 15; *MHUG*, p. 13; *CWD*, pp. 38 – 39; *CWHC*, pp. 112, 718; *HTIE*, pp. 33 - 34.

3. *GIB*, p. 15; *MHUG*, p. 13; *CWD*, p. 39; *CWHC*, pp. 112 – 113, 706, 710, 732; *HTIE*, p. 34; *OR*, vol. 30, part 4, p. 386.

4. *GIB*, pp. 15 – 16; *MHUG*, p. 13; *CWD*, p. 39; *CWHC*, p. 113; *HTIE*, p. 34.

Joseph Jackson Bartlett

1. *GIB*, p. 23; *MHUG*, p. 21; *CWD*, p. 48; *CWHC*, p. 119; *HTIE*, p. 42; *GG*, p. 108; *CWG*, pp. 87, 224. Warner, Welsh, Boatner, Eicher, Faust, Tagg, and Spencer all state that General Bartlett was born in 1834, however, the inscription on his grave marker indicates that he was born in 1833. Warner states that he obtained November 21, 1834, as the date of Bartlett's birth from the general's obituary in the Washington *Post* of January 15, 1893, and that the information in the obituary was presumably provided by the general's brother, Reverend W. A. Bartlett of Washington, D.C. *GIB*, p. 614 (note 17).

2. *GIB*, pp. 23 – 24; *MHUG*, p. 21; *CWD*, p. 48; *CWHC*, p. 119; *HTIE*, pp. 42 – 43; *CWR*, p. 1414; *GG*, pp. 108 –109; *OR*, vol. 2, pp. 386, 388 – 389.

3. *GIB*, p. 24; *MHUG*, p. 21; *CWD*, p. 48; *CWHC*, pp. 119, 718; *HTIE*, p. 43; *GG*, p. 109; *OR*, vol. 19, part 1, p. 381; *OR*, vol. 25, part 1, p. 569.

4. *GIB*, p. 24; *MHUG*, p. 21; *CWD*, p. 48; *CWHC*, pp. 119, 710; *HTIE*, p. 43; *GG*, p. 109.

William Worth Belknap

1. *GIB*, p. 29; *MHUG*, p. 25; *CWD*, p. 57; *CWHC*, p. 126; *HTIE*, p. 53; *ANC*, p. 49.

2. *GIB*, p. 29; *MHUG*, pp. 25 – 26; *CWD*, p. 57; *CWHC*, pp. 126, 710, 718; *HTIE*, p. 53; *CWR*, p. 1171; *ANC*, pp. 49 - 50. Both Warner and Welsh incorrectly state that

General Belknap commanded a division during the Atlanta Campaign, the March to the Sea, and the Carolinas Campaign. Actually, he commanded a brigade throughout those three campaigns, except for a six week period after the capture of Atlanta when he did temporarily command his division, from September 20 to October 31, 1864.

3. *GIB*, p. 29; *MHUG*, p. 26; *CWD*, p. 57; *CWHC*, p. 126; *HTIE*, p. 53; *ANC*, p. 50.

4. *GIB*, pp. 29 – 30; *MHUG*, p. 26; *CWD*, p. 57; *CWHC*, p. 126; *HTIE*, p. 53; *ANC*, p. 50.

Luther Prentice Bradley

1. *GIB*, pp. 40 – 41; *MHUG*, p. 33; *CWD*, p. 77; *CWHC*, p. 140.

2. *GIB*, p. 41; *MHUG*, pp. 33 – 34; *CWD*, p. 77; *CWHC*, p. 140; *CWR*, p. 1069.

3. *GIB*, p. 41; *MHUG*, p. 34; *CWD*, p. 77; *CWHC*, pp. 140, 718. Both Warner and Boatner incorrectly state that General Bradley was wounded during the Battle of Franklin, which occurred on November 30, 1864. The records are clear that Bradley was wounded the day before during fighting at Spring Hill and that the senior colonel in the brigade, Joseph Conrad, commanded the brigade at the Battles of Franklin and Nashville. *OR*, vol. 45, part 1, pp. 230, 269 – 274.

4. *GIB*, p. 41; *MHUG*, p. 34; *CWD*, p. 77; *CWHC*, pp. 140, 732.

John Rutter Brooke

1. *GIB*, p. 46; *MHUG*, p. 39; *CWD*, p. 88; *CWHC*, p. 145; *CWR*, p. 1578; *GG*, pp. 42 – 43.

2. *GIB*, p. 46; *MHUG*, p. 39; *CWD*, p. 88; *CWHC*, p. 145; *GG*, pp. 43 – 44; *CWR*, p. 1592.

3. *GIB*, p. 46; *MHUG*, p. 39; *CWD*, p. 88; *CWHC*, pp. 145, 711, 718; *GG*, p. 44.

4. *GIB*, pp. 46 - 47; *MHUG*, p. 39; *CWD*, p. 88; *CWHC*, pp. 145, 732.

Stephen Gano Burbridge

1. *GIB*, p. 54; *MHUG*, p. 44; *CWD*, p. 106; *CWHC*, pp. 154, 719; *HTIE*, p. 95; *CWR*, p. 1208.

2. *GIB*, p. 54; *MHUG*, p. 44; *CWD*, p. 106; *CWHC*, p. 154; *HTIE*, p. 95.

3. *GIB*, pp. 54 - 55; *CWD*, p. 106; *CWHC*, p. 154; *HTIE*, p. 95. Both Warner and Faust incorrectly state that General Burbridge was relieved of his command in Kentucky in January 1865, whereas he held that command until February 22, 1865.

4. *GIB*, p. 54; *CWD*, p. 106; *CWHC*, pp. 154, 711; *HTIE*, pp. 95, 654.

5. *GIB*, p. 55; *MHUG*, p. 44; *CWHC*, p. 154; *HTIE*, p. 95; *CWG*, pp. 186, 229. Warner, Eicher, Faust, and Spencer all state that General Burbridge died on December 2, 1894. Welsh states that he died on November 30, 1894, which matches the date inscribed on his grave marker.

William Wallace Burns

1. *GIB*, p. 56; *MHUG*, p. 45; *CWD*, p. 107; *CWHC*, p.155; *HTIE*, p. 96.

2. *GIB*, p. 56; *MHUG*, pp. 45 – 46; *CWD*, p. 107; *CWHC*, pp. 155, 719; *HTIE*, p. 96; Robert U. Johnson and Clarence C. Buel, editors, *Battles and Leaders of the Civil War*, 4 vols. (New York: The Century Company, 1887 – 1888; reprint, New York: Thomas Yoseloff, Inc, 1956), vol. 2, p. 374.

3. *GIB*, p. 56; *MHUG*, p. 46; *CWD*, p. 107; *CWHC*, pp. 155, 732; *HTIE*, p. 96.

4. *GIB*, p. 56; *MHUG*, p. 46; *CWD*, p. 107; *CWHC*, p. 155; *HTIE*, p. 96.

Cyrus Bussey

1. *GIB*, pp. 58 – 59; *MHUG*, p. 47; *CWD*, p. 109; *CWHC*, p. 156; *HTIE*, p. 98.

2. *GIB*, p. 59; *HTIE*, p. 98; *CWR*, p. 1160; William L. Shea and Earl J. Hess, *Pea Ridge: Civil War Campaign in the West* (Chapel Hill, NC: The University of North Carolina Press, 1992), pp. 90, 282; *OR*, vol. 8, pp. 232 – 235. Warner incorrectly states that General Bussey was mustered into the Federal service on August 10, 1861, as colonel

of the Third Iowa Cavalry. Actually he was named colonel of the Third Iowa Infantry on that date and colonel of the Third Iowa Cavalry on September 5, 1861.

3. *GIB*, p. 59; *CWD*, p. 109; *CWHC*, pp. 156, 711, 719; *HTIE*, p. 98.

4. *GIB*, p. 59; *CWD*, p. 109; *CWHC*, p. 156; *HTIE*, p. 98.

William Thomas Clark

1. *GIB*, pp. 82 – 83; *MHUG*, p. 69; *CWD*, p. 157; *CWHC*, p. 175.

2. *GIB*, p. 83; *MHUG*, p. 69; *CWD*, p. 157; *CWHC*, pp. 175, 719, 742.

3. *CWD*, p. 157; *CWHC*, pp. 175, 711, 719.

4. *GIB*, p. 83; *MHUG*, p. 69; *CWD*, p. 157; *CWHC*, p. 175.

Powell Clayton

1. *GIB*, p. 84; *MHUG*, p. 70; *CWD*, p. 158; *CWHC*, p. 176; *CWR*, pp. 1181, 1186; William Garrett Piston and Richard W. Hatcher III, *Wilson's Creek: The Second Battle of the Civil War and the Men Who Fought It* (Chapel Hill, NC: The University of North Carolina Press, 2000), pp. 61 - 62, 243 – 244.

2. *GIB*, p. 84; *CWD*, p. 158; *CWHC*, pp. 176, 719.

3. *GIB*, pp. 84 – 85; *CWD*, p. 158; *CWHC*, p. 176.

4. *GIB*, p. 85; *CWD*, p. 158; *CWHC*, p. 176.

Thomas Turpin Crittenden

1. *GIB*, p. 101; *MHUG*, p. 82; *CWD*, pp. 208 – 209; *CWHC*, p. 191.

2. *GIB*, p. 101; *MHUG* p. 82; *CWD*, p. 209; *CWHC*, pp. 191, 720; *CWR*, p. 1119.

3. *GIB*, p. 101; *CWD*, p. 209; *CWHC*, p. 191; *OR*, vol. 16, part 1, pp. 792 – 798; *OR*, vol. 52, part 1, p. 261.

4. *GIB*, pp. 101 – 102, 618 (note 82); *MHUG*, p. 83; *CWD*, p. 209; *CWHC*, p. 191.

George Crook

1. *GIB*, p. 102; *MHUG*, p. 83; *CWD*, p. 209; *CWHC*, p. 191; *HTIE*, p. 193; *CWG*, pp. 64, 83, 237; *ANC*, p. 67. There is no agreement among the standard sources as to the place or date of birth for General Crook. Warner and Faust state that he was born near Dayton on September 8, 1828. Welsh states that he was born near Dayton on September 8, 1829, and Welsh states that on a form submitted by Crook to the adjutant general in 1881 Crook indicated that he was born in 1829. Boatner states that he was born in 1829. Eicher states that he was born in Taylorsville, Ohio on September 8, 1828. Spencer lists Dayton as his hometown and September 8, 1828, as his date of birth. Peters states that he was born in Dayton on September 9, 1830. And to further confuse things, Crook's grave marker indicates that he was born in Dayton on September 8, 1830.

2. *GIB*, pp. 102 – 103; *MHUG*, pp. 83 – 84; *CWD*, p. 209; *CWHC*, p. 191; *HTIE*, p. 193; *ANC*, pp. 67 - 68.

3. *GIB*, p. 103; *MHUG*, p. 84; *CWD*, p. 209; *CWHC*, pp. 191, 720; *HTIE*, p. 193; *CWR*, p. 1513; *ANC*, p. 68.

4. *GIB*, p. 103; *CWD*, p. 209; *CWHC*, pp. 192, 703, 711, 720; *HTIE*, p. 193; *ANC*, p. 68. Warner incorrectly states that General Crook was commissioned brigadier general of volunteers in August 1862. He was appointed on September 7, 1862, and confirmed on March 11, 1863. His commission ranked from September 7, 1862.

5. *GIB*, pp. 103 – 104; *CWD*, p. 209; *CWHC*, pp. 192, 707, 733; *HTIE*, pp. 193 – 194; *ANC*, pp. 68 -69.

John Wynn Davidson

1. *GIB*, p. 112; *MHUG*, p. 90; *CWD*, p. 223; *CWHC*, pp. 199 – 200.

2. *GIB*, p. 112; *MHUG*, pp. 90 – 91; *CWD*, p. 223; *CWHC*, pp. 200, 720.

3. *GIB*, p. 112; *CWD*, p. 223; *CWHC*, pp. 200, 707, 711, 733.

4. *GIB*, p. 112; *MHUG*, pp. 91 – 92; *CWD*, p. 223; *CWHC*, p. 200.

Frederick Tracy Dent

1. *GIB*, p. 119; *MHUG*, p. 95; *CWD*, p. 233; *CWHC*, p. 206; *HTIE*, p. 215.

2. *GIB*, p. 119; *MHUG*, p. 95; *CWD*, p. 233; *CWHC*, pp. 206, 720, 733; *HTIE*, pp. 215 – 216; *CWR*, p. 1712; *OR*, vol. 29, part 2, pp. 123, 145. Most of the top aides who served on Grant's staff in the last year of the war (such as Orville Babcock, Adam Badeau, Cyrus Comstock, Ely Parker, and Horace Porter) were brevetted brigadier generals, but they did not receive a commission as a substantive brigadier general. The fact that Frederick Dent was commissioned a substantive brigadier general is conspicuously different, and can only be explained by referencing his familial relationship with Grant.

3. *GIB*, pp. 119 – 120; *MHUG*, p. 95; *CWD*, p. 233; *CWHC*, pp. 206 – 207, 720; *HTIE*, p. 216. Warner incorrectly states that General Dent served as Grant's military secretary until 1873. He served as Grant's aide-de-camp until Grant became president on March 4, 1869, and then he served as Sherman's aide-de-camp.

Abner Doubleday

1. *GIB*, p. 129; *MHUG*, p. 101; *CWD*, p. 244; *CWHC*, p. 213; *HTIE*, p. 224; *GG*, p. 26; *ANC*, p. 79.

2. *GIB*, pp. 129 – 130; *MHUG*, pp. 101 – 102; *CWD*, p. 244; *CWHC*, pp. 213, 720; *HTIE*, p. 224; *GG*, p. 26; *ANC*, p. 79.

3. *GIB*, p. 130; *CWD*, p. 244; *CWHC*, pp. 213, 703; *HTIE*, p. 224; *GG*, pp. 26 – 27; *ANC*, p. 79.

4. *GIB*, pp. 129 – 130; *MHUG*, p. 102; *CWD*, p. 244; *CWHC*, pp. 213, 707, 733; *HTIE*, p. 224; *GG*, p. 27; *ANC*, pp. 79 – 80.

Alexander Brydie Dyer

1. *GIB*, pp. 135 – 136; *MHUG*, p. 106; *CWD*, p. 254; *CWHC*, p. 220; *HTIE*, p. 232.

2. *GIB*, p. 136; *MHUG*, p. 106; *CWD*, p. 254; *CWHC*, pp. 220, 707, 716; *HTIE*, p. 232. In his bio sketch of General Dyer, Warner implies that Dyer replaced James W. Ripley as Ordnance Chief when Ripley retired, which is incorrect. Interestingly, in his bio sketch of General Ramsay, Warner correctly states that George D. Ramsay replaced

Ripley when Ripley retired in September 1863 and that Ramsay held that position for one year. *GIB*, pp. 136, 389.

3. *GIB*, p. 136; *MHUG*, p. 106; *CWD*, p. 254; *CWHC*, p. 220; *HTIE*, p. 232.

John Edwards

1. *GIB*, pp. 137 – 138; *MHUG*, p. 107; *CWD*, p. 261; *CWHC*, p. 223.

2. *GIB*, p. 138; *MHUG*, p. 107; *CWD*, p. 261; *CWHC*, pp. 223, 721; *CWR*, p. 1172.

3. *GIB*, p. 138; *MHUG*, p. 107; *CWD*, p. 261; *CWHC*, p. 223.

Charles Ewing

1. *GIB*, p. 145; *MHUG*, p. 110; *CWD*, p. 269; *CWHC*, p. 229.

2. *GIB*, p. 145; *CWD*, p. 269; *CWHC*, p. 229; *CWR*, p. 1713; *OR*, vol. 24, part 2, p. 264.

3. *GIB*, p. 145; *CWD*, p. 269; *CWHC*, pp. 229, 721.

4. *GIB*, p. 145; *MHUG*, p. 110; *CWD*, p. 269; *CWHC*, p. 229.

George Washington Getty

1. *GIB*, p. 170; *MHUG*, p. 128; *CWD*, p. 329; *CWHC*, p. 252; *HTIE*, p. 305.

2. *GIB*, pp. 170 - 171; *MHUG*, p. 128; *CWD*, pp. 329 – 330; *CWHC*, pp. 252, 721; *HTIE*, p. 305. Welsh incorrectly states that General Getty served at Gettysburg. At the time of that battle Getty was in southeastern Virginia in command of his Seventh Corps division.

3. *GIB*, p. 171; *MHUG*, pp. 128 – 129; *CWD*, p. 329; *CWHC*, pp. 252, 707, 712, 734; *HTIE*, p. 305.

4. *GIB*, p. 171; *MHUG*, p. 129; *CWD*, p. 329; *CWHC*, p. 252; *HTIE*, p. 305.

John Gibbon

1. *GIB*, p. 171; *MHUG*, p. 129; *CWD*, p. 340; *CWHC*, p. 253; *HTIE*, p. 309; *GG*, p. 45.

2. *GIB*, p. 171; *MHUG*, p. 129; *CWD*, p. 340; *CWHC*, pp. 253, 721; *HTIE*, p. 309; *GG*, p. 45.

3. *GIB*, pp. 171 – 172; *MHUG*, p. 129; *CWD*, p. 340; *CWHC*, p. 253; *HTIE*, p. 309; *GG*, pp. 45 - 46.

4. *GIB*, p. 172; *CWD*, p. 340; *CWHC*, pp. 253, 703, 707, 734; *HTIE*, p. 309; *GG*, p. 46.

5. *GIB*, p. 172; *MHUG*, pp. 129 – 130; *CWD*, p. 340; *CWHC*, p. 253; *HTIE*, p. 309; *GG*, p. 46.

Lawrence Pike Graham

1. *GIB*, p. 180; *MHUG*, p. 135; *CWD*, p. 350; *CWHC*, p. 262.

2. *GIB*, p. 180; *MHUG*, p. 135; *CWD*, p. 350; *CWHC*, pp. 262, 722, 734.

3. *GIB*, pp. 180 – 181; *MHUG*, p. 135; *CWD*, p. 350; *CWHC*, p. 262.

Walter Quintin Gresham

1. *GIB*, pp. 188 – 189; *MHUG*, p. 141; *CWD*, p. 358; *CWHC*, p. 268; *CWR*, pp. 1134, 1139 - 1140.

2. *GIB*, p. 189; *MHUG*, p. 141; *CWD*, p. 358; *CWHC*, pp. 268, 712, 722; *CWR*, pp. 1139 - 1140.

3. *GIB*, p. 189; *CWD*, p. 358; *CWHC*, p. 268.

William Alexander Hammond

1. *GIB*, pp. 201 – 202; *MHUG*, p. 149; *CWD*, p. 370; *CWHC*, p. 277; *HTIE*, p. 334.

2. *GIB*, p. 202; *MHUG*, p. 149; *CWD*, p. 370; *CWHC*, pp. 277, 716; *HTIE*, p. 334.

3. *GIB*, p. 202; *MHUG*, p. 149; *CWD*, p. 370; *CWHC*, pp. 277, 716; *HTIE*, p. 334.

4. *GIB*, p. 202; *MHUG*, p. 149; *CWD*, p. 370; *CWHC*, pp. 277, 716; *HTIE*, p. 334.

William Selby Harney

1. *GIB*, pp. 208 – 209; *MHUG*, p. 153; *CWD*, pp. 376, 716; *CWHC*, p. 281.

2. *GIB*, p. 209; *MHUG*, p. 153; *CWD*, p. 376; *CWHC*, p. 281.

3. *GIB*, p. 209; *MHUG*, p. 153; *CWD*, p. 376; *CWHC*, p. 281.

Joseph Abel Haskin

1. *GIB*, p. 214; *MHUG*, p. 158; *CWD*, p. 383; *CWHC*, p. 286; *HTIE*, p. 349.

2. *GIB*, pp. 214 – 215; *MHUG*, p. 158; *CWD*, p. 383; *CWHC*, pp. 286, 722, 734; *HTIE*, p. 349.

3. *GIB*, p. 215; *MHUG*, p. 158; *CWD*, pp. 383 - 384; *CWHC*, p. 286; *HTIE*, p. 349.

John Porter Hatch

1. *GIB*, pp. 216 – 217; *MHUG*, p. 159; *CWD*, p. 384; *CWHC*, p. 287; *HTIE*, p. 349.

2. *GIB*, p. 217; *MHUG*, p. 159; *CWD*, p. 384; *CWHC*, pp. 287, 722; *HTIE*, p. 349.

3. *GIB*, p. 217; *MHUG*, pp. 159 – 160; *CWD*, p. 384; *CWHC*, pp. 287, 712, 734; *HTIE*, pp. 349 – 350.

4. *GIB*, p. 217; *MHUG*, p. 160; *CWD*, p. 384; *CWHC*, p. 287; *HTIE*, p. 350.

William Babcock Hazen

1. *GIB*, pp. 225 – 226; *MHUG*, p. 165; *CWD*, p. 390; *CWHC*, p. 291; *HTIE*, pp. 354 – 355.

2. *GIB*, p. 226; *MHUG*, p. 165; *CWD*, p. 390; *CWHC*, pp. 291, 723; *HTIE*, p. 355; *CWR*, pp. 1515 - 1516. Both Warner and Welsh state that General Hazen was promoted brigadier general in April 1863. Although his appointment did date from April 4, 1863, his nomination was confirmed on March 9, 1863, and his commission ranked from November 29, 1862.

3. *GIB*, p. 226; *MHUG*, pp. 165 – 166; *CWD*, p. 390; *CWHC*, pp. 291, 703, 707, 734; *HTIE*, p. 355. Both Warner and Welsh state that General Hazen was promoted major general in April 1865. Although his appointment did date from April 20, 1865, his nomination was confirmed on February 14, 1865, and his commission ranked from December 13, 1864.

Charles Edward Hovey

1. *GIB*, p. 236; *MHUG*, p. 173; *CWD*, p. 412; *CWHC*, p. 305.

2. *GIB*, p. 236; *MHUG*, pp. 173 – 174; *CWD*, p. 412; *CWHC*, p. 305; *CWR*, p. 1060.

3. *GIB*, pp. 236 – 237; *CWD*, p. 412; *CWHC*, pp. 305, 712.

Rufus Ingalls

1. *GIB*, pp. 245 – 246; *MHUG*, p. 180; *CWD*, p. 425; *CWHC*, p. 313; *HTIE*, p. 383.

2. *GIB*, p. 246; *MHUG*, p. 180; *CWD*, p. 425; *CWHC*, pp. 313, 708, 713, 723, 734; *HTIE*, p. 383. Welsh incorrectly states that General Ingalls was appointed chief quartermaster of the Army of the Potomac at the start of the Civil War. Faust incorrectly states that he was named chief quartermaster of that army in September 1861. He was named chief quartermaster of the Army of the Potomac on July 10, 1862, upon the removal, at his own request, of Brig. Gen. Stewart Van Vliet. *OR*, vol. 11, part 3, pp. 312 - 313.

3. *GIB*, p. 246; *MHUG*, p. 180; *CWD*, p. 425; *CWHC*, p. 313; *HTIE*, p. 383.

August Valentine Kautz

1. *GIB*, p. 257; *MHUG*, p. 187; *CWD*, p. 448; *CWHC*, p. 327; *HTIE*, p. 408.

2. *GIB*, pp. 257 –258; *MHUG*, pp. 187 – 188; *CWD*, pp. 448 – 449; *CWHC*, p. 327; *HTIE*, p. 408; *CWR*, pp. 1473 – 1474.

3. *GIB*, p. 258; *MHUG*, p. 188; *CWD*, p. 449; *CWHC*, pp. 327 – 328, 708, 713, 723, 735; *HTIE*, p. 408.

4. *GIB*, p. 258; *MHUG*, p. 188; *CWD*, p. 449; *CWHC*, p. 328; *HTIE*, p. 408.

Philip Kearny

1. *GIB*, p. 258; *MHUG*, p. 188; *CWD*, p. 449; *CWHC*, p. 328; *HTIE*, p. 408; *CWG*, pp. 74, 260; *ANC*, p. 111. Warner, Welsh, Eicher, Faust, and Spencer all state that General Kearny was born on June 2, 1815. Boatner states that he was born in 1814. Peters states that he was born on June 1, 1814, which is the date indicated on General Kearny's grave marker.

2. *GIB*, p. 258; *CWD*, p. 449; *CWHC*, p. 328; *HTIE*, p. 408; *ANC*, p. 111.

3. *GIB*, pp. 258 – 259; *MHUG*, p. 188; *CWD*, p. 449; *CWHC*, p. 328; *HTIE*, p. 408; *ANC*, pp. 111 - 112.

4. *GIB*, p. 259; *MHUG*, pp. 188 – 189; *CWD*, p. 449; *CWHC*, pp. 328, 704, 723; *HTIE*, pp. 408 – 409; *ANC*, pp. 74 – 75, 112 - 113. Peters incorrectly states that General Kearny was killed just prior to the Battle of Second Manassas, whereas he was killed on September 1, 1862, at Chantilly, just <u>after</u> the Battle of Second Manassas. The other equestrian statue at Arlington marks the grave site of Sir John Dill in Section 32. He served as chief of the British Joint Mission to the United States and as senior British representative on the Combined Chiefs of Staff during World War II, until his death in Washington, D.C. on November 4, 1944.

5. *GIB*, p. 259; *CWD*, p. 37; *CWHC*, p. 328; *HTIE*, p. 184.

Benjamin Franklin Kelley

1. *GIB*, p. 260; *MHUG*, p. 189; *CWD*, p. 450; *CWHC*, pp. 328 – 329, 723; *HTIE*, p. 410; *CWR*, p. 1660; *OR*, vol. 2, pp. 64 – 68.

2. *GIB*, pp. 260 – 261; *CWD*, p. 450; *CWHC*, pp. 329, 713; *HTIE*, p. 410; *OR*, vol. 37, part 1, pp. 188 - 189; *OR*, vol. 43, part 1, pp. 2 - 3.

3. *GIB*, p. 261; *MHUG*, p. 190; *CWD*, p. 450; *CWHC*, p. 329; *HTIE*, p. 410.

John Haskell King

1. *GIB*, p. 268; *MHUG*, p. 195; *CWD*, p. 463; *CWHC*, p. 333; Mark W. Johnson, *That Body of Brave Men: The U. S. Regular Infantry and the Civil War in the West* (Cambridge, MA: Da Capo Press, 2003), pp. xxiii – xxxiv.

2. *GIB*, p. 268; *MHUG*, p. 195; *CWD*, p. 463; *CWHC*, pp. 333, 724; *CWR*, p. 1714; Johnson, *That Body of Brave Men*, pp. 43 – 46, 64 – 65, 96 – 98, 102 – 103, 105 – 106, 118 – 119, 121 – 122, 124, 174, 261, 276 – 278, 282, 295, 311, 333.

3. *GIB*, pp. 268 – 269; *MHUG*, p. 195; *CWD*, p. 463; *CWHC*, p. 333; Johnson, *That Body of Brave Men*, pp. 352 – 354, 384, 387 – 394, 397, 400, 403 – 404, 409 – 412, 416 – 422, 434, 444.

4. *GIB*, p. 269; *MHUG*, p. 195; *CWD*, p. 463; *CWHC*, pp. 333, 708, 713, 735; Johnson, *That Body of Brave Men*, pp. 486 – 500, 510 – 511, 518, 521, 528 – 529.

Wladimir Bonawentura Krzyzanowski

1. *GIB*, p. 273; *MHUG*, p. 197; *CWHC*, p. 336; *HTIE*, p. 421; *CWG*, pp. 80, 262. Warner, Welsh, Eicher, and Faust all state that General Krzyzanowski was born on July 8, 1824, in Raznova, Prussia, however, the inscription on his grave marker indicates that he was born in Roznowo, Poland on June 9, 1824. At the time of his birth the Polish city of Raznova was within the borders of Prussia.

2. *GIB*, p. 273; *MHUG*, p. 197; *CWD*, p. 469; *CWHC*, pp. 336 – 337; *HTIE*, p. 421; *CWR*, p. 1426; *GG*, pp. 140 – 141.

3. *GIB*, p. 273; *MHUG*, p. 197; *CWD*, p. 469; *CWHC*, p. 337; *HTIE*, p. 421; *GG*, p. 141. It has been reported that Carl Schurz, a fellow immigrant and a major general in the Eleventh Corps, stated that the Senate failed to act on General Krzyzanowski's nomination because no Senator could pronounce his name. Even if Schurz said such a thing, it must have been as a joke. The Senate confirmed the nominations of many other immigrants with hard to pronounce names, such as Alexander Schimmelfennig and Adolph von Steinwehr, and in March 1865 the Senate had no difficulty confirming Krzyzanowski's nomination as a brevet brigadier general of volunteers. *GIB*, pp. 637 – 638 (note 318); *CWD*, p. 469; *HTIE*, p. 421; *GG*, p. 141.

4. *GIB*, pp. 273 – 274; *MHUG*, pp. 197 – 198; *CWD*, p. 469; *CWHC*, pp. 337, 750; *HTIE*, p. 421; *GG*, pp. 141 – 142.

5. *GIB*, p. 274; *MHUG*, p. 198; *CWD*, p. 469; *CWHC*, p. 337; *HTIE*, p. 421; *GG*, p. 142; Jeffrey I. Richman, *Final Camping Ground: Civil War Veterans at Brooklyn's Green-*

Wood Cemetery, in Their Own Words (Brooklyn, NY: The Green-Wood Cemetery, 2007), p. 334 of the accompanying illustrated biographical dictionary on CD.

John Sanford Mason

1. *GIB*, pp. 313 – 314; *MHUG*, p. 223; *CWD*, p. 516; *CWHC*, p. 367.

2. *GIB*, p. 314; *MHUG*, p. 223; *CWD*, p. 516; *CWHC*, pp. 367, 724; *CWR*, p. 1497; *OR*, vol. 21, pp. 289 – 293.

3. *GIB*, p. 314; *MHUG*, p. 223; *CWD*, p. 516; *CWHC*, pp. 367, 735.

4. *GIB*, p. 314; *MHUG*, pp. 223 – 224; *CWD*, p. 516; *CWHC*, p. 367.

James Winning McMillan

1. *GIB*, p. 305; *MHUG*, p. 217; *CWD*, p. 537; *CWHC*, p. 382; *HTIE*, p. 464.

2. *GIB*, p. 305; *MHUG*, p. 217; *CWD*, p. 537; *CWHC*, pp. 382, 725; *HTIE*, p. 464; *CWR*, pp. 1110 – 1111. Warner incorrectly states that General McMillan was promoted brigadier general on April 4, 1863, to rank from November 29, 1862. He was appointed on March 4, 1863, and the Senate confirmed his nomination five days later, with his commission to rank from November 29, 1862.

3. *GIB*, p. 305; *MHUG*, pp. 217 – 218; *CWD*, p. 537; *CWHC*, pp. 382, 713; *HTIE*, p. 464. Warner incorrectly states that General McMillan was in permanent command of his division throughout the 1864 Shenandoah Campaign. Actually the only time he commanded his division during that campaign was temporarily from October 15 to 24, 1864.

4. *GIB*, pp. 305 – 306; *MHUG*, p. 218; *CWHC*, p. 382; *HTIE*, p. 464. Both Warner and Welsh state that General McMillan was appointed to the pension review board in 1875, however, Faust states that the appointment occurred in 1871.

Montgomery Cunningham Meigs

1. *GIB*, p. 318; *MHUG*, p. 227; *CWD*, p. 542; *CWHC*, p. 386; *HTIE*, p. 485; *ANC*, pp. 152 – 153.

2. *GIB*, pp. 318 – 319; *MHUG*, p. 227; *CWD*, p. 542; *CWHC*, pp. 386, 708, 716; *HTIE*, p. 485; *CWR*, pp. 1712 – 1713; *ANC*, p. 153.

3. *GIB*, p. 319; *MHUG*, p. 227; *CWD*, p. 542; *CWHC*, p. 386; *HTIE*, p. 485; *ANC*, p. 154.

Nelson Appleton Miles

1. *GIB*, pp. 322 – 323; *MHUG*, p. 229; *CWD*, p. 550; *CWHC*, p. 389; *HTIE*, p. 492; *CWR*, pp. 1255, 1427; *ANC*, p. 155.

2. *GIB*, p. 323; *MHUG*, pp. 229 – 230; *CWD*, p. 550; *CWHC*, pp. 389, 704, 713, 725; *HTIE*, p. 492; *OR*, vol. 21, p. 230; *CWR*, p. 1427; *ANC*, p. 155.

3. *GIB*, pp. 323 – 324; *MHUG*, p. 230; *CWD*, p. 550; *CWHC*, pp. 389, 708, 735; *HTIE*, p. 492; *ANC*, pp. 155 – 157. The only other family mausoleum at Arlington (for the family of Brig. Gen. Thomas Crook Sullivan) is located in Section 1. *ANC*, p. 157.

John Franklin Miller

1. *GIB*, p. 324; *MHUG*, p. 230; *CWD*, p. 551; *CWHC*, p. 390.

2. *GIB*, p. 324; *MHUG*, pp. 230 – 231; *CWD*, p. 551; *CWHC*, pp. 390, 725; *CWR*, p. 1130; *OR*, vol. 16, part 1, pp. 252, 267, 753, 808, 817; *OR*, vol. 16, part 2, pp. 121, 430 – 431, 563, 989; *OR*, vol. 20, part 1, pp. 211, 431 – 436; *OR*, vol. 23, part 1, p. 484. Warner implies that General Miller was present at and in command of his regiment at Shiloh. Welsh states that Miller commanded a brigade at Shiloh and Corinth. Both are incorrect, for Miller was not present at either battle. Indeed, Miller's name never shows up in either volume 10 (Shiloh) or volume 16 (Iuka/Corinth) of the *Official Records*. The after action report of Brig. Gen. Alexander M. McCook concerning the Battle of Shiloh (*OR*, vol. 10, part 1, p. 305) clearly states that Lt. Col. David M. Dunn commanded the 29th Indiana during that battle. Also, the standard sources all overlook the fact that Miller commanded the post at Nashville in July and August 1862. Warner implies that Miller was with his regiment during the Perryville Campaign, but that is not correct.

3. *GIB*, pp. 324 – 325; *MHUG*, p. 231; *CWD*, p. 551; *CWHC*, pp. 390, 713; *OR*, vol. 45, part 1, pp. 95, 508.

Robert Byington Mitchell

1. *GIB*, pp. 328 – 329; *MHUG*, p. 233; *CWD*, p. 557; *CWHC*, p. 392.

2. *GIB*, p. 329; *MHUG*, p. 233; *CWD*, pp. 557 - 558; *CWHC*, pp. 392, 725; *CWR*, p. 1187; *OR*, vol. 20, part 1, p. 372.

3. *GIB*, p. 329; *MHUG*, p. 233; *CWD*, p. 558; *CWHC*, p. 392; *OR*, vol. 30, part 1, pp. 890 – 894. Welsh states that General Mitchell was sick at Nashville in January and February 1863, and then he states that Mitchell was on sick leave until September 1863. The latter point is incorrect. The records are clear that although he was ill, Mitchell commanded his forces in the field from March until September 1863. Mitchell filed reports of his involvement in fighting at Brentwood and the Little Harpeth River on March 25, 1863, Green Hill on April 6, 1863, and Middle Tennessee from June 23 until July 3, 1863. *OR*, vol. 23, part 1, pp. 185 – 186, 214 – 215, 542 – 546. In a message from the field dated June 24, 1863, Mitchell stated that recently he had been very sick. *OR*, vol. 23, part 1, p. 532.

Joseph Anthony Mower

1. *GIB*, p. 338; *MHUG*, p. 238; *CWD*, p. 573; *CWHC*, p. 401; *HTIE*, pp. 515 – 516.

2. *GIB*, pp. 338 - 339; *MHUG*, p. 238; *CWD*, p. 573; *CWHC*, p. 401; *HTIE*, p. 516; *CWR*, pp. 1327 - 1328. The standard sources have the facts wrong concerning General Mower's capture and escape at Corinth. Warner states that he was captured, he escaped, and he was recaptured. Welsh states that he was captured, but that the Confederates left him in a Confederate field hospital because of the severity of his wound. Boatner states that he was captured and recaptured. Faust states that he was captured, he escaped, he was recaptured, and he was held until paroled. Eicher states that he was captured and was recovered by U. S. forces later that day. In his own after action report dated October 15, 1862, Mower stated that he was wounded while trying to get away from the enemy and that he "fell into their hands. Their precipitate retreat, however, in the subsequent part of the day left me free, and sundown found me again in camp." *OR*, vol. 17, part 1, p. 198.

3. *GIB*, p. 339; *MHUG*, p. 238; *CWD*, p. 573; *CWHC*, pp. 401, 704, 708, 725, 736; *HTIE*, p. 516. Warner states that General Mower was promoted to brigadier general on March 16, 1863, and Welsh states that he was so promoted in March 1863. Although his appointment did date from March 16, 1863, he was confirmed on March 13, 1863, and his commission ranked from November 29, 1862.

4. *GIB*, p. 339; *MHUG*, p. 238; *CWD*, p. 573; *CWHC*, p. 401; *HTIE*, p. 516.

Edward Otho Cresap Ord

1. *GIB*, pp. 349 – 350; *MHUG*, p. 244; *CWD*, p. 609; *CWHC*, pp. 409, 726; *HTIE*, pp. 547 – 548.

2. *GIB*, p. 350; *MHUG*, p. 245; *CWD*, p. 609; *CWHC*, pp. 409 - 410, 704, 726; *HTIE*, p. 548.

3. *GIB*, p. 350; *MHUG*, p. 245; *CWD*, pp. 609 – 610; *CWHC*, pp. 410, 708, 736; *HTIE*, p. 548.

4. *GIB*, p. 350; *MHUG*, p. 245; *CWD*, p. 610; *CWHC*, p. 410; *HTIE*, p. 548; Bernarr Cresap, *Appomattox Commander: The Story of General E. O. C. Ord* (New York: A. S. Barnes & Company, Inc., 1981), pp. 341 – 343. Warner states that General Ord was stricken with yellow fever on board a ship bound from New York to Vera Cruz, which does not make much sense. Welsh and Cresap state that he was on a boat bound from Vera Cruz to New York, which makes sense, because one or more of the persons on the boat must have contracted yellow fever while in Mexico.

Thomas Ogden Osborn

1. *GIB*, pp. 351 – 352; *MHUG*, p. 246; *CWD*, p. 613; *CWHC*, p. 411; *CWR*, p. 1063.

2. *GIB*, p. 352; *CWD*, p. 613; *CWHC*, p. 411; *CWR*, p. 1063.

3. *GIB*, p. 352; *MHUG*, p. 246; *CWD*, p. 613; *CWHC*, pp. 411, 714, 726, 754; *CWR*, p. 1063.

4. *GIB*, p. 352; *MHUG*, p. 246; *CWD*, p. 613; *CWHC*, p. 411.

Halbert Eleazer Paine

1. *GIB*, p. 356; *MHUG*, p. 249; *CWD*, p. 616; *CWHC*, p. 413; *HTIE*, p. 553.

2. *GIB*, p. 357; *MHUG*, p. 249; *CWD*, p. 616; *CWHC*, pp. 413, 726; *HTIE*, pp. 553 – 554; *CWR*, p. 1668. Warner states that General Paine was promoted to brigadier general on April 9, 1863. Although his appointment did date from April 9, 1863, he was confirmed on March 13, 1863, and his commission ranked from March 13, 1863.

3. *GIB*, p. 357; *MHUG*, p. 249; *CWD*, p. 616; *CWHC*, pp. 413, 714; *HTIE*, p. 554.

4. *GIB*, p. 357; *MHUG*, p. 249; *CWD*, p. 616; *CWHC*, p. 413; *HTIE*, p. 554.

Innis Newton Palmer

1. *GIB*, pp. 357 – 358; *MHUG*, p. 250; *CWD*, p. 616; *CWHC*, p. 414; *HTIE*, p. 554.

2. *GIB*, p. 358; *MHUG*, p. 250; *CWD*, pp. 616 – 617; *CWHC*, pp. 414, 726; *HTIE*, p. 554.

3. *GIB*, p. 358; *CWD*, p. 617; *CWHC*, pp. 414, 714, 736; *HTIE*, p. 554; *OR*, vol. 47, part 1, pp. 980 – 983.

4. *GIB*, p. 358; *MHUG*, p. 250; *CWD*, p. 617; *CWHC*, p. 414; *HTIE*, p. 554.

Gabriel Rene Paul

1. *GIB*, p. 363; *MHUG*, p. 253; *CWD*, p. 624; *CWHC*, p. 419; *GG*, p. 22.

2. *GIB*, pp. 363 – 364, 649 – 650 (note 466); *MHUG*, p. 253; *CWD*, p. 624; *CWHC*, pp. 419, 726; *CWR*, p. 1367; *GG*, p. 23; *OR*, vol. 4, p. 85; *OR*, vol. 9, p. 552. Warner, Welsh, and Boatner all erroneously state that General Paul commanded his brigade at Fredericksburg. Paul's absence from command of his brigade during the fighting at Fredericksburg is curious. Col. William F. Rogers of the 21st New York Infantry commanded the brigade during the battle. In their after action reports, both Rogers and Brig. Gen. Abner Doubleday, the division commander, state that Paul was in Washington, D.C. at the time of the battle because of "severe domestic affliction." I assume that is a euphemism for something, but I do not know what. Doubleday did state that, although Paul was not present during the fighting of December 13, Paul later "arrived…in time to take command of his brigade and lead it off the field." Unfortunately it is unclear exactly when Paul took command of the brigade, for in his report Rogers says nothing about Paul returning and commanding the brigade when it left the field. *OR*, vol. 21, pp. 57, 465, 473.

3. *GIB*, p. 364; *MHUG*, pp. 253 – 254; *CWD*, p. 624; *CWHC*, pp. 419, 726; *GG*, p. 23.

4. *GIB*, p. 364; *MHUG*, p. 254; *CWD*, p. 624; *CWHC*, pp. 419, 736; *GG*, p. 23.

William Henry Penrose

1. *GIB*, p. 366; *MHUG*, pp. 255 – 256; *CWD*, p. 640; *CWHC*, p. 425; *CWR*, p. 1710; *OR*, vol. 11, part 2, pp. 361 – 364; *OR*, vol. 12, part 2, pp. 489 – 491; *OR*, vol. 21, pp. 420 – 421.

2. *GIB*, pp. 366 – 367; *MHUG*, p. 256; *CWD*, p. 640; *CWHC*, pp. 425, 754; *CWR*, pp. 1362 – 1363.

3. *GIB*, p. 367; *MHUG*, pp. 256 – 257; *CWD*, p. 640; *CWHC*, pp. 425, 726, 736.

Thomas Gamble Pitcher

1. *GIB*, p. 372; *MHUG*, p. 259; *CWD*, p. 654; *CWHC*, p. 431; *CWG*, pp. 81, 276. Warner, Welsh, Eicher, and Spencer all state that General Pitcher was born on October 23, 1824. Boatner states that he was born in 1824. The inscription on his grave marker indicates that he was born on October 23, 1825.

2. *GIB*, p. 372; *MHUG*, p. 259; *CWD*, p. 654; *CWHC*, p. 431.

3. *GIB*, p. 372; *MHUG*, p. 259; *CWD*, p. 654; *CWHC*, pp. 431, 726; *CWR*, pp. 1711 – 1712; *OR*, vol. 12, part 2, pp. 158 - 159. Warner states that General Pitcher was promoted on March 20, 1863, to rank from November 29, 1862. Although his appointment did date from March 20, 1863, his nomination was confirmed on March 10, 1863. Eicher states that General Pitcher was captured at Cedar Mountain and was exchanged in January 1863. None of the other standard sources mention his being captured and exchanged, and there is nothing in the *Official Records* concerning his capture. If he had been captured, one would think that General Augur would have mentioned it in his after action report at the same time he was praising Pitcher's performance and recommending his promotion. Welsh states that after the battle Pitcher was first sent to Culpeper, Virginia, and then to Washington, D.C., "where he remained confined to his room until November 19, 1862, when he proceeded to New York City for duty." *MHUG*, p. 259. Boatner states that Pitcher was "on convalescent leave until 10 Jan. '63." *CWD*, p. 654.

4. *GIB*, pp. 372 – 373; *MHUG*, pp. 259 – 260; *CWD*, pp. 654 – 655; *CWHC*, pp. 431, 736. Warner incorrectly states that General Pitcher served as superintendent at West Point until September 1, 1870. *GIB*, p. 650 (note 475). Actually he served until September 1, 1871. And Warner incorrectly states that Pitcher served as governor of the Soldiers' Home until 1877. *GIB*, p. 373. He served until 1878.

Joseph Bennett Plummer

1. *GIB*, p. 374; *MHUG*, p. 261; *CWD*, p. 656; *CWHC*, p. 431; *CWG*, pp. 75, 276. Warner, Welsh, Eicher, and Spencer all state that General Plummer was born on November 15, 1816. Boatner states that he was born in 1820. The inscription on his grave marker indicates that he was 43 years old when he died, which would mean that he was born in 1818. Warner states that he obtained November 15, 1816, as the date of birth from "the vital records of Barre, Massachusetts" and he states that Plummer "seems to have taken a few years off his age…so as not to endanger an appointment to the Military Academy which he sought for at least two years." *GIB*, p. 374. Warner states that most sources he consulted stated that Plummer was born in either 1819 or 1820, and that in a letter dated March 7, 1836, Plummer himself wrote that he was born in November 1817. *GIB*, pp. 650 – 651 (Endnote 479).

2. *GIB*, p. 374; *MHUG*, p. 261; *CWD*, p. 656; *CWHC*, p. 431.

3. *GIB*, pp. 374 – 375; *MHUG*, p. 261; *CWD*, p. 656; *CWHC*, pp. 431, 726; *CWR*, p. 1327; *OR*, vol. 3, pp. 60, 61, 65, 66, 72 – 73, 203, 206 – 209; *OR*, vol. 8, pp. 113 – 115.

4. *GIB*, p. 375; *MHUG*, p. 261; *CWD*, p. 656; *CWHC*, pp. 431 – 432. It is certain that General Plummer was not originally buried at Arlington National Cemetery, because the first burial at Arlington occurred on May 13, 1864. *ANC*, p. 26. Warner states that he was unable to determine where Plummer was originally buried, even with the assistance of the staff at Arlington National Cemetery. *GIB*, p. 651 (Endnote 480).

Orlando Metcalfe Poe

1. *GIB*, p. 375; *MHUG*, pp. 261 – 262; *CWD*, p. 656; *CWHC*, p. 432; *HTIE*, p. 588.

2. *GIB*, p. 375; *MHUG*, p. 262; *CWD*, pp. 656 – 657; *CWHC*, p. 432; *HTIE*, p. 588; *CWR*, pp. 1281 - 1282.

3. *GIB*, pp. 375 – 376; *MHUG*, p. 262; *CWD*, p. 657; *CWHC*, pp. 432, 736; *HTIE*, p. 588.

4. *GIB*, p. 376; *MHUG*, p. 262; *CWD*, p. 657; *CWHC*, p. 432; *HTIE*, p. 588.

Green Berry Raum

1. *GIB*, p. 390; *MHUG*, p. 271; *CWD*, p. 681; *CWHC*, p. 446.

2. *GIB*, pp. 390 – 391; *MHUG*, p. 271; *CWD*, p. 681; *CWHC*, p. 446; *CWR*, p. 1071; *OR*, vol. 17, part 1, pp. 228, 232 - 234.

3. *GIB*, p. 391; *MHUG*, p. 271; *CWD*, p. 681; *CWHC*, pp. 446, 727, 755. Warner states that General Raum was given the full rank of brigadier general on February 28, 1865, to rank from February 15, 1865. Although his appointment did date from February 28, 1865, he was confirmed on February 23, 1865.

4. *GIB*, p. 391; *MHUG*, p. 271; *CWD*, p. 681; *CWHC*, p. 446.

John Aaron Rawlins

1. *GIB*, p. 391; *MHUG*, p. 272; *CWD*, p. 681; *CWHC*, p. 447; *HTIE*, p. 616.

2. *GIB*, pp. 391 – 392; *MHUG*, p. 272; *CWD*, pp. 681 – 682; *CWHC*, pp. 447, 708, 714, 716, 727; *HTIE*, p. 616.

3. *GIB*, p. 392; *MHUG*, p. 272; *CWD*, p. 682; *CWHC*, p. 447; *HTIE*, p. 616.

Joseph Jones Reynolds

1. *GIB*, pp. 397 – 398; *MHUG*, p. 275; *CWD*, p. 694; *CWHC*, p. 451; *HTIE*, p. 626.

2. *GIB*, p. 398; *MHUG*, p. 275; *CWD*, p. 694; *CWHC*, pp. 451, 705, 727; *HTIE*, p. 626.

3. *GIB*, p. 398; *MHUG*, pp. 275 – 276; *CWD*, p. 694; *CWHC*, pp. 451, 705, 727; *HTIE*, p. 626; *OR*, vol. 20, part 1, pp. 179, 371 - 372.

4. *GIB*, p. 398; *MHUG*, p. 276; *CWD*, pp. 694 – 695; *CWHC*, pp. 451, 708, 736; *HTIE*, p. 626.

Americus Vespucius Rice

1. *GIB*, pp. 398 – 399; *MHUG*, p. 276; *CWD*, p. 695; *CWHC*, p. 451; *CWR*, p. 1506.

2. *GIB*, p. 399; *MHUG*, p. 276; *CWD*, p. 695; *CWHC*, p. 451; *CWR*, p. 1523; *OR*, vol. 10, part 1, pp. 263 – 264, 856; *OR*, vol. 17, part 1, pp. 637, 721, 776; *OR*, vol. 24, part 2, pp. 280 - 281. Boatner states that General Rice "fought at Missionary Ridge" during

the fighting at Chattanooga, Tennessee on November 25, 1863. The other standard sources do not mention Rice being present during the fighting at Chattanooga in late November 1863 and there is no mention of Rice in the *Official Records* concerning Chattanooga or Missionary Ridge. Welsh states that Rice "did not return to duty until February 1864." *MHUG*, p. 276.

3. *GIB*, p. 399; *MHUG*, p. 276; *CWD*, p. 695; *CWHC*, pp. 451 – 452, 727; *CWR*, p. 1523; *OR*, vol. 38, part 3, pp. 178, 188, 194, 216.

4. *GIB*, p. 399; *MHUG*, p. 276; *CWD*, p. 695; *CWHC*, p. 452.

James Brewerton Ricketts

1. *GIB*, pp. 403 – 404; *MHUG*, p. 279; *CWD*, p. 699; *CWHC*, p. 453; *HTIE*, p. 633.

2. *GIB*, p. 404; *MHUG*, p. 279; *CWD*, p. 699; *CWHC*, pp. 453, 727; *HTIE*, pp. 633 – 634. Warner states that General Ricketts was promoted to brigadier general of volunteers on April 30, 1862, to rank from July 21, 1861. Although his appointment did date from April 30, 1862, he was confirmed on April 28, 1862.

3. *GIB*, p. 404; *MHUG*, p. 279; *CWD*, p. 699; *CWHC*, pp. 453, 708, 714, 736; *HTIE*, pp. 633 – 634.

4. *GIB*, p. 404; *MHUG*, p. 279; *CWD*, pp. 699 – 700; *CWHC*, p. 453; *HTIE*, p. 634.

William Starke Rosecrans

1. *GIB*, p. 410; *MHUG*, p. 283; *CWD*, p. 708; *CWHC*, p. 461; *HTIE*, p. 642; *ANC*, p. 199. Peters incorrectly states that Rosecrans graduated from West Point in 1841. He graduated in 1842.

2. *GIB*, p. 410; *MHUG*, p. 283; *CWD*, p. 708; *CWHC*, pp. 461, 717; *HTIE*, p. 642.

3. *GIB*, pp. 410 – 411; *MHUG*, p. 283; *CWD*, p. 708; *CWHC*, pp. 461, 705, 708; *HTIE*, pp. 642 – 643.

4. *GIB*, p. 411; *MHUG*, p. 283; *CWD*, p. 708; *CWHC*, p. 461; *HTIE*, p. 643; *ANC*, p. 199.

Lovell Harrison Rousseau

1. *GIB*, pp. 412 – 413; *MHUG*, p. 284; *CWD*, p. 710; *CWHC*, p. 463; *HTIE*, p. 645.

2. *GIB*, p. 413; *MHUG*, p. 284; *CWD*, p. 710; *CWHC*, pp. 463, 705, 727; *HTIE*, p. 645. Welsh incorrectly states that General Rousseau was promoted to brigadier general and major general in October 1862. His commission as brigadier general ranked from October 1, 1861, and his commission as major general ranked from October 8, 1862.

3. *GIB*, p. 413; *MHUG*, p. 284; *CWD*, p. 710; *CWHC*, pp. 463, 709, 717; *HTIE*, p. 645; *CWG*, pp. 76, 178, 282. Warner, Welsh, Eicher, Faust, and Spencer all state that General Rousseau was born on August 4, 1818 and died on January 7, 1869. Boatner states that he was born in 1818 and died in 1869. That would mean that he was fifty years old when he died. The inscription on his grave marker indicates that he died on January 9, 1869, and that he was 56 years old when he died, which would mean that he was born in 1812.

Daniel Henry Rucker

1. *GIB*, pp. 414 – 415; *MHUG*, p. 285; *CWD*, p. 711; *CWHC*, p. 464.

2. *GIB*, p. 415; *MHUG*, p. 285; *CWD*, p. 711; *CWHC*, pp. 464, 709, 714, 727, 736; *OR*, Series 3, vol. 4, p. 897. Eicher incorrectly states that General Rucker was chief quartermaster of the Department of Washington, D.C. from April 29 until September 1861, and from August 1862 until January 1863. A review of all the pertinent pages in the *Official Records* clearly shows that Rucker held this command throughout the entire war. Furthermore, Eicher incorrectly states that Rucker was an aide-de-camp (in charge of supply trains) for Maj. Gen. George B. McClellan from September 28, 1861, to July 10, 1862, and that he was chief quartermaster of the Army of the Potomac from July 10 until August 1862. The records are clear that Rufus Ingalls became chief quartermaster of the Army of the Potomac on July 10, 1862, upon the removal of Stewart Van Vliet, and that Ingalls held that position throughout the remainder of the war. There is nothing in the *Official Records* indicating that Rucker was an aide-de-camp on McClellan's staff or that he was in charge of McClellan's supply trains at any time during the war.

3. *GIB*, p. 415; *MHUG*, p. 285; *CWD*, p. 711; *CWHC*, p. 464.

Rufus Saxton

1. *GIB*, pp. 420 – 421; *MHUG*, p. 287; *CWD*, p. 722; *CWHC*, p. 470; *HTIE*, p. 659.

2. *GIB*, p. 421; *MHUG*, p. 287; *CWD*, p. 722; *CWHC*, pp. 470, 727; *HTIE*, p. 659; *OR*, vol. 12, part 1, pp. 626 – 642.

3. *GIB*, p. 421; *CWD*, pp. 722 – 723; *CWHC*, pp. 470, 714, 737; *HTIE*, p. 659.

4. *GIB*, p. 421; *MHUG*, pp. 287 – 288; *CWD*, p. 723; *CWHC*, p. 470; *HTIE*, p. 659.

John McAllister Schofield

1. *GIB*, p. 425; *MHUG*, p. 291; *CWD*, p. 726; *CWHC*, pp. 472 – 473; *HTIE*, p. 661; *ANC*, p. 204.

2. *GIB*, pp. 425 – 426; *MHUG*, p. 291; *CWD*, p. 726; *CWHC*, pp. 473, 727; *HTIE*, p. 661; *CWR*, p. 1321.

3. *GIB*, p. 426; *MHUG*, p. 291; *CWD*, pp. 726 – 727; *CWHC*, pp. 473, 705, 709, 717, 727.

4. *GIB*, p. 426; *MHUG*, p. 291; *CWD*, p. 727; *CWHC*, p. 473; *HTIE*, p. 661; *ANC*, p. 205.

Philip Henry Sheridan

1. *GIB*, p. 437; *MHUG*, p. 298; *CWD*, p. 747; *CWHC*, p. 483; *HTIE*, p. 679; *CWG*, pp. 61, 85, 285; *ANC*, p. 209. Warner, Welsh, Faust, Spencer, and Peters all state that General Sheridan was born on March 6, 1831, in Albany, New York. Boatner states that he was born in New York in 1831. Eicher states that he was probably born in Albany, New York on March 6, 1831, and that it is less likely that he was born either in Somerset, Ohio on September 6, 1831, or aboard a ship going from Ireland to New York. In his memoirs Sheridan stated that he was born in Albany, New York on March 6, 1831. Philip H. Sheridan, *Personal Memoirs of P. H. Sheridan* (New York: Charles L. Webster & Company, 1888; reprint, Wilmington, NC: Broadfoot Publishing Company, 1992), vol. 1, p. 2. Warner states that the place and date of Sheridan's birth is uncertain and that "Sheridan stated at times that he was born in Massachusetts and at other times, in Somerset, Ohio. When he entered West Point he indicated that he was born in 1830, but, in 1864 when he accepted his commission as brigadier general in the Regular Army, he moved the year of his birth to 1832. Some historians believe he was born at sea en route to America on a vessel flying the British flag, others, that he was born in Ireland. Perhaps Sheridan himself did not know, but for obvious reasons wished it to be known that he was native-born." *GIB*, pp. 658 – 659 (Endnote 578).

2. *GIB*, p. 437; *MHUG*, p. 298; *CWD*, p. 747; *CWHC*, p. 483; *HTIE*, p. 679; *ANC* p. 209; Sheridan, *Personal Memoirs*, vol. 1, pp. 11 - 12.

3. *GIB*, pp. 437 – 438; *MHUG*, p. 298; *CWD*, p. 747; *CWHC*, pp. 483, 728; *HTIE*, p. 679; *ANC*, p. 209; Sheridan, *Personal Memoirs*, vol. 1, pp. 121 - 125. Both Warner and Faust state that General Sheridan was made a brigadier general of volunteers on September 13, 1862, to rank from July 1, 1862. Although his appointment did date from September 13, 1862, he was nominated on July 14, 1862, and confirmed on March 10, 1863.

4. *GIB*, p. 438; *CWD*, pp. 747 – 748; *CWHC*, pp. 483, 705, 728; *HTIE*, p. 679; *ANC*, pp. 209 – 210. Both Warner and Faust state that General Sheridan was promoted to major general on March 16, 1863, to rank from December 31, 1862. Although his appointment did date from March 16, 1863, he was nominated on March 7, 1863, and confirmed on March 10, 1863. Faust incorrectly states that Sheridan commanded the Twentieth Corps at Chickamauga. He commanded a Twentieth Corps division during that battle.

5. *GIB*, pp. 438 – 439; *MHUG*, p. 298; *CWD*, p. 748; *CWHC*, pp. 483 - 484, 702, 717; *HTIE*, pp. 679 – 680; *ANC*, p. 210.

6. *GIB*, p. 439; *MHUG*, p. 298; *CWD*, p. 748; *CWHC*, p. 484; *HTIE*, p. 680; *ANC*, pp. 210 – 211. Peters incorrectly states that General Sheridan became general-in-chief of the army in 1884, after the death of William T. Sherman. Sheridan became general-in-chief when Sherman stepped down from that position on November 1, 1883. Sherman retired from the army on February 8, 1884, having reached the mandatory retirement age of sixty-four, and he died on February 14, 1891.

Daniel Edgar Sickles

1. *GIB*, p. 446; *MHUG*, p. 302; *CWD*, p. 760; *CWHC*, p. 488; *HTIE*, p. 688; *GG*, pp. 61 – 62.

2. *GIB*, pp. 446 – 447; *MHUG*, pp. 302 – 303; *CWD*, p. 760; *CWHC*, pp. 488, 705, 728; *HTIE*, p. 688; *GG*, p. 62. Warner, Welsh, Boatner, and Faust all incorrectly state that General Sickles fought at Antietam. He and the Third Corps were not there. The Third Corps had been left behind to man the Washington, D.C. defenses when the reorganized Army of the Potomac advanced into Maryland in September 1862 and fought the Army of Northern Virginia at South Mountain and Antietam.

3. *GIB*, p. 447; *MHUG*, p. 303; *CWD*, p. 760; *CWHC*, p. 488; *HTIE*, p. 688; *GG*, pp. 63 – 64.

4. *GIB*, p. 447; *MHUG*, p. 303; *CWD*, p. 760; *CWHC*, pp. 488, 709, 737; *HTIE*, p. 688; *GG*, p. 64.

Green Clay Smith

1. *GIB*, p. 457; *MHUG*, p. 309; *CWD*, p. 771; *CWHC*, p. 495; *CWG*, pp. 82, 287. Warner, Welsh, Eicher, and Spencer all state that General Smith was born on July 4, 1826, although Eicher does list July 2, 1832, as an alternate date of birth. Boatner states that he was born in 1832. The inscription on his grave marker indicates that he was born in 1832. As Warner points out, it is very unlikely that Smith was born on July 2, 1832, because that would mean that he was made a second lieutenant in the First Kentucky Infantry during the Mexican War before his fourteenth birthday. *GIB*, pp. 660 – 661 (Endnote 607).

2. *GIB*, p. 457; *MHUG*, p. 309; *CWD*, p. 771; *CWHC*, p. 495. Warner states that General Smith graduated from Transylvania University at the age of eighteen, which would be 1844, and that he took his degree from the Lexington Law School three years later, which would be 1847. It seems unlikely that he would have graduated from law school in 1847, considering the fact that he was in the army from June 1846 until June 1847. Eicher lists three possible years (1844, 1849, and 1850) for his graduation from Transylvania University and Eicher lists 1853 as the date of his graduation from law school.

3. *GIB*, p. 457; *MHUG*, p. 309; *CWD*, p. 771; *CWHC*, pp. 495, 728; *CWR*, p. 1191. Warner and Eicher state that General Smith was a private in 1861 without naming a regiment and Eicher lists him as a major in the Third Kentucky (Union) Cavalry without any dates.

4. *GIB*, p. 457; *MHUG*, p. 309; *CWD*, p. 771; *CWHC*, pp. 495, 715; *OR*, vol. 10, part 1, p. 884; *OR*, vol. 16, part 1, pp. 743, 745 – 752, 759 – 762; *OR*, vol. 23, part 1, pp. 7, 142 – 144, 177 – 182, 222 – 227. Warner incorrectly states that General Smith resigned from the army on December 4, 1863. He resigned on December 1, 1863.

5. *GIB*, pp. 457 – 458; *MHUG*, p. 309; *CWD*, p. 771; *CWHC*, p. 495.

Morgan Lewis Smith

1. *GIB*, p. 460; *MHUG*, p. 311; *CWD*, p. 773; *CWHC*, p. 498; *CWG*, pp. 78, 287. Warner, Welsh, Eicher, and Spencer all state that General Smith was born on March 8, 1821. Boatner states that he was born in 1821. The inscription on his grave marker indicates that he was born on March 8, 1822.

2. *GIB*, p. 460; *MHUG*, p. 311; *CWD*, p. 773; *CWHC*, p. 498.

3. *GIB*, p. 460; *MHUG*, p. 311; *CWD*, p, 773; *CWHC*, pp. 498, 728; *CWR*, p. 1326.

4. *GIB*, p. 460; *MHUG*, p. 311; *CWD*, pp. 773 – 774; *CWHC*, p. 498.

5. *GIB*, p. 460; *MHUG*, p. 311; *CWD*, p. 774; *CWHC*, p. 498.

William Farrar Smith

1. *GIB*, pp. 462 – 463; *MHUG*, p. 313; *CWD*, p. 775; *CWHC*, p. 499; *HTIE*, p. 699.

2. *GIB*, p. 463; *MHUG*, p. 313; *CWD*, p. 775; *CWHC*, pp. 499 – 500, 728; *HTIE*, p. 699; *CWR*, p. 1650.

3. *GIB*, p. 463; *CWD*, p. 775; *CWHC*, pp. 499 – 500, 705; *HTIE*, p. 699.

4. *GIB*, pp. 463 - 464; *MHUG*, p. 313; *CWD*, pp. 775 – 776; *CWHC*, pp. 500, 709, 737; *HTIE*, p. 699.

5. *GIB*, p. 464; *MHUG*, pp. 313 – 314; *CWHC*, p. 500; *HTIE*, p. 699.

Julius Stahel

1. *GIB*, p. 469; *MHUG*, p. 316; *CWD*, pp. 790 – 791; *CWHC*, p. 504; *HTIE*, p. 711. The standard sources do not agree on whether General Stahel fled to Berlin first and then London, or vice versa. Warner, Welsh, and Faust all state that he fled to London and then to Berlin, whereas Boatner and Eicher state the opposite. And the standard sources do not agree on the year Stahel moved to the United States. Warner, Welsh, and Faust all state that he came to America in 1859, whereas Eicher states that he moved to New York in 1856. Boatner does not state a year for his move to New York.

2. *GIB*, p. 469; *MHUG*, p. 316; *CWD*, p. 791; *CWHC*, pp. 504, 728; *HTIE*, p. 711; *CWR*, p. 1408.

3. *GIB*, p. 469; *MHUG*, p. 316; *CWD*, p. 791; *CWHC*, pp. 504, 705; *HTIE*, p. 711. Warner states that General Stahel was promoted to major general of volunteers on March 17, 1863. Although his appointment did date from March 17, 1863, he was nominated and confirmed on March 14, 1863, and his commission ranked from March 14, 1863.

4. *GIB*, pp. 469 – 470; *MHUG*, pp. 316 – 317; *CWD*, p. 791; *CWHC*, p. 504; *HTIE*, pp. 711 – 712.

Charles John Stolbrand

1. *GIB*, pp. 479, 663 (Endnote 641); *MHUG*, p. 322; *CWD*, pp. 799 – 800; *CWHC*, p. 513; *HTIE*, pp. 719 – 720.

2. *GIB*, p. 479; *MHUG*, p. 322; *CWD*, p. 800; *CWHC*, p. 513; *HTIE*, p. 720; *OR*, vol. 8, p. 117; *OR*, vol. 17, part 2, pp. 212 – 213, 514; *OR*, vol. 24, part 1, pp. 644, 649; *OR*, vol. 24, part 2, pp. 292 – 293.

3. *GIB*, p. 479; *CWD*, p. 800; *CWHC*, pp. 513, 729; *HTIE*, p. 720; *OR*, vol. 38, part 1, p. 103; *OR*, vol. 38, part 3, p. 95; *OR*, vol. 39, part 3, pp. 271, 399, 565, 752; *OR*, vol. 44, pp. 20, 850; *OR*, vol. 47, part 1, p. 102.

4. *GIB*, pp. 479 – 480; *MHUG*, p. 322; *CWD*, p. 800; *CWHC*, p. 513; *HTIE*, p. 720.

Samuel Davis Sturgis

1. *GIB*, pp. 486 – 487; *MHUG*, p. 326; *CWD*, p. 816; *CWHC*, p. 518; *HTIE*, p. 729.

2. *GIB*, p. 487; *MHUG*, p. 326; *CWD*, p. 816; *CWHC*, pp. 518, 729; *HTIE*, p. 729; *OR*, vol. 1, pp. 650 – 652; *OR*, vol. 3, pp. 64 - 71.

3. *GIB*, p. 487; *MHUG*, p. 326; *CWD*, p. 816; *CWHC*, pp. 518, 709, 737; *HTIE*, pp. 729 – 730; *OR*, vol. 12, part 1, pp. 3, 169, 174, 244; *OR*, vol. 12, part 2, pp. 20, 42, 48, 257; *OR*, vol. 12, part 3, pp. 313, 408, 435, 585; *OR*, vol. 39, part 1, pp. 87 – 89, 147 – 220.

4. *GIB*, p. 487; *MHUG*, p. 326; *CWD*, pp. 816 – 817; *CWHC*, p. 518; *HTIE*, p. 730.

Wager Swayne

1. *GIB*, pp. 490 – 491; *MHUG*, p. 329; *CWD*, p. 822; *CWHC*, p. 519.

2. *GIB*, p. 491; *MHUG*, p. 329; *CWD*, p. 822; *CWHC*, p. 519; *CWR*, pp. 1516 – 1517; *OR*, vol. 17, part 1, pp. 181, 185, 186, 190 – 191.

3. *GIB*, p. 491; *MHUG*, p. 329; *CWD*, pp. 822 – 823; *CWHC*, pp. 519, 705, 709, 715, 729, 737, 759; *CWR*, pp. 1516 – 1517. Warner states that General Swayne was advanced to major general of volunteers on May 1, 1866, to rank from June 20, 1865. Although his appointment did date from May 1, 1866, he was nominated on March 31, 1866, and confirmed on April 26, 1866.

4. *GIB*, p. 491; *MHUG*, pp. 329 – 330; *CWD*, p. 823; *CWHC*, p. 519.

Stewart Van Vliet

1. *GIB*, p. 524; *MHUG*, p. 351; *CWD*, p. 867; *CWHC*, p. 543.

2. *GIB*, pp. 524, 667 (Endnote 707); *MHUG*, p. 351; *CWD*, pp. 867 – 868; *CWHC*, p. 543; *OR*, vol. 11, part 3, pp. 258, 262 – 263, 312 – 313. The flap concerned General Van Vliet's poorly phrased request that navy vessels escort army vessels, which were laden with provisions and forage, up the James River. In his message to Goldsborough Van Vliet stated that "the general commanding [Maj. Gen. George B. McClellan] desires that these vessels be convoyed up the James." In his message Van Vliet did not order Goldsborough to do anything, but he also failed to state that the army was requesting Goldsborough's cooperation and assistance. As Warner stated, this was indeed a "tempest in a teapot." *GIB*, p. 667 (Endnote 707). But it is difficult to avoid the belief that Van Vliet's request to be removed as chief quartermaster was motivated by this flap and the embarrassment it caused George B. McClellan.

3. *GIB*, pp. 524, 667 (Endnote 707); *MHUG*, p. 351; *CWD*, p. 868; *CWHC*, pp. 543, 709, 715, 730, 738.

4. *GIB*, p. 524; *MHUG*, p. 351; *CWD*, p. 868; *CWHC*, p. 543.

Louis Douglass Watkins

1. *GIB*, p. 543; *MHUG*, p. 360; *CWD*, p. 895; *CWHC*, p. 556. Warner, Welsh, and Eicher all state that General Watkins was born on November 29, 1833. Boatner states that he was born in 1835. Warner states that "there is considerable discrepancy in various sources in regard to the date of Watkins' birth, as well as to the place and date of his death." *GIB*, p. 669 (Endnote 731). To further confuse matters, the inscription on his grave marker indicates that Watkins was 39 years old when he died, which would place his birth in 1829. Inexplicably General Watkins is not included in Spencer's book.

2. *GIB*, pp. 543 – 544; *MHUG*, pp. 360 – 361; *CWD*, p. 895; *CWHC*, p. 556; *OR*, vol. 11, part 2, pp. 46 – 47.

3. *GIB*, p. 544; *MHUG*, p. 361; *CWD*, p. 895; *CWHC*, p. 556; *CWR*, p. 1192; *OR*, vol. 20, part 1, pp. 88 – 92.

4. *GIB*, p. 544; *MHUG*, p. 361; *CWD*, p. 895; *CWHC*, pp. 556, 730, 738, 760; *OR*, vol. 38, part 2, pp. 792 – 795.

5. *GIB*, p. 544; *MHUG*, p. 361; *CWD*, p. 895; *CWHC*, p. 556. Warner, Welsh, and Eicher all state that General Watkins died on March 29, 1868. Boatner states that he died in 1868. The inscription on his grave marker indicates that he died on March 24, 1868.

Joseph Rodman West

1. *GIB*, p. 552; *MHUG*, p. 365; *CWD*, p. 902; *CWHC*, p. 562; *HTIE*, p. 814.

2. *GIB*, p. 552; *CWD*, pp. 114, 902; *CWHC*, p. 562; *CWR*, p. 1002; *HTIE*, pp. 106, 814; *OR*, vol. 9, pp. 553, 555, 569.

3. *GIB*, p. 552; *CWD*, p. 902; *CWHC*, pp. 562, 730; *HTIE*, p. 814; *OR*, vol. 9, p. 581; *OR*, vol. 34, part 1, pp. 930 – 932; *OR*, vol. 41, part 1, pp. 221 – 224, 296 – 298, 897, 976.

4. *GIB*, pp. 552 – 553; *MHUG*, p. 365; *CWD*, p. 902; *CWHC*, p. 562; *HTIE*, p. 814.

Frank Wheaton

1. *GIB*, p. 553; *MHUG*, p. 365; *CWD*, p. 910; *CWHC*, p. 563; *GG*, p. 115.

2. *GIB*, p. 553; *MHUG*, p. 365; *CWD*, p. 910; *CWHC*, pp. 563, 730; *GG*, p. 115; *CWR*, p. 1634; *OR*, vol. 2, pp. 399, 400. Tagg incorrectly states that two days after the Battle of Fredericksburg, which would be December 15, 1862, General Wheaton's promotion was approved and he was given command of a Sixth Corps brigade. His nomination was not confirmed until March 9, 1863, although he was indeed given command of a Sixth Corps brigade on December 15, 1862, based on his appointment as brigadier general of volunteers two weeks earlier.

3. *GIB*, p. 553; *MHUG*, p. 365; *CWD*, p. 910; *CWHC*, pp. 563, 709, 715, 738; *GG*, pp. 115 – 116. Warner incorrectly states that General Wheaton was in command of a division when the Sixth Corps was sent to Washington, D. C. in July 1864. At that time he was still in command of his brigade. He advanced to command of his division on September 21, 1864.

4. *GIB*, pp. 553 – 554; *MHUG*, p. 366; *CWD*, p. 910; *CWHC*, p. 563; *GG*, p. 116.

Joseph Wheeler

1. *GIG*, p. 332; *MHCG*, p. 232; *CWD*, p. 910; *CWHC*, p. 563; *HTIE*, p. 818; *ANC*, pp. 238 – 239.

2. *GIG*, pp. 332 – 333; *MHCG*, p. 232; *CWD*, p. 910; *CWHC*, pp. 563, 790, 799; *HTIE*, p. 818; *ANC*, p. 239; *OR*, vol. 10, part 1, pp. 468, 524, 535, 558 – 560; *OR*, vol. 16, part 2, pp. 824, 940. Many of the standard sources provide the wrong date for General Wheeler's advancement to chief of cavalry for the Army of Mississippi. Warner gives July 13, 1862, as the date. Boatner incorrectly states that Wheeler led a cavalry brigade at Stones River and he gives July 18, 1863, as the date Wheeler was named cavalry chief. Both Faust and Peters give July 1862 as the date. The order naming Wheeler chief of cavalry, dated October 13, 1862, is located in the *Official Records*. *OR*, vol. 16, part 2, p. 940. Eicher correctly gives October 1862 as the date.

3. *GIG*, p. 333; *MHCG*, p. 232; *CWD*, p. 910; *CWHC*, pp. 563, 790; *HTIE*, pp. 818 – 819; *ANC*, p. 239. Peters incorrectly states that Wheeler attained the grade of lieutenant general. The other standard sources do not make this mistake. In his Introduction and in his Endnotes Warner discusses the fact that, despite what some sources might contend, Wheeler was not promoted to lieutenant general. *GIG*, pp. xvii, 398 (Endnote 530).

4. *GIG*, p. 333; *MHCG*, pp. 232 – 233; *CWD*, p. 910; *CWHC*, p. 563; *HTIE*, p. 819; *ANC*, pp. 239 – 240. Warner, Welsh, and Peters all incorrectly state that General Wheeler served eight terms in the United States House of Representatives, whereas in fact he only served for a total time of less than seven years.

William Denison Whipple

1. *GIB*, p. 555; *MHUG*, p. 366; *CWD*, p. 912; *CWHC*, p. 564; *HTIE*, p. 819.

2. *GIB*, p. 555; *MHUG*, p. 366; *CWD*, p. 912; *CWHC*, pp. 564, 730; *HTIE*, pp. 819 - 820.

3. *GIB*, p. 555; *CWD*, p. 912; *CWHC*, pp. 564, 709, 730, 738; *HTIE*, p. 820.

4. *GIB*, p. 555; *MHUG*, pp. 366 – 367; *CWD*, p. 912; *CWHC*, p. 564; *HTIE*, p. 820. Warner incorrectly states that General Whipple served as an aide-de-camp to general-in-chief William T. Sherman for five years. Actually, it was for a period of eight years.

Orlando Bolivar Willcox

1. *GIB*, p. 558; *MHUG*, p. 369; *CWD*, p. 926; *CWHC*, p. 570; *HTIE*, p. 828; *CWG*, pp. 79, 301. Warner, Welsh, Eicher, Faust, and Spencer all state that General Willcox was born on April 16, 1823. Boatner states that he was born in 1823. The inscription on his grave marker indicates that he was born on April 26, 1823. The fact that he retired from the army on April 16, 1887, which is presumably his sixty-fourth birthday, makes it likely that he was born on April 16 and not April 26.

2. *GIB*, p. 558; *MHUG*, p. 369; *CWD*, p. 926; *CWHC*, p. 570; *HTIE*, p. 828. Faust incorrectly states that General Willcox commanded his regiment at First Manassas. He commanded the second brigade of Brig. Gen. Samuel P. Heintzelman's division at First Manassas. *OR*, vol. 2, pp. 315, 408 – 409. Both Warner and Faust state that Willcox was commissioned a brigadier general of volunteers on August 19, 1862, to rank from July 21, 1861. Although his appointment did date from August 19, 1862, he was not confirmed until March 11, 1863.

3. *GIB*, pp. 558 – 559; *MHUG*, p. 369; *CWD*, pp. 265, 926; *CWHC*, pp. 570, 731; *HTIE*, p. 828. Welsh incorrectly states that General Willcox was commissioned a brigadier general of volunteers in August 1862, to rank from April 1861. He was appointed on August 19, 1862, and confirmed on March 11, 1863. His commission ranked from July 21, 1861.

4. *GIB*, p. 559; *CWD*, p. 926; *CWHC*, pp. 570, 715, 731; *HTIE*, p. 828.

5. *GIB*, p. 559; *MHUG*, p. 369; *CWD*, p. 926; *CWHC*, pp. 570, 709, 738; *HTIE*, p. 828.

Horatio Gouverneur Wright

1. *GIB*, p. 575; *MHUG*, p. 380; *CWD*, p. 949; *CWHC*, p. 583; *HTIE*, p. 844; *ANC*, p. 244.

2. *GIB*, pp. 575, 672 (Endnote 768); *CWD*, p. 949; *CWHC*, pp. 583, 706, 731; *HTIE*, p. 844; *ANC*, p. 244. Warner incorrectly states that General Wright was made a brigadier general of volunteers on September 16, 1861. He was appointed on September 14, 1861, he was confirmed on February 3, 1862, and his commission ranked from September 14, 1861. Warner persuasively contends that Wright's appointment as a major general of volunteers was based on his assignment to department command and that the negation and revocation of his nomination was based on his removal from department command. *GIB*, p. 672 (Endnote 768).

3. *GIB*, pp. 575 – 576; *MHUG*, p. 380; *CWD*, pp. 949 – 950; *CWHC*, pp. 583, 706, 710, 738; *HTIE*, p. 844; *ANC*, pp. 244 – 245.

4. *GIB*, p. 576; *MHUG*, p. 380; *CWD*, p. 950; *CWHC*, p. 583; *HTIE*, p. 844; *ANC*, p. 245.

Marcus Joseph Wright

1. *GIG*, p. 346; *MHCG*, p. 240; *CWD*, p. 950; *CWHC*, p. 583; *HTIE*, p. 844; *OR*, vol. 7, pp. 436, 857; *OR*, vol. 10, part 1, pp. 437, 449, 450 – 452.

2. *GIG*, p. 346; *MHCG*, pp. 240 – 241; *CWD*, p. 950; *CWHC*, pp. 583 – 584, 800; *HTIE*, p. 844.

3. *GIG*, pp. 346 – 347; *MHCG*, p. 241; *CWD*, p. 950; *CWHC*, p. 584; *HTIE*, p. 844.

BIBLIOGRAPHY

Arnold, Phil, editor. *Grave Matters*. "Welcome Home, General!" Volume 5, No. 1. (Summer 1995). Fallbrook, CA, 1995.

Boatner, Mark M. III. *The Civil War Dictionary*. New York: David McKay Company, Inc., 1959.

Cresap, Bernarr. *Appomattox Commander: The Story of General E. O. C. Ord*. New York: A. S. Barnes & Company, Inc., 1981.

Dyer, Frederick H. *A Compendium of the War of the Rebellion*. Des Moines, IA: The Dyer Publishing Company, 1908; reprint, Dayton, OH: Morningside, 1979.

Eicher, John H. and David J. Eicher. *Civil War High Commands*. Stanford, CA: Stanford University Press, 2001.

Faust, Patricia L., editor. *Historical Times Illustrated Encyclopedia of the Civil War*. New York: Harper & Row, 1986.

Hinkel, John V. *Arlington: Monument to Heroes*. Englewood Cliffs, NJ: Prentice – Hall, Inc., 1970.

Hunt, Roger D. and Jack R. Brown. *Brevet Brigadier Generals in Blue*. Gaithersburg, MD: Olde Soldiers Books, Inc., Revised Edition, 1997.

Johnson, Mark. *That Body of Brave Men: The U. S. Regular Infantry and the Civil War in the West*. Cambridge, MA: Da Capo Press, 2003.

Johnson, Robert U. and Clarence C. Buel, editors. *Battles and Leaders of the Civil War*. Vol. 2. New York: The Century Company, 1887 – 1888; reprint, New York: Thomas Yoseloff, Inc., 1956.

Peters, James Edward. *Arlington National Cemetery: Shrine to America's Heroes*. Kensington, MD: Woodbine House, 1986.

Piston, William Garrett and Richard W. Hatcher III. *Wilson's Creek: The Second Battle of the Civil War and the Men Who Fought It*. Chapel Hill, NC: The University of North Carolina Press, 2000.

Richman, Jeffrey I. *Final Camping Ground: Civil War Veterans at Brooklyn's Green-Wood Cemetery, in Their Own Words*. Brooklyn, NY: The Green-Wood Cemetery, 2007.

Shea, William L. and Earl J. Hess. *Pea Ridge: Civil War Campaign in the West*. Chapel Hill, NC: The University of North Carolina Press, 1992.

Sheridan, Philip H. *Personal Memoirs of P. H. Sheridan*. Vol. 1. New York: Charles L. Webster & Company, 1888; reprint, Wilmington, NC: Broadfoot Publishing Company, 1992.

Spencer, James, compiler. *Civil War Generals: Categorical Listings and Biographical Directory*. New York: Greenwood Press, 1986.

Tagg, Larry. *The Generals of Gettysburg: The Leaders of America's Greatest Battle*. Campbell, CA: Savas Publishing Company, 1998.

United States War Department. *The War of the Rebellion: A Compilation of the Official Records of the Union and Confederate Armies*, 70 vols. in 128 parts. Washington, D.C.: U.S. Government Printing Office, 1880-1901.

Warner, Ezra J. *Generals in Blue: Lives of the Union Commanders*. Baton Rouge, LA: Louisiana State University Press, 1964.

Warner, Ezra J. *Generals in Gray: Lives of the Confederate Commanders*. Baton Rouge, LA: Louisiana State University Press, 1959.

Welsh, Jack D. *Medical Histories of Confederate Generals*. Kent, OH: The Kent State University Press, 1995.

Welsh, Jack D. *Medical Histories of Union Generals*. Kent, OH: The Kent State University Press, 1996.

ABOUT THE AUTHOR

David L. Callihan was born in Pittsburgh and raised in Charlotte, North Carolina. He received a BA in history from Duke University in 1977 and a JD from the Dickinson School of Law in 1980. He is a life-long Civil War enthusiast and former licensed battlefield guide at Gettysburg National Military Park. After working as an attorney in Pennsylvania for nineteen years, David decided to devote his full time to studying and writing about the Civil War. His first two books also dealt with Civil War generals' grave sites: *They Did Their Work Bravely: Civil War Generals Buried in Pennsylvania* (Heritage Books, 2004) and *Lest We Forget: The Grave Sites of the Union Civil War Generals Buried in the United States* (Author House, 2007). David has authored nine articles published in *The Gettysburg Magazine* and is also the editor/publisher of *Grave Matters* (www.gravematters.net), a newsletter about Civil War grave sites. David resides in Dryden, New York with his wife Jean.